TYPING SKILLS
Book I

CM01390417

KM 14 1

By the same author and available from ST(P):
OFFICE SKILLS
TELEPHONE AND RECEPTION SKILLS

Also available from ST(P):
HOW TO TYPE MATHEMATICS AND SCIENCE
Marion Smith and Graham Taylor

TYPING SKILLS

Book I

Thelma J Foster

Formerly Senior Lecturer, Business Studies Department,
Worcester Technical College

Stanley Thornes (Publishers) Ltd

First published 1984 by
Stanley Thornes (Publishers) Ltd
Educa House
Old Station Drive
Leckhampton Road
CHELTENHAM GL53 0DN

British Library Cataloguing in Publication Data

Foster, Thelma J
Typing skills I
1. Typewriting
I. Title
652.3   Z49

ISBN 0-85950-127-2

Typeset by Quadraset Ltd, Combe End, Radstock, Bath, Avon
Printed and bound in Great Britain by Bell & Bain Ltd, Thornliebank, Glasgow

CONTENTS

FOR YOUR TYPING FOLDER EXERCISES

ACCURACY/SPEED PASSAGES

PROGRESS TESTS

ABBREVIATIONS USED IN THIS BOOK

AA	Automobile Association		m/c	machine; machinery
abt	about		m/cs	machines
a/c	account		memo	memorandum
advert	advertisement		memos	memoranda
am	ante meridiem (before noon)		Messrs	Messieurs
amp	ampere		Middx	Middlesex
&	and		mm	millimetre(s)
asap	as soon as possible		Mon	Monday
@	at		MP	Member of Parliament
			Mr	Master
BA	Bachelor of Arts		Mrs	Mistress
Beds	Bedfordshire			
Berks	Berkshire		NCR	no carbon required
bn	been		NP	new paragraph
			No	number
caps	capitals		Northants	Northamptonshire
cat	catalogue		Nov	November
cc	copy circulated; carbon copy			
cd	could		OBE	Officer of the Order of the British
cm	centimetre(s)			Empire
Co	company; county		Oxon	Oxfordshire
cwt	hundredweight		oz	ounce(s) (imperial weight)
dept	department		PIN	personal identification number
Dr	Doctor		PLC	Public Limited Company
			pm	post meridiem (afternoon)
ea	each		POP	Post Office Preferred (size of envelope)
EEC	European Economic Community		PS	postscript
EFT	electronic funds transmission			
eg	exempli gratia (for example)		qty	quantity
enc	enclosure			
encls	enclosures		RAC	Royal Automobile Club
encs	enclosures		Rd	road
Esq	Esquire		recd	received
etc	et cetera		rect	receipt
E & OE	errors and omissions excepted		ref	reference
ext	(telephone) extension		reg	registered
			reqd	required
f	for		Rev	Reverend
ffly	faithfully			
fr	from		shd	should; shorthand
Fri	Friday		sp caps	spaced capitals
ft	foot; feet		St	street; saint
g	gram(s)		tab	tabulator
gd	good		tel	telephone
gds	goods		th	that
Glos	Gloucestershire		trs	transpose
			Thurs	Thursday
Herts	Hertfordshire		Tues	Tuesday
hrs	hours		TV	television
hv	have			
			uc	upper case
ie	id est (that is)		UK	United Kingdom
in	inch(es)		us	underscore
inc	include; included; including			
info	information		VAT	Value Added Tax
			VDU	visual display unit
JP	Justice of the Peace (a magistrate)			
			w	with
kg	kilogram(s)		wd	would
			Wed	Wednesday
ℓ	litre		wh	which
Lancs	Lancashire		wk	week; work
lb	pound(s) (imperial weight)		wks	weeks; works
lc	lower case		Worcs	Worcestershire
Ltd	limited (company)			
ltr	letter		yd	yard(s)
			yr	your
m	metre(s)		yrs	yours
MA	Master of Arts			

INTRODUCTION

This book has several new features – the main one being that it is linked to office practice wherever it is possible. Typewriting is a part of so many office jobs that it should never be taught in isolation from office practice, yet so often the typewriting teacher does not teach the same group for office practice and finds it difficult to organise correlation of the two subjects. A great deal of work that would normally be typed in offices (ink stencils, spirit masters, completion of forms) is carried out by hand in office practice lessons. Very often, too, these lessons take place in rooms without even a single typewriter, which is totally unrealistic. Many regional examining boards have tried at least to partly remedy this by combining office practice and typewriting in one examination, which is a step in the right direction. I hope that this book will take realism a stage further.

As every teacher of office practice will endorse, any reinforcement of the subject from whatever angle is useful and, with this in mind, I have used office practice topics (wherever possible) for speed and accuracy drills, varied by the occasional interesting general knowledge passage. Most typewriting textbooks provide mainly irrelevant material for speed and accuracy practice, which must mean very little to typewriting students.

Many evening class students learn to type without office practice training, and *Typing Skills Book I* will also be useful to them, as an insight into the business world.

At intervals, I have introduced brief revision exercises which could be kept by pupils/students in a separate Typing Folder, together with the relevant specimen typed exercises. These exercises will help students to remember some of the many points of typewriting theory which they find so confusing in the early stages of learning to type.

In addition, there are Progress Tests which will enable teachers and pupils/students alike to check on the latest points of theory taught.

Throughout Book I, blocked letter layout is described and illustrated together with open punctuation. At this stage in learning to type it simplifies life immensely if the other letter layouts are left until later on (they will be introduced at the beginning of Book II). Similarly, full punctuation will be introduced in Book II, with practice on both full and open punctuation given at regular intervals. I appreciate that many employers still prefer the traditional letter layout and punctuation, and, after all, pupils/students are going to use their typewriting skills in offices – the examinations they hope to pass are but a preliminary hurdle and should not be allowed to dictate the "right" or "wrong" way of typing punctuation or setting out letters. All teachers must make it clear that employers have the right to ask their typists to follow the "house style".

Speed and accuracy passages have been combined. As they are all numbered in the right hand margin with the number of words in each line (based on a 5-stroke word count) these passages can be used for either speed or accuracy, or both. They are not introduced until page 67, as until then accuracy is the major consideration, but of course there is no reason why teachers should not compose their own speed/accuracy passages based on the stage reached on the keyboard, if they prefer to do so.

Similarly, there are no suggested timings for exercises or Progress Tests in Book I, as so many pupils/students find it extremely difficult to master new points of theory *and* work against the clock to produce error-free exercises. In Book II, a time limit will be introduced, as obviously this is an important factor in passing typewriting examinations, and must be practised. The leisurely approach has to be discouraged!

Another important feature of *Typing Skills Book I* is correlation with English – also an area that is often difficult to organise in schools and colleges. Long experience has shown me that all age groups (and ability levels) have difficulty with the same problems when learning to type, and I have introduced simple exercises at regular intervals in the hope that constant practice will improve standards.

Typing Skills Book I covers approximately 1 year's teaching for CSE pupils, dependent on the amount of time allocated to typing lessons each week. (In an ideal world, this should be at least 5 hours, with 2 hours on one day to be used as a double period, but I am very well aware that most schools have considerably less time than 5 hours a week allocated to them for typing.) *Typing Skills Book I* also covers the Royal Society of Arts (Elementary) Typewriting Syllabus.

Typing Skills Book II will cover CSE typewriting syllabuses (which are many, varied and wide, as far as I am able to judge) and the Royal Society of Arts Stage II (Intermediate) Typewriting Syllabus.

Typing Skills Book III will cover the Royal Society of Arts Stage III (Advanced) Typewriting Syllabus, as well as useful practice for audio typists and teleprinter operators.

T J Foster

ACKNOWLEDGMENTS TO:

Marion Smith
Tony Edwards
Staff of Stanley Thornes (Publishers) Ltd

Letterheading is rarely available either in schools or colleges and when it is, it has to be used economically. Also, the students are usually restricted to a few firms' names printed on the letterheading, which are not often appropriate for most of the exercises in the typewriting textbook.

Although it is not essential to use printed letterheading for every practice letter typed by students, it is obviously desirable that they should use it at regular intervals, otherwise practice in typing business letters will not be realistic and examination work will be affected.

I have tried to do something about this problem by:

a) restricting the number of firms' names in *Typing Skills Book 1 to 9*;

b) including sufficient exercises based on typing business letters which can be used on *any* printed letterheading without confusing students (ie I have omitted the name of the firm after ''Yours faithfully'').

Teachers using my book *Office Skills* may find it useful to know that the names asterisked on the list below are used in filing practice in the chapter on filing. It would, therefore, be a useful exercise to include the letters and carbon copies typed during a typing lesson for demonstrating the various points of the alphabetical filing rules.

*The Midland Secretarial Agency
Frederick Road
Edgbaston
Birmingham
B15 4NX

*WTC Transport Co Ltd
Grovebury Road
Leighton Buzzard
Beds
LU7 8SL

*Lamb's Furniture Co Ltd
35 Old Bedford Road
Luton
Beds
LU2 7HQ

*GPR Developments Ltd
78 East Square
Chelmsford
Essex
CM1 1JN

*A L Carter & Co Ltd
Trentham Trading Estate
High Street
Kirkcaldy
Fife
KY1 1LR

Office Equipment Supply Co Ltd
Knightley Road
Bromswood
Lancs
T45 7BC

Shaw & Short Ltd, Wholesalers
Whitaker Street
Manchester
M96 8TB

Barwest Bank PLC
Edgware Road
Westminster
London
W2 47F

Brickfield Building Society
Grainger St
Newcastle upon Type
NE3 4JU

Typing Skills

PAGES 1 to 120

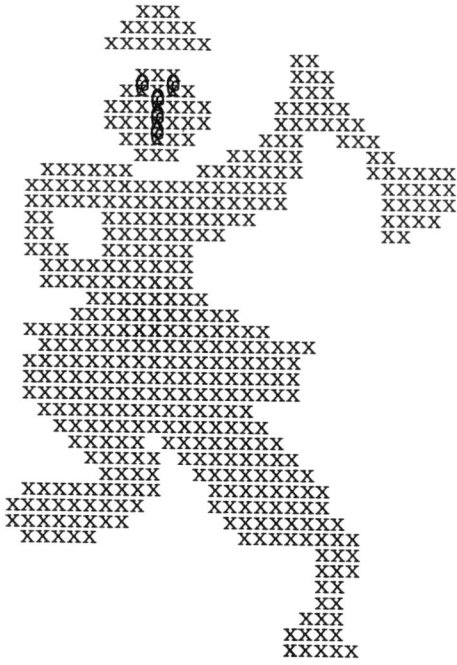

The clown

A donkey

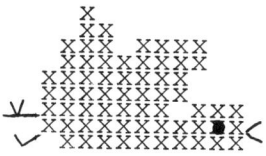

Easter chicks

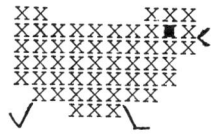

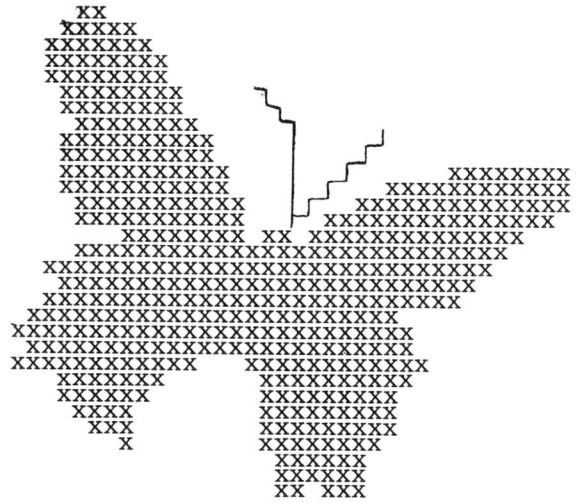

A butterfly

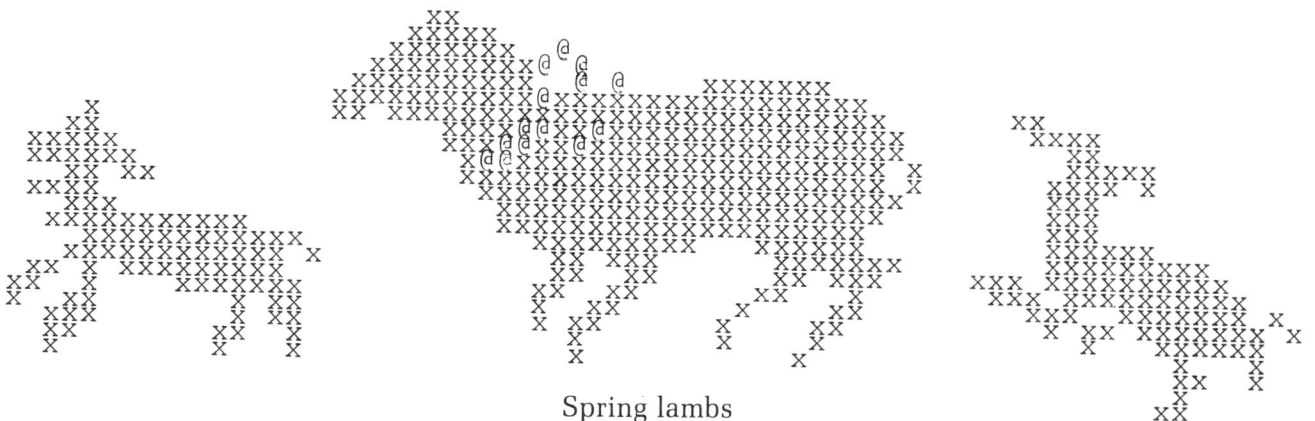

Spring lambs

SECTION 1

You and Your Typewriter

Occasionally, it is necessary to add small finishing touches with a ball-point pen.

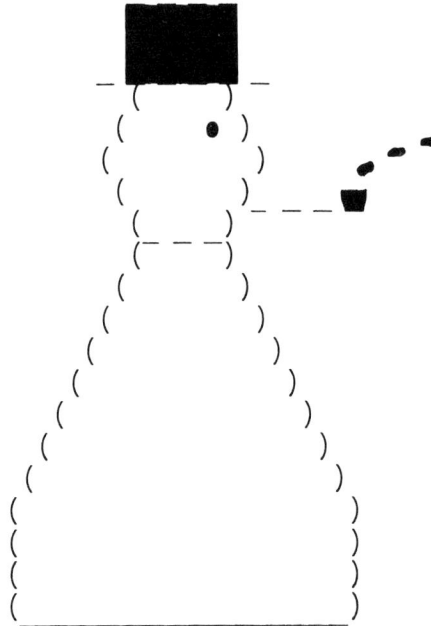

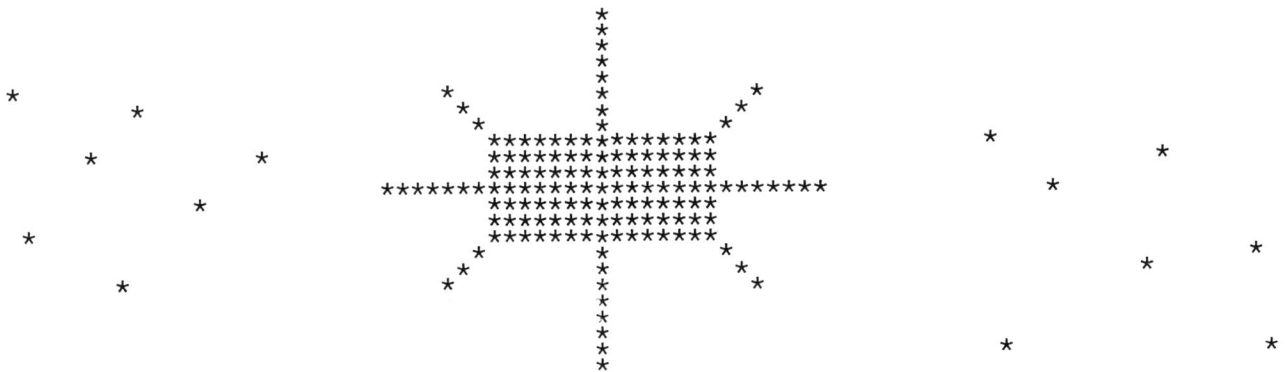

X M A S   G R E E T I N G S

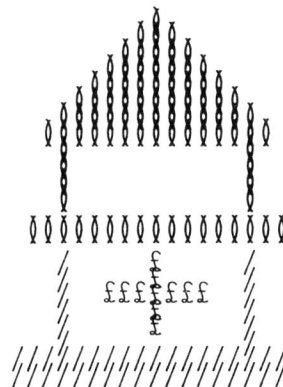

HOW THE TYPEWRITER BEGAN

The typewriter as we know it today was slow in gaining recognition. For a long time it was regarded as a great curiosity, of little practical use. The very early typewriters embossed words on the paper and were designed so that blind people could both read and write. The braille system in use today had its origins in the first typewriters, invented in the early 1800s. Eventually, a typewriter was invented which was faster than writing by hand and began to be considered seriously. By 1878 the shift key, which enabled operators to type upper and lower case letters, was added. The typewriter brought about greater efficiency in offices and, at the same time, it brought about another dramatic change – women office workers. Prior to the invention of the typewriter, most office workers, including secretaries, had been men. However, early typewriting classes were filled with women, and gradually the typists in offices were nearly all women. Typewriting, together with shorthand, has had an enormous effect on the emancipation of women.

Over the years, typewriters have been continually changing. The first electric machines came into use in the 1930s and in 1961 an electric typewriter was introduced with a "golfball" head which replaced the type basket. With the golfball the carriage remains stationary while the golfball moves along the paper. Some of these golfball typewriters justified (straightened) the right hand margin, and also produced work with proportional spacing, which closely resembled printed work.

Word processor, VDU and printer

Automatic typewriters were manufactured, operated by punched tape, which typed letters looking like top copies without the necessity for a typist. These were the forerunners of today's word processors and "memory" typewriters, which can edit text on a visual display unit (VDU) screen so that the typist can check the layout before it is printed at a speed of 500 words per minute. The golfball head has now been replaced on these latest typewriters by the "daisy wheel", made of plastic, which operates on the same principle – the carriage is stationary while the daisy wheel moves along the typing paper.

Start at the top of the picture and work downwards.

Mark each line lightly in pencil as you complete it, or you may lose your place.

Letters that are symmetrical in shape are used for "drawing" on the typewriter, otherwise the picture will be too long and too thin.

Examples of symmetrical letters are:

    x   e   m   o   s w   z

In the picture of the monkey below, the letter "x" has been used, but it could be done with any of the letters above.

The eyes are two "o's" typed over the "x's" which outline its face, and the mouth is formed by 3 "z's" similarly typed over.

Single line spacing is used.

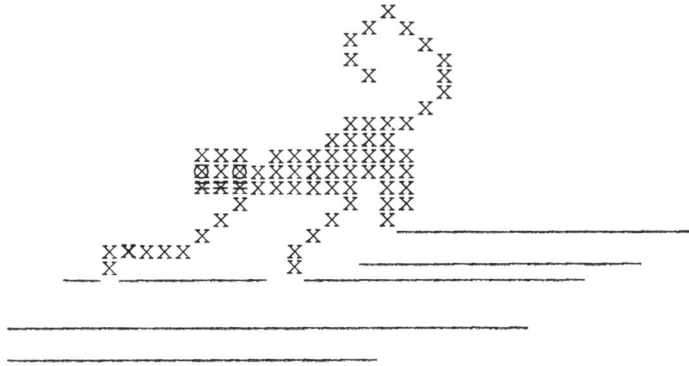

A monkey

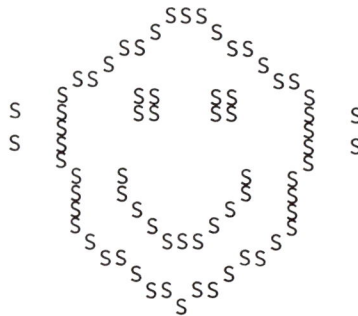

Smile, please!

In "Smile, please!", half line spacing is used.

DIFFERENT TYPEWRITERS

There are two kinds of typewriter in general use in offices – electric and manual. In addition, there are what are known as "special-purpose" typewriters which are used in offices where the work is highly specialised.

Manual typewriters

There are three different kinds of manual typewriter:

- Standard length carriage used in most offices (14")
- Specially long carriage for typing wide documents
- Portable typewriters – extra-light to carry so that they can be moved easily.

Manual typewriters are cheaper than electric typewriters, they need no power point, and are much less heavy than electric machines.

Manual typewriter

Electric typewriters

These produce very good-quality work, when used by a well-trained typist, because of the evenness of touch. It is not possible to "bang" too hard on electric typewriters. They are less tiring than manual typewriters for this reason, and also because of the "repeater" keys on the machine – usually for underscore and fullstop. The carriage return is automatic, too, and helps to speed up the typing.

Some electric typewriters will produce more carbon copies than manual machines (a manual will produce about 6). With very thin carbon and typing paper, an electric machine, with pressure adjusted to maximum, may produce up to 12 carbon copies.

It is also possible to change the typeface on some electric machines – by means of a removable "golfball" on which the characters are mounted or by means of a moulded segment. These interchangeable typefaces enable the typist to change the "pitch" of the machine (ie the number of characters the machine produces per inch – pica is 10 pitch and elite is 12 pitch) and also provide a different typestyle for display work. In addition, some foreign languages (Russian for example) have different characters and an interchangeable typeface would have to be used for these.

SECTION 7

Typing for Fun

Up to the present, electric typewriters which have been in general use have keyboards and carriage movements driven by an electric motor – the action is mechanical.

Electronic typewriters

It is now possible to buy a truly electronic typewriter – the keyboard is controlled from an electrical impulse through a circuit board (with silicon "chips"). The weight of an electronic typewriter is about half that of an electric typewriter, and repairs are much easier and quicker to carry out, as it consists of only seven components, each of which can be replaced when necessary. The faulty part can be repaired and stored by the mechanic until required to repair another faulty machine.

The electronic typewriter is almost identical in operation to an electric typewriter except that it has a small "memory" of eight characters which can be used to:

● backspace
● correct automatically
● adjust layout of headings.

The touch required on an electronic typewriter is feather light – even less than on the traditional electric typewriter.

The price of the two machines is almost the same.

The typing element is called a "daisy wheel" because it is shaped like the petals on a daisy. The daisy wheel is interchangeable to give different pitch and characters.

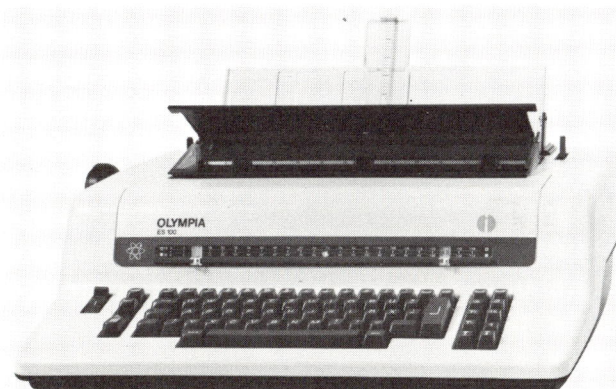

Daisy
wheel

H

Harassed
Height
Heroes
Honorary
Humour
   Humorous
Hungry
Hurriedly
Hypocrisy
Hypothesis
   Hypotheses

I

Immigrate
   Immigrant
Incidentally
Incipient
Indispensable
Influential
Inoculate
   Inoculation
Install (or: instal)
   Instalment
Intelligence
Irrelevant
Irreparable
Irresistible

K

Knowledge

L

Leisure
Liaison
Livelihood
Lose
Lounge

M

Maintenance
Manoeuvre
Marriage
Medicine
Mediterranean
Miniature
Minutes
Movable
Murmur

N

Necessary
Negotiate
   Negotiable
Niece

O

Occurred
   Occurrence
Omitted
   Omission
Opinion

P

Paid
Parallel
   Paralleled
Parliament
Pastime
Penicillin
Permanent
Permissible
Perseverance
Physical
Pleasant
Pleasure
Possess
   Possessive
Potential
Predecessor
Preference
   Preferred
Preliminary
Prestige
Procedure
Professional
Professor
Pronunciation
Proprietary
Psychology

R

Really
Received
Recommend
Relieved
Repetition
Responsibility

S

Seize
Sentence
Separate
Severely
Shining
Similar
Statutory
Substitute
Subtle
   Subtlety
Successful
   Successfully
Summary
Summery
Supersede
Suppression
Surprise
Synonym
   Synonymous

T

Technical
Technological
Tendency
Training
Transfer
Transient
Twelfth

U

Uncomfortable
Unconscious
Underrate
Unfortunately
Unnecessary
Until
Usual

V

Vaccinate
Video

W

Wednesday
Weird
Wield
Withhold
Woollen

Y

Yield

Memory typewriter

This can store up to 200 000 characters (about 200 pages of A4 typing). The characters are not just the letters printed on the paper, but also include instructions to the machine regarding line spacing, headings, etc. A copy of each letter or document stored in the memory must be kept in a folder so that it is possible to refer to them for reference and retyping when required.

Word processor (or text processor)

This is the more sophisticated development of the memory typewriter, where the storage of the typed material is outside the machine and may be on magnetic card, tape or floppy disks (called "floppy" because they are limp). A word processor also has a visual display unit (VDU) on which the typist can see what is being typed as it happens. It is printed out only when text and layout are satisfactory. Whole sections can be moved out, revised, added, deleted or enlarged. Only the new material will need to be retyped. On some word processors a high-speed independent "printer" (a typewriter without a keyboard) prints out the work once it has been approved, from the memory, at 500 words per minute without possibility of errors – a perfect "top" copy every time.

A word processor will produce all the repetitive work of a typist – circulars, reports, minutes, legal documents – much faster and with complete accuracy, and of a sufficiently high quality to be suitable for sending out to other firms or organisations.

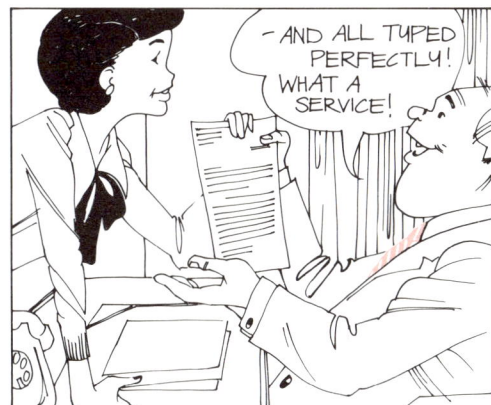

COMMONLY MISSPELT WORDS

A

Absence
Absorption
Accessible
Accidental
  Accidentally
Accommodation
Achieve
  Achieved
  Achievement
Acknowledge
Acquiesce
  Acquiescence
Acquire
  Acquisition
Addresses
Aerial
Aggravate
Agreeable
All right
Amateur
Among
Analysis
  Analyses
Ancillary
Antarctic
Anxiety
Apparent
Appearance
Appropriate
Arctic
Argument
Arrangement
Association
Athletic
Audio
Awful

B

Bachelor
Bargain
Benefited
Breathe
  Breathing
Budgeted
Bureau
  Bureaucracy
Business

C

Careful
Category
Ceiling
Certainly
Chaos
  Chaotic
Cheque
Choice
Clothes
Colleagues
College
Committee
Comparative
Compatible
Competent
  Competence
Completely
Confident
Confirmation
Connoisseur
Conscientious
Conscious
Consequence
Consistent
Contribute
Convenience
Correspondent
  Correspondence
Corroborate
Courteous
Courtesy
Criticism

D

Deceive
Decision
Deficient
Desirable
Desperate
Deterrent
Disappeared
Disappoint
Disastrous
Discipline
Discrepancy
Dissatisfied
Distributor

E

Economics
Efficient
  Efficiency
Eighth
Eliminated
Embarrassed
  Embarrassment
Enthusiasm
Equipped
  Equipment
Erroneous
Essential
Exaggerated
Excellent
Exercise
Exhausted
Experience

F

Familiar
Favourite
Feasible
February
Field
Financial
Foreign
Fortunately
Forty
Fulfilled
  Fulfilment

G

Garage
Gauge
Genius
Genuine
Gesture
Glamorous
Government
Grammar
Grief
Grievance
Guarantee
Guard
  Guardian
Guillotine
Gymnasium

TYPEFACES – ELITE AND PICA

"Elite" and "pica" are two different sizes of typeface or pitch. The "typeface" is the typewriter key which actually strikes your paper and prints the character. Elite (12 pitch, ie 12 characters to the inch) is slightly smaller than pica (10 pitch), and therefore if your machine is elite, you can type more letters across the paper than if your machine is pica. An easy way to check for yourself is to measure across the scale at the back of your typewriter with a piece of A4 paper, keeping the left hand edge on zero (where your paper guide should be). An elite pitch means that the right hand edge of the A4 paper is on 100 on the scale, and pica pitch means that the right hand edge is on 82.

12☐ 0 6   138 Elite

10☐ 0 5   115 Pica

TYPEWRITER RIBBONS

Typewriter ribbons are made of nylon, silk, cotton or carbon. "Carbon" ribbons, sometimes called "film" ribbons, are in fact made of carbon-coated plastic film. Nylon and silk ribbons produce work of very good appearance but carbon ribbons produce the best and sharpest imprint of all. The finer the fabric, the sharper the imprint. Unfortunately, carbon ribbons can be used once only, and so are very expensive. Two-colour ribbons are available (called bi-chrome) – usually red and black – and correcting ribbons, which switch from normal black to white, so that the error is typed over in white, made invisible, and the correction typed over in black.

There are also "lift-off" correcting ribbons, which lift off a mistake from the typed page on to the (white) correcting ribbon, leaving the paper clear for the correct character to be typed in.

The latest electric and electronic typewriters have ribbons in the form of cassettes, which are easy to change and avoid the typist's hands coming into contact with the ribbon itself – only the outside of the cassette is handled.

Fabric ribbons gradually become fainter and fainter with constant use and must be changed before the imprint becomes too pale.

The ribbon mechanism on a typewriter operates by automatically reversing the ribbon when one spool becomes full and the other is empty. If for some reason the reversing mechanism is not working, a hole will appear in the ribbon – you will need to call a mechanic to correct the fault.

Typewriters have a ribbon switch (see page 10) which enables the typist to use either the top half of the ribbon or the bottom half. In addition, there is a switch which disengages the ribbon completely, so that the typeface strikes the paper over the top of the ribbon. This is for typing ink stencils (see Book II).

Accuracy/speed practice

1 There are two main types of carbon paper – single is coated on 12
one side and double on both sides. Single carbon paper is the 25
one most widely used and is available in various "weights" ie 38
thicknesses. 41

2 Most firms today use what is known as "long-life" carbon paper 13
which is plastic coated and is clean, easy to handle and less 25
likely to curl or crease. Carbon paper is available in a 37
variety of strong colours. 42

3 Carbon paper should be stored flat, preferably in a box, away 12
from radiators, in a cool place. Creased carbon paper produces 25
"trees" on the carbon copies. A "treed" carbon copy is the sign 39
of a careless typist. 44

4 Careful erasing prolongs the life of carbon paper. Rubber dust 13
should be brushed off the carbon paper after erasing, away from 26
the type basket on to the desk. The typewriter carriage should 39
be moved as far as possible to left or right before rubbing out. 52

5 One-time carbons are a thin, inexpensive type of carbon paper, 12
often used for interleaving documents supplied in sets – tele- 25
printer rolls, computer stationery, invoices, statements, etc, 38
and after removal from the documents are scrapped. 48

6 NCR in connection with making copies means "no carbon required" 13
and produces copies by the use of chemicals, either on the back 26
of the paper or on the back and front. NCR paper is supplied 38
in sets, lightly attached at the top and thus saves the typist 51
inserting and removing carbons. 57

7 NCR paper is clean to handle, quicker for the typist and less 12
storage space is required in the stationery store cupboard for 25
boxes of carbon paper. NCR is, however, more expensive than 38
ordinary paper plus carbon paper. 45

8 NCR paper is often used for continuous stationery. Continuous 13
stationery consists of sets of documents which are fed into a 25
typewriter by a special attachment. After each document has 37
been typed, it can be torn off the roll by means of 48
perforations, and the next document is brought into the 59
machine, ready for typing. 65

CARE OF YOUR TYPEWRITER

Each new typewriter is supplied with a cleaning kit in a wallet. It usually consists of a soft duster, and two brushes (one with soft bristles and one with stiff bristles) with long handles. In addition, an efficient cleaning kit for a manual typewriter should contain a small bottle of methylated spirits.

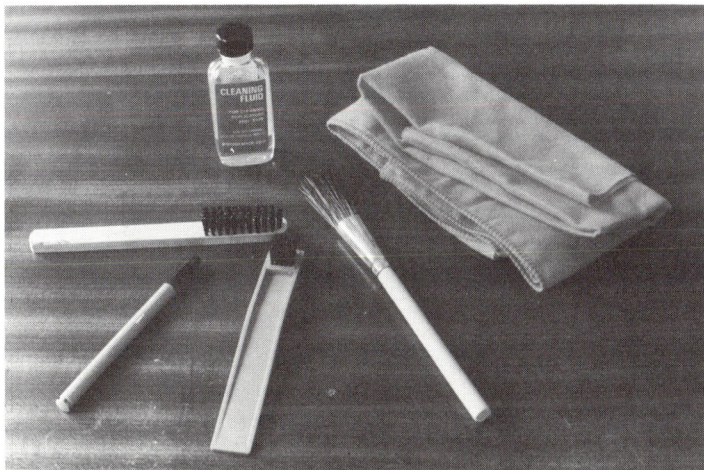

Typewriter cleaning kit

Daily routine

Remove dust (preferably first thing in the morning), especially underneath, as this will rise into the machine and clog it.

Make sure the typewriter is never left near the edge of a desk where it could be easily knocked off.

Never leave a typewriter near a hot radiator – this will dry out the oil in the machine.

If a typewriter has to be moved, move both margins to the centre so that the carriage will not slide along, and lift from *underneath*, with the back of the machine towards you.

When typing single copies, use a backing sheet (see page 12) – this improves the look of the typing as well as protecting the roller (platen) from wear and tear. Always rub out carefully (see page 45).

Always replace the typewriter cover at the end of the day, or after use.

Accuracy/speed practice

1 Some firms will employ school leavers as office juniors.   11
An office junior will learn to do many different jobs.   23

2 Someone new to the office may be introduced to audio typing.   12
An audio typist listens to a cassette through headphones and   24
types what is heard.   29

3 Copy typists type from handwritten or corrected typescript.   12
Their typing speeds vary. A junior typist may be sent on a   24
day-release course.   28

4 A shorthand typist has to have a good typing speed and also   12
be able to write shorthand quickly. In addition, a good   23
knowledge of English is needed.   30

5 Many school leavers are attracted by the idea of becoming   11
receptionists. A receptionist in a firm is the first person   24
a caller may speak to.   29

6 Another important key post in a firm is that of the telephon-   12
ist or switchboard operator. Many of these are trained by   24
British Telecom.   28

Accuracy/speed practice

1 As a business letter is sent from one firm to another, it is   12
very important that the typing is neat and accurate, and that   24
spelling and punctuation are excellent.   33

2 However carefully a business letter is typed, all the effort   12
is wasted if the envelope in which it is posted is wrongly   24
addressed and it is wrongly delivered.   32

3 A circular letter is one of which many copies are sent out.   12
Usually, circular letters are sent for advertising purposes,   24
to inform potential customers about new products.   34

4 Form letters are business letters sent from one firm to   11
another, or to members of the public. Form letters are pre-   23
printed on letter headings, without name or address.   34

5 Postcards are sometimes sent in place of form letters;   11
as they do not require envelopes they save time and money.   24
The name of the firm is printed at the top.   32

Remove the front of the typewriter and cover the keys with a duster. Brush the typeface with the stiff brush dipped in methylated spirits to remove surplus ink which eventually clogs letters such as p's, o's, b's, g's and c's. Clean fingermarks off the machine with meths, and remove rubber dust with the soft brush. Wipe the roller (platen) with a duster dampened with meths.

There is now available a specially treated paper which is coated with a layer containing a special cleaning fluid. This fluid is released when the surface is struck by the typeface, whereupon it dissolves away the surplus ink. The fluid is then re-absorbed into the sheet. This is a very effective and clean way to deal with clogged typeface, but the specially treated paper is quite expensive, and has a limited life.

Golfball heads and daisy wheels have to be cleaned by using the specially treated paper; the typewriter is switched to "stencil" before using it (see page 6).

Never use oil on a typewriter – it will get on to the typing paper and ruin the work.

Always send for a mechanic if your typewriter goes wrong – don't try to mend it yourself.

Accuracy/speed practice

CHILD SAFETY IN CARS

	Words
When a car crashes, it stops very suddenly, but those inside don't	13
stop at the same time. They go on moving forward at the car's speed	28
until they in turn hit something. That "something" can be the	41
steering column, the dashboard, the windscreen or some other part	54
of the inside of the car. It is this second collision which causes	68
injury or even death.	72
In crashes, small children become flying missiles. A crash at 25	86
miles per hour into something stationary like a lamp post, is likely	100
to be as bad as dropping a child 20 feet on to the ground. A crash	114
with an oncoming car at normal traffic speed could be very much	126
worse.	128

Accuracy/speed practice

PASSING A DRIVING TEST

	Words
Many young people pass their driving tests quite soon after their	13
seventeenth birthdays - but many more fail their first test and	26
several subsequent tests, too. Examiners complain that many people	40
(not just young people) take their driving tests far too quickly after	54
first starting to learn to drive. They seem to think that a course of	69
lessons with a qualified instructor, a few hours on the road with a	82
friend or parent, and they are safe to be out on their own in a car.	96
In addition to formal instruction, constant practice under all types	110
of weather conditions, winter and summer, is essential so that confi-	124
dence builds up and the learner-driver is gradually able to cope with	138
any unexpected situation.	143
The other factor that causes failure of the driving test is nerves.	157
Many people, quite capable of driving sensibly and competently, lose	171
their heads when under the eyes of the examiner and behave in a	184
manner that is totally unlike their normal pattern. The only answer	198
to this state of near-panic is to be so confident beforehand that	211
the right manoeuvres are carried out automatically.	222

SECTION 2

Typewriting Technique

Accuracy/speed practice

1 Most firms large enough to be divided into departments have a 12

mail room where letters and parcels are delivered by the postman. 26

2 Staff working in a mail room are trained by a supervisor and are 13

efficient and (eventually) experienced, so that mail is dealt 26

with promptly. 29

3 A well-organised mail room contains scales (two types) for 12

weighing both letters and parcels, a franking machine and other 25

equipment. 27

4 Mail arriving at a firm may include many different documents 12

besides letters. There may be invoices, quotations, estimates 25

and orders. 27

5 In some firms, it is usual to divide incoming mail into first 12

and second-class, opening the first-class mail first, as it is 25

generally more important. 30

6 Not all letters come by post. Some are delivered by the firm's 13

messengers and are internal mail. Letters between offices and 26

branches are known as "memos". 33

7 Mail for posting may arrive at any time during the day, but the 13

afternoons are the busiest times in the mail room, and to avoid 25

a sudden rush, a system of regular collection from every office 38

should be organised. 43

8 Trays marked "outgoing mail" placed where the messenger from the 13

mail room can conveniently collect the mail at frequent intervals, 27

ensure that letters for posting are dealt with promptly. 38

9 It is necessary to weigh a bulky letter, as letters which are 12

understamped are handed to recipients with a request for twice 25

the missing postage. 29

10 Other letters which must be weighed are letters going abroad, 12

whether by airmail or surface mail. Airmail is expensive, but 25

special thin paper and envelopes cut the cost down. 36

11 There is an airmail letter form available at The Post Office 13

which is the cheapest way to send letters by air. This is 25

called an "aerogramme". "Surface" mail is carried by train, 38

ship, or van and is cheaper than airmail but slower. 48

PARTS OF THE TYPEWRITER

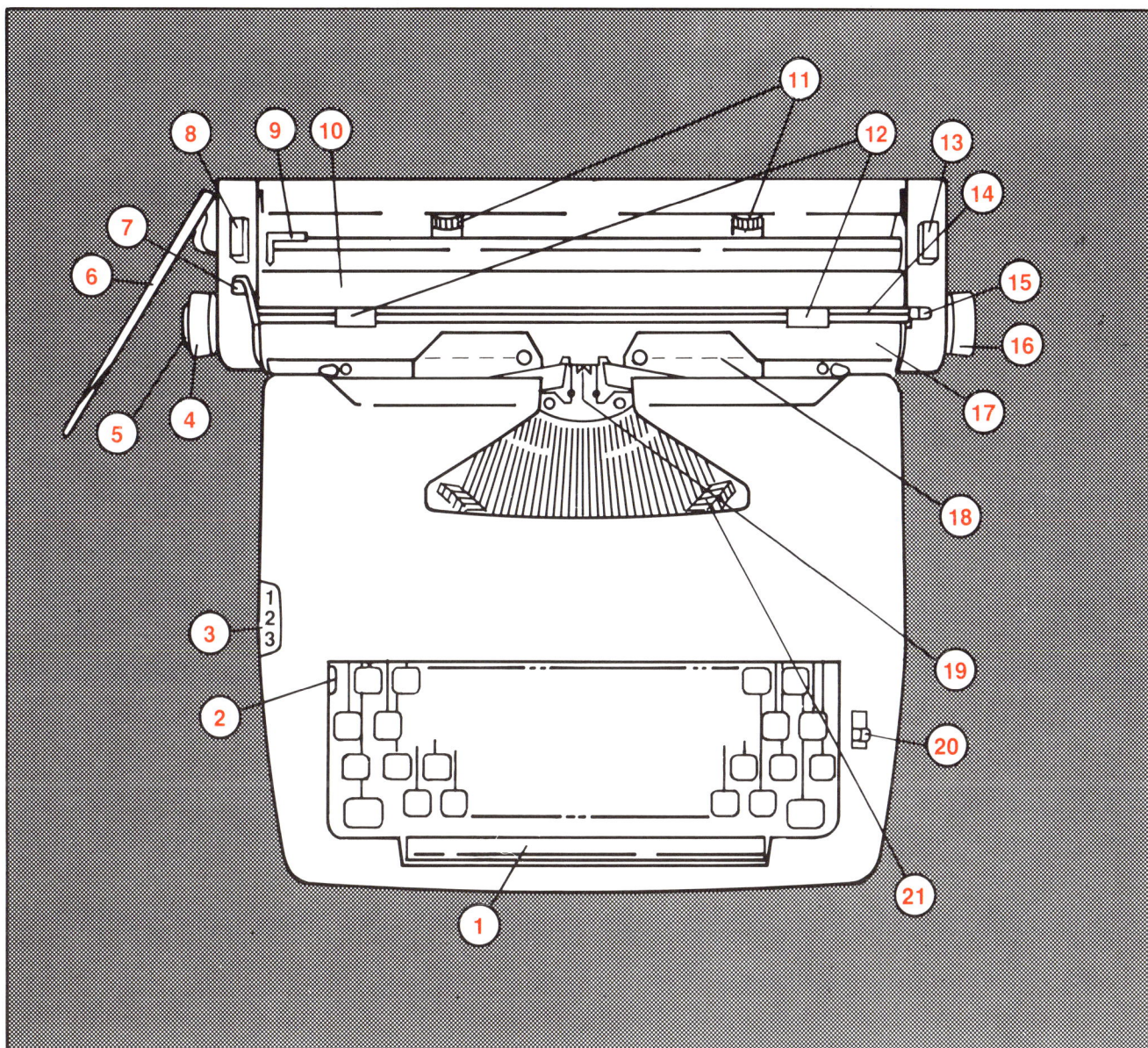

1 Space Bar	**8** Carriage Release Lever	**15** Paper Release Lever
2 Touch Regulator	**9** Paper Guide	**16** Platen Turning Knob
3 Line Space Indicator	**10** Erasure Table	**17** Platen (Roller)
4 Platen Turning Knob	**11** Margin Set	**18** Alignment Scale
5 Variable Line Spacer	**12** Bail Bar Rollers	**19** Typing Point
6 Carriage Return Lever	**13** Carriage Release Lever	**20** Ribbon Switch
7 Interliner Lever	**14** Bail Bar	**21** Type Basket

Preparation for accuracy/speed practice

micro-processors micro-processors micro-processors micro-processors

technology technology technology technology technology technology technology

aeroplane aeroplane aeroplane aeroplane aeroplane aeroplane aeroplane aeroplane

complicated complicated complicated complicated complicated complicated

instantaneous instantaneous instantaneous instantaneous instantaneous

inter-office inter-office inter-office inter-office inter-office inter-office

musicians musicians musicians musicians musicians musicians musicians musicians

builders builders builders builders builders builders builders builders

Accuracy/speed practice

INFORMATION TECHNOLOGY

	Words
Incredible quantities of information, stored by micro-processors,	13
are available in a split second at the touch of a button. This	26
is what information technology means.	34
Information technology is getting cheaper and cheaper, as the equip-	48
ment becomes smaller. Six or seven years ago, pocket calculators	61
were 50 times dearer than they are today and were used by only a few	75
people. Now they're as common as pencils and not much larger. If	89
the aeroplane had developed at the same rate, it would be possible	102
to fly around the world now in 7 seconds for under £1!	114
A home computer costs under £50, plugs into a portable television	128
set and can do complicated tasks which as recently as 1962 would	141
have required a computer the size of the Albert Hall.	152
For today's children, computers are becoming as familiar in the	165
classrooms as desks and blackboards. At home, too, children are	179
using computers as a natural, everyday part of their lives.	191
In offices, a desk-top computer can not only provide instantaneous	204
information or calculation, but also an inter-office communications	218
system that makes the telephone look like jungle drums.	229
Information technology is not just for business use; theatres use	243
it for bookings, musicians to create sounds, and farmers, publicans	256
and builders are all starting to wonder how they ever did without it.	271

PAPER SIZES

There are two sizes of paper most commonly used in offices: A4 which is 210 mm × 297 mm (8¼″ × 11¾″ approximately) and A5, which is half the size of A4 – 210 mm × 148 mm (8¼″ × 5⅞″ approximately). A5 paper can be turned and used with the shorter edge inserted into the typewriter. A4 paper is usually inserted into the machine with the shorter edge horizontal.

BEFORE STARTING TO TYPE:

CHECK:

how you are sitting (your posture):

Feet should be flat on the floor, one foot slightly in front of the other. (If you are very short, you may need a footrest to feel comfortable.)

DO NOT EVER CROSS YOUR KNEES (this restricts your circulation, causing problems later in life).

Elbows should be slightly away from your sides – adopt a relaxed position.

Wrists low, just above the typewriter, in a straight line from elbows to knuckles.

Fingers curved – try to imagine you are going to grasp a thick pole.

ADJUST:

your chair so that your back is supported and your knees are comfortably under your desk. Draw your chair up to your desk so that you are OVER your typewriter keyboard and not leaning towards it. *The lower edge of the typewriter should be parallel with the front edge of the desk.*

BOOK (or copy):

should be on the right of your typewriter, and either on your copyholder, or supported by another book so that it slopes slightly towards you.

Preparation for accuracy/speed practice

compulsory compulsory compulsory compulsory compulsory compulsory compulsory
Magistrates' Magistrates' Magistrates' Magistrates' Magistrates' Magistrates'
Association Association Association Association Association Association
recommended recommended recommended recommended recommended recommended
passenger passenger passenger passenger passenger passenger passenger passenger
conviction conviction conviction conviction conviction conviction conviction
endorsed endorsed endorsed endorsed endorsed endorsed endorsed endorsed endorsed
licence licence licence licence licence licence licence licence licence licence
entitled entitled entitled entitled entitled entitled entitled entitled entitled
exemption exemption exemption exemption exemption exemption exemption exemption
patients patients patients patients patients patients patients patients patients
Medical Medical Medical Medical Medical Medical Medical Medical Medical Medical

Accuracy/speed practice

SEAT BELTS IN CARS

	Words
On 31 January 1983, the wearing of seat belts in cars became	12
compulsory. The penalty for not wearing seat belts by the driver or	26
front seat passenger is a maximum of a fine of £50. The fine that is	40
recommended by the Magistrates' Association is £10. A driver of a car	56
will not be held responsible if the passenger does not wear a seat	69
belt. A seat belt conviction will not be endorsed on a motorist's	83
driving licence.	86
Drivers entitled to exemption include taxi drivers, milkmen and postmen,	101
as well as driving examiners. Nobody is expected to wear seat belts	115
while reversing their cars. Policemen are expected to wear seat belts	130
(except when escorting prisoners!) to set an example.	141
Doctors charge £19 to patients who seek exemption from wearing a seat	155
belt on medical grounds. The Medical Commission on Accident Prevention	171
has said that anyone fit enough to drive a car is generally fit enough	185
to wear a belt. Pregnant women, very fat people and those with neck,	199
shoulder or abdominal injuries, would all be safer belted than unbelted.	214
Arrangements are being made for the disabled and those on low incomes	228
seeking exemption to be examined free through the Department of Health	243
and Social Security.	247

Rule up a backing sheet (A4 size) preferably using coloured paper, so that you do not type on it by mistake – it will last you several weeks. Rule a line one inch from the top from edge to edge of the paper, and one inch from the bottom from edge to edge of the paper. The backing sheet is used to protect the roller (platen) on your typewriter, and also to improve the appearance of your typing, by providing a "buffer" between paper and platen.

Place your backing sheet at the back of your typing paper, which will also be A4 size.

The following should be routine before **every** typing lesson:

● Make sure your paper guide is on zero

● Set your line spacer for single line spacing (unless instructed otherwise, later on)

● Set your margins as instructed at the beginning of each page or exercise

Lift the bail bar forwards, away from the machine.

Move the interliner lever forwards and insert the paper, with the left hand edge of the paper close against the paper guide. Using the interliner lever for paper insertion means that it is a noiseless process – no competent typist ever inserts paper without disengaging the line spacer (which is what happens when the interliner lever is used). Try putting your paper in without using it (once!) and see what a difference it makes.

Turn both sheets of paper into your machine, with the coloured backing sheet towards you.

Straighten the paper by using the paper release lever.

Line the top edge of the paper exactly with the alignment scale.

Turn up 7 line spaces from the top edge of the paper with the carriage return lever. This will bring your first line of typing level with the line ruled on your backing sheet (which you will be able to see through your typing paper). There are 6 typing lines to one inch. The seventh line is your typing line.

Return the bail bar so that the rollers rest on either side of the paper, about ½″ in from the right and left hand edges.

Make sure your interliner lever has been returned to normal. Make sure your paper release lever (if you used it) has been returned to normal.

YOU ARE NOW READY TO START TYPING.

Preparation for accuracy/speed practice

American American American American American American American American American
piece piece piece piece piece piece piece piece piece piece piece piece piece
safety safety safety safety safety safety safety safety safety safety safety
remembered remembered remembered remembered remembered remembered remembered
Bronze Bronze Bronze Bronze Bronze Bronze Bronze Bronze Bronze Bronze Bronze
sheath sheath sheath sheath sheath sheath sheath sheath sheath sheath sheath
didn't didn't didn't didn't didn't didn't didn't didn't didn't didn't didn't
gadgets gadgets gadgets gadgets gadgets gadgets gadgets gadgets gadgets gadgets
Monopoly Monopoly Monopoly Monopoly Monopoly Monopoly Monopoly Monopoly
umbrellas umbrellas umbrellas umbrellas umbrellas umbrellas umbrellas umbrellas
margarine margarine margarine margarine margarine margarine margarine margarine
cat's-eyes cat's-eyes cat's-eyes cat's-eyes cat's-eyes cat's-eyes cat's-eyes
invention invention invention invention invention invention invention invention

Accuracy/speed practice

THE SAFETY PIN

	Words
One day in 1849 an American called Walter Hunt fiddled around with	14
a piece of wire for a couple of hours and - invented the safety pin!	28
It wasn't his only invention - among other things he designed a	41
special type of shoe to enable people to walk safely up walls - but	55
it is the one for which he is remembered.	63
People have been using pins to fasten their clothes since the	76
Bronze Age, but only Walter Hunt had the idea of fitting a sheath	90
so that the sharp end of the pin didn't stick into you.	101
Mr Hunt himself wasn't too sharp - about money at least. He dreamt	116
up the safety pin to pay off a debt and made only about £200 from it.	130
We are all surrounded by wonderful ideas and gadgets that we just	144
take for granted, but how did they start? What's the story behind	157
tin openers, zips, ballpoint pens, Monopoly, umbrellas, margarine	171
and many, many more? And, more recently, what about cat's-eyes in	185
the road, which have probably contributed more to road safety in	198
recent years than any other invention?	216

MANUAL TYPEWRITERS

Strike each key briskly with the tips of the fingers. Don't push at the keys, or the letters you type will have a "fuzzy" look with a slight shadow.

Carriage return   Hold the fingers of the left hand flat and almost close together, and strike the lever between the first and second joints of the first finger. Don't push or drag the carriage return lever across the typewriter, as this wastes energy, breaks the typing rhythm and causes mistakes.

Return the fingers to the "home keys" at once after returning the carriage.

ELECTRIC TYPEWRITERS

Use a light, tapping stroke, bringing fingers down gently to tap the keys. Don't hit the keys, as this will cancel out the advantages of easy electric keyboard striking.

Carriage return   Touch the carriage return key with a flicking motion of the right little finger and instantly return the finger to its "home key" (semi-colon) position. Don't punch the carriage return key or linger on it; don't start typing before the carriage has fully returned to the margin.

The conventional electric typewriter has a slightly higher keyboard than the manual and needs a slightly more sloping forearm position.

The electronic typewriter keyboard is approximately the same height as that of a manual.

LINE SPACING

```
This is an example of
typing in single line
spacing.
```

```
This is an example of

typing in 1½ line

spacing.
```

```
This is an example of

typing in double line

spacing.
```

MARGINS

These set the starting point on the left of your typing paper and the stopping point on the right of your typing paper. They are used to give a "frame" of plain paper around your typing, to give it an attractive appearance.

A bell rings several spaces before the right hand margin stop, to warn you that you have only a few spaces left in which to type. It is important to listen for your bell and find out how many spaces your typewriter gives you before the margin stops you. The number of spaces varies on different makes of typewriter. On all typewriters there is a "margin release" which (later on) you will need to use so that you are able to complete a short word.

Listen for the bell

Preparation for accuracy/speed practice

Micro-electronics Micro-electronics Micro-electronics Micro-electronics

laser laser laser laser laser laser laser laser laser laser laser laser laser

registration registration registration registration registration registration

interesting interesting interesting interesting interesting interesting

terminals terminals terminals terminals terminals terminals terminals terminals

withdrawing withdrawing withdrawing withdrawing withdrawing withdrawing

identification identification identification identification identification

Accuracy/speed practice

THE CASHLESS SOCIETY

	Words
The truly "cashless" society may never completely come to pass,	13
but if the present plans of the banks go ahead, payments by	25
plastic card may become the norm, rather than the exception as	38
at present.	40
In 1982, the Office of Fair Trading published a report entitled	54
"Micro-electronics and Retailing". In addition to examining the	68
production of till slips in supermarkets by the laser scanning of	81
bar-coded goods, rather than the manual registration of prices by	94
the cashier, it also gives an interesting glimpse into banking in	107
the future.	110
The banks have already introduced electronic funds transfer (EFT)	123
internally and on an inter-bank basis. Now, their customers can	137
obtain cash by inserting a plastic card into a cash dispenser and	150
keying in their personal identification number (PIN).	161
From this it is not too far a step to allow account holders to pay	175
for goods at the corner shop, supermarket or department store by	188
installing EFT terminals at the point of sale. The customer	201
would place the card into the terminal, key in the PIN and instead	215
of receiving cash, the retailer's account would be credited with	228
the amount of the transaction and the customer's account debited.	241
The customer will be charged for each transaction, just as a	254
charge is made at present for withdrawing money from a current	266
account by way of a cheque.	272

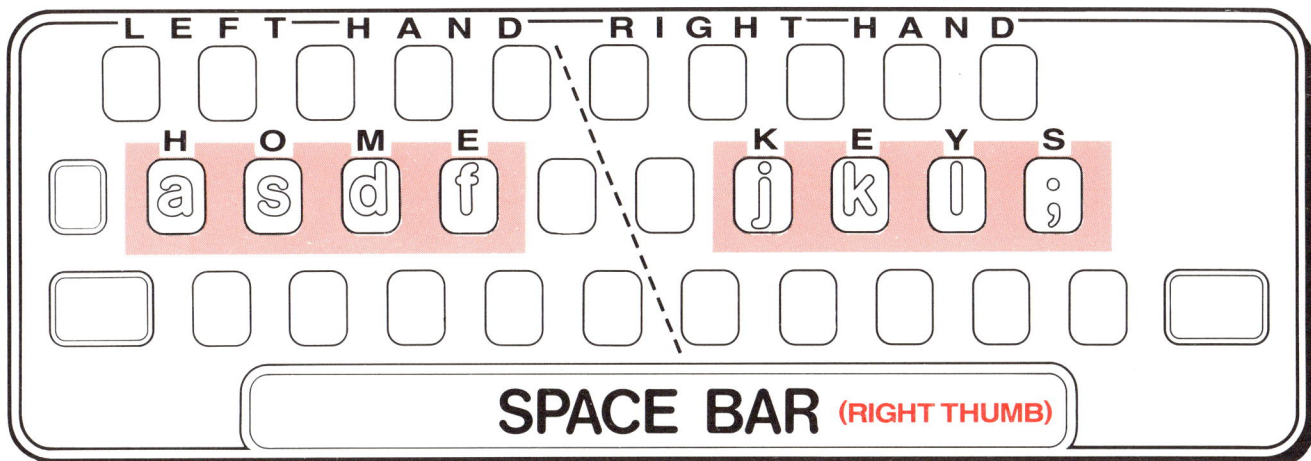

LEFT HAND **RIGHT HAND**

HOME **KEYS**

a s d f j k l ;

SPACE BAR (RIGHT THUMB)

THE HOME KEYS

Practise finding the home keys WITHOUT LOOKING

The home keys are:

a s d f (left hand)   j k l ; (right hand)

From these eight keys all the other keys are found on the typewriter keyboard. First finger keys on each hand are: (left) "f" and (right) "j". Place your two first (index) fingers on these keys and your other fingers on the remaining six keys. Your hands are now in the "home position". You have to train your fingers to find this position each time you start to type. Eventually, you will be able to start typing without having to start with the home position but you will have to use it for a long time yet.

Finding the home position

Without looking (keep your eyes on the chart at the top of this page or on the wallchart in your classroom), place your fingers on the space bar, then move them, lightly, to the bottom row of keys. From there, move gently to the "home row". Adjust your fingers so that when you move your first fingers to right and left you can feel the keys for "g" and "h". If you cannot, take your hands away from the keyboard, and start again. When you think your hands are in the correct position, *then* look down to check. Repeat this several times until it begins to feel easy.

THE SPACE BAR

Use your **right thumb** for pressing down the space bar, unless you are left-handed, in which case use your left thumb, if you find it easier; but **always use the same thumb** – whichever one you prefer.

A space is made on your typing paper by depressing the space bar once. This is the space shown between each group of letters, and later, between each word.

14

Preparation for accuracy/speed practice

pioneer pioneer pioneer pioneer pioneer pioneer pioneer pioneer pioneer pioneer

displayed displayed displayed displayed displayed displayed displayed displayed

friends friends friends friends friends friends friends friends friends friends

mathematics mathematics mathematics mathematics mathematics mathematics

graduating graduating graduating graduating graduating graduating graduating

industrial industrial industrial industrial industrial industrial industrial

structure structure structure structure structure structure structure structure

society's society's society's society's society's society's society's society's

mechanical mechanical mechanical mechanical mechanical mechanical mechanical

calculating calculating calculating calculating calculating calculating

forerunners forerunners forerunners forerunners forerunners forerunners

engineer engineer engineer engineer engineer engineer engineer engineer engineer

Isambard Brunel Isambard Brunel Isambard Brunel Isambard Brunel Isambard Brunel

profit-sharing profit-sharing profit-sharing profit-sharing profit-sharing

stimulate stimulate stimulate stimulate stimulate stimulate stimulate stimulate

Accuracy/speed practice

CHARLES BABBAGE

	Words
Charles Babbage, pioneer of the computer, was born in 1791. He	13
was the son of a banker, and displayed his practical skill when	26
he was very young. As a student at Cambridge, Babbage and his	39
friends set out to reform English mathematics. After graduating in	53
1814, he devoted himself mainly to reforming society's industrial	66
structure until 1820, when he became more and more interested in	79
mechanical means of calculating tables of figures, and, eventually,	93
the forerunners of the modern computer. One of Babbage's friends	107
was Isambard Brunel, a famous engineer of the times.	118
Babbage also became interested in the factory workers of his age,	131
and proposed a simple form of profit-sharing to help improve	144
workers' rates of pay and stimulate their interest in the prosperity	158
of their employers. The latter were not very interested in Babbage's	172
scheme.	174
Babbage's experiences were used by Charles Dickens in some of the	188
office scenes in LITTLE DORRIT.	194

SPACE BAR

Set your margins on A4 paper as follows: elite left hand 19   right hand 81
pica left hand 10   right hand 72

Margins

Typing home key "f"

Practise finding the home keys several times, then type the lines below. Leave one space (tap space bar once) between each group of letters. Do not attempt to type the numbers at the beginning of each line.

When you make a mistake, just ignore it and repeat the group of letters.

Do not type over a mistake, either now or at any other time.

1	fff fff fff fff fff fff fff fff fff fff fff fff fff fff fff ff
2	ffff ffff ffff ffff ffff ffff ffff ffff ffff ffff ffff ffff ff
3	ff ff ff ff ff ff ff ff ff ff ff ff ff ff ff ff ff ff ff ff
4	ff fff ff fff ff fff ff fff ff fff ff fff ff fff ff fff ff fff

New key

Say the letters quietly

Typing home key "j"

Practise finding the home keys several times. Then type the lines below.

5	jjj jjj jjj jjj jjj jjj jjj jjj jjj jjj jjj jjj jjj jjj jjj jj
6	jjjj jjjj jjjj jjjj jjjj jjjj jjjj jjjj jjjj jjjj jjjj jjjj jj
7	jj jj jj jj jj jj jj jj jj jj jj jj jj jj jj jj jj jj jj jj
8	jj jjj jj jjj jj jjj jj jjj jj jjj jj jjj jj jjj jj jjj jj jjj

New key

TAP keys lightly DO NOT hold them down

Typing home keys "f" and "j"

9	jjj fff jjj fff jjj fff jjj fff jjj fff jjj fff jjj fff jjj ff
10	jfj jfj jfj jfj jfj jfj jfj jfj jfj jfj jfj jfj jfj jfj jfj jf
11	fjf fjf fjf fjf fjf fjf fjf fjf fjf fjf fjf fjf fjf fjf fjf fj
12	jffj jffj jffj jffj jffj jffj jffj jffj jffj jffj jffj jffj jf
13	fjfj fjfj fjfj fjfj fjfj fjfj fjfj fjfj fjfj fjfj fjfj fjfj fj
14	jfjf jfjf jfjf jfjf jfjf jfjf jfjf jfjf jfjf jfjf jfjf jfjf jf

Listen for the bell

15

Preparation for accuracy/speed practice

particular particular particular particular particular particular particular
representative representative representative representative representative
subscriptions subscriptions subscriptions subscriptions subscriptions
privileges privileges privileges privileges privileges privileges privileges
entitled entitled entitled entitled entitled entitled entitled entitled entitled
conditions conditions conditions conditions conditions conditions conditions
policy policy policy policy policy policy policy policy policy policy policy
affects affects affects affects affects affects affects affects affects affects
attached attached attached attached attached attached attached attached attached
views views views views views views views views views views views views views
officials officials officials officials officials officials officials officials
decisions decisions decisions decisions decisions decisions decisions decisions
majority majority majority majority majority majority majority majority majority
accepted accepted accepted accepted accepted accepted accepted accepted accepted

Accuracy/speed practice

THE TRADE UNION AND THE INDIVIDUAL

	Words
If you go to work for a large firm, where a particular trade union	13
is represented, you may be asked to join that union by the union	26
representative who also works for the firm - his wages are paid by	40
the employer, not by the trade union. He (or she) is elected as a	54
representative by the trade union members. The representative may	67
be called a shop steward, and is the link between the union and its	81
members at the particular workplace. He will give you details of	94
subscriptions and rights and privileges to which you are entitled.	108
He is also the person to whom you should apply if you feel that	121
your pay and/or conditions of work need to be improved. The shop	134
steward will also keep you informed of union policy as it affects	147
you.	149
As a union member, you will be attached to a local "branch" of the	163
union. Here you make your views known about any aspect of your	176
local working conditions to the branch officials. A vote is taken	189
on all issues and decisions discussed at the branch meeting, with	202
the majority view being accepted.	209

SPACE BAR

A4

Margin 19 elite / 10 pica   **Margin** 81 elite / 72 pica

Practise keys learned

1   fff jjj jfj fjf jffj fjjf jjj fff jfj fjf jffj fjjf jjj fff fj

2   fjfj fjfj jfjf jfjf ffff jjjj ffjj jjff ffff jjjj ffjj jjff jf

First finger reach from home key "f" to top row key "r"

New key

3   fff rrr fff rrr fff rrr fff rrr fff rrr fff rrr fff rrr fff rr

4   frf frf frf frf frf frf frf frf frf frf frf frf frf frf frf fr

5   frr frr frr frr frr frr frr frr frr frr frr frr frr frr frr fr

6   frfr frfr frfr frfr frfr frfr frfr frfr frfr frfr frfr frfr fr

7   frrf frrf frrf frrf frrf frrf frrf frrf frrf frrf frrf frrf fr

8   rffr rffr rffr rffr rffr rffr rffr rffr rffr rffr rffr rffr rf

9   fff rrr frf frfr frrf rffr fff rrr frf frfr frrf rffr fff rrrr

10 frf rfr ffrr rrff rffr frrf ffrr rrff rffr frrf ffrr rrff rffr

Wrists UP!

Feet flat!

First finger reach from home key "j" to top row key "u"

New key

11 jjj uuu jjj uuu jjj uuu jjj uuu jjj uuu jjj uuu jjj uuu jjj uu

12 juj juj juj juj juj juj juj juj juj juj juj juj juj juj juj ju

13 juu juu juu juu juu juu juu juu juu juu juu juu juu juu juu ju

14 juju juju juju juju juju juju juju juju juju juju juju juju ju

15 ruuj ruuj ruuj ruuj ruuj ruuj ruuj ruuj ruuj ruuj ruuj ruuj ru

16 fruj fruj fruj fruj fruj fruj fruj fruj fruj fruj fruj fruj fr

17 jurf jurf jurf jurf jurf jurf jurf jurf jurf jurf jurf jurf jr

TAP keys lightly

Eyes on book

Repeat keys learned

18 fjfj fjfj jfjf jfjf ffjj ffjj fffj jjjf fjfj jfjf ffjj jjff jj

19 frf frf frfr frfr frrf frrf rffr rffr fff rrr frf frfr frrf rf

20 juju juju ruuj ruuj fruj fruj jurf jurf juju ruuj fruj jurf ju

21 jjjj uuuu juju juju ruuj fruj jurf uuuu jjjj juju juuu juju jr

Twelve-second drills

1 I do not think they will stay very long.
2 This is a rule known to all the men here.
3 They own the land by the fork in the road.
4 If we do a job, we like to do it very well.
5 A bird in the hand is worth two in the bush.

6 We shall be glad to learn if it is all right.
7 Just now it is not wise to ask him to go away.
8 In a few days we shall return the goods to you.
9 On the day we shall be at the start of the road.
10 The morning was long but the afternoon was short.

11 I find that I like to know a lot about my friends.
12 We are glad that you will take care of this matter.
13 You are doing your work to the best of your ability.
14 They are the ones on whom we shall call for more tea.
15 I wanted to start the job as soon as I possibly could.

16 Every man wishes to live long, but no man would be old.
17 We shall be very glad if he can get the new ones for us.
18 They were not pleased to hear that we shall not be there.
19 He thinks she can manage to get the letter signed clearly.
20 If the dresses are made well, the girl will buy them often.

21 Send it to us if they do not want to spend the money for it.
22 He wonders where he may go after he gets well enough to work.
23 They want to finish the job today, so try to give them a hand.
24 This is quite a good game, and it does not need much equipment.
25 They own the land by the fork in the road, near the pretty farm.

26 Most of them will come in later on, when they have done the jobs.
27 The pair made a very big hit, and many boys and girls came to see.
28 This man is the head of a huge firm and he needs a new office girl.
29 This girl may try for the job but she may find it too far from home.
30 But in any case, she may ring up first to ask if he wants to see her.

31 We may not always find the things that are worth doing, easy at first.
32 To do the things we most want to do, we need to study most of each day.
33 It is up to us to build our skill little by little with daily practices.
34 From the work you have done so far you know how easy it is to do it well.
35 It should be a simple thing for you to work until you can type quite fast.

36 It is the only one of its kind, and it should not be used by all the girls.
37 Try to let us know as soon as you can if it will be ready for us on the day.
38 Put it on top of the box when you get it so that I can see it when I come in.
39 I hope you will be able to come early so that we shall not lose too much time.
40 Let me know the date it might be, and then I can write it down in the notebook.

41 I want the man to go with me when I start the new job as he knows the way there.
42 It may be better to go on the bus when we are ready because the car is not ready.
43 We may not be able to tell at first, but if it looks nice, we can take it with us.
44 Do not try to do a great deal on the first day, or you will find you are too tired.
45 Come and stay with us when you can, and we will see to it that you have a nice time.

SPACE BAR

A4	**Margin** 19 elite / 10 pica	**Margin** 81 elite / 72 pica

Practise keys learned

1 fjjf fjjf fjfj fjfj ffjj ffjj ffrr ffrr frrf frrf rffr rffr fr

2 rju rju frju frju ujrf ujrf jur jur fur fur ruff ruff fur fur

Practise finding the home keys WITHOUT LOOKING

Typing home key "d"

New key

3 ddd fff ddd fff ddd fff ddd fff ddd fff ddd fff ddd fff ddd ff

4 fdf fdf fdf fdf fdf fdf fdf fdf fdf fdf fdf fdf fdf fdf fdf fd

5 fdd fdd fdd fdd fdd fdd fdd fdd fdd fdd fdd fdd fdd fdd fdd fd

6 dfd dfd dfd dfd dfd dfd dfd dfd dfd dfd dfd dfd dfd dfd dfd df

Repeat keys learned

7 dfjj dfjj dfjj jfdd jfdd jfdd djru drju drju dujrf dujrf dujrf

8 fjdd fjdd fjdd ujrd ujrd ujrd ffdd ffdd jjdd jjdd uudd uudd uj

9 fur fur fur fur fur fur ruff ruff ruff duff duff duff frju frj

Say "space bar" quietly in between groups of letters

Second finger reach from home key "d" to top row key "e"

New key

10 ddd eee ddd eee ddd eee ddd eee ddd eee ddd eee ddd eee ddd ee

11 ded ded ded ded ded ded ded ded ded ded ded ded ded ded ded de

12 deed deed deed deed deed deed deed deed deed deed deed deed

13 feed feed feed feed feed feed fed fed fed fed fed fed fed fed

14 deer deer deer deer deer deer reed reed reed reed reed reed

15 jeer jeer jeer jeer jeer jeer jeered jeered jeered jeered jeer

16 err err err err err erred erred erred erred erred erred erred

17 fur fur furred furred furred furred furred ruff ruffed ruffed

18 due due due dude dude dude rude rude rude free free free freed

19 referee referee referee refereed refereed freed freed freed

20 defer defer defer deferred deferred deferred deferred deferred

Feet flat!

Remove paper from machine with the paper release lever

17

Exercise 113

Type the following sentences (including the number at the beginning of each sentence), inserting an apostrophe where it has been omitted. Each exercise has *one* apostrophe missing.

1   For practice, we normally type on white A4 bank paper, but today its all gone, so we are using blue A4 bank.

2   Typing paper is sold in reams. A ream contains 500 sheets of A4. Usually, typing paper is ordered, in a firm, by one of the Chief Buyers assistants.

3   Good-quality typing paper, known as bond, is expensive and not to be wasted. Its in two sizes – A4 and A5.

4   Bank paper is generally used for carbon copies, as its thinner than bond. Its main advantage, though, is its cheapness.

5   Kates job is to issue typing paper on Mondays and Thursdays.

6   Re-cycled paper is paper that has been used once and is pulped and re-made into a cheaper type of paper. Its uses are many – paper bags, newspapers. Peoples homes often contain re-cycled paper.

7   Carbon papers are manufactured in several different colours. Coloured carbon copies are useful for identification of departments, branches, areas or sections. A typists time can be saved by using coloured carbons.

8   An offices paper economy is important and money may be saved by the co-operation of all the typists.

9   Cheaper paper should be used for inter-office communications known as memos but not for letters to outside firms. Theirs should always be on letter-heading printed on bond. Theres no need to use bond for memos.

10   The Post Office Preferred sizes of envelopes are given in the Post Office Guide.

Exercise 114

Complete the following sentences with one of the two words in brackets. Type on A4 paper, in single line spacing with double between sentences. Type numbers at the margin and leave 2 spaces after numbers before starting sentences.

1   In an attempt to find (whose/who's) van was blocking his entrance, our neighbouring firm's director telephoned all the offices in the road.

2   Twist, Swindle and Dunnem, solicitors, are anxious to trace any relatives of John Jennings (deceased/diseased).

3   For some time (passed/past) the staff in the Reception Area have been arriving later and later.

4   We shall all (loose/lose) our places in the queue if we do not hurry to the theatre.

5   There is an ancient (rite/right) or ceremony in connection with the opening of Parliament.

6   The bottles of wine had to be stored very carefully in the (cellar/seller) because the contents are affected by temperature.

7   We shall set (sail/sale) to the islands as soon as the ship is seaworthy.

SPACE BAR

A4

Practise keys learned

1 fee fee fee feed feed feed fed fed fed free free free freed

2 fur furred ruff ruffed deer reed reeded err erred jeer jeered

3 refer refer refer referred referred referred defer defer defer

4 defer deferred deferred deferred rude dude feud feud feud feud

Practise finding the home keys WITHOUT LOOKING

First finger reach from home key "j" to "h"

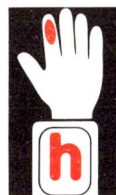

New key

5 jjj hhh jjj hhh jjj hhh jjj hhh jjj hhh jjj hhh jjj hhh jjj hh

6 jhj jhj jhj jhj jhj jhj jhj jhj jhj jhj jhj jhj jhj jhj jhj jh

7 jhh jhh jhh jhh jhh jhh jhh jhh jhh jhh jhh jhh jhh jhh jh

8 jhjh jhjh jhjh jhjh jhjh jhjh jhjh jhjh jhjh jhjh jhjh jh

9 fhhj fhhj fhhj fhhj fhhj fhhj fhhj fhhj fhhj fhhj fhhj fh

10 jhju jhju jhju jhju jhju jhju jhju jhju jhju jhju jhju jh

11 her her her here here here herd herd herd herded herded herded

12 hue hue hue hued hued hued heed heed heed heeded heeded heeded

Say the letters quietly to yourself as you type

Repeat keys learned

13 fur furred defer deferred ruff ruffed huff huffed deed freed

14 her here herd herded hue hued refer referred defer deferred

Wrists UP!

First finger reach from home key "f" to "g"

New key

15 fff ggg fff ggg fff ggg fff ggg fff ggg fff ggg fff ggg fff gg

16 fgf fgf fgf fgf fgf fgf fgf fgf fgf fgf fgf fgf fgf fgf fgf fg

17 fgg fgg fgg fgg fgg fgg fgg fgg fgg fgg fgg fgg fgg fgg fgg fg

18 fgfg fgfg fgfg fgfg fgfg fgfg fgfg fgfg fgfg fgfg fgfg fg

19 fggf fggf fggf fggf fggf fggf fggf fggf fggf fggf fggf fg

20 fgfr fgfr fgfr fgfr fgfr fgfr fgfr fgfr fgfr fgfr fgfr fg

Feet flat!

18

Exercise 111

Words that sound the same but are spelt differently are called *homophones*. Type the following sentences (including the number at the beginning of each sentence), and insert in the spaces the correct word from the two given in brackets. *Use your dictionary to check them.*

1   Personal letters are those we (right, write) to our friends.

2   The (Personal, Personnel) Department is the one in a firm which deals with appointing new employees.

3   Money may be withdrawn from a current account by making out a (check, cheque) to cash, or to self.

4   Continuous (stationery, stationary) is used for sets of forms such as invoices and orders.

5   All the employees in the firm will be (effected, affected) by the recession.

6   The typist typed a (draft, draught) of the important letter before it was finally approved.

7   We all felt (confidant, confident) that the outcome of the meeting would be favourable.

8   The balance sheet showed that the firm had made very little (profit, prophet) during the preceding financial year.

9   The clerk's handwriting was so (elegible, illegible) that it was almost impossible to read it.

10 The account that pays no interest is the (currant, current) account.

11 The (licence/license) required for a black and white television set is less expensive than that required for a colour television.

12 Modern oven (ware/wear) has become so attractive that it is quite suitable for bringing on to the table.

13 Evergreen trees are those which do not shed (their/there) leaves.

Exercise 112

Type the following list of words, choosing the one that is correctly spelt in each case.

receive/recieve
necessary/neccesary
accommodated/accomodated
possesion/possession
separate/seperate
foreign/foriegn
langauge/language
reccurred/recurred
occurred/occured
referances/references
paid/payed
assessed/assesed

SPACE BAR

A4

Margin 19 elite
10 pica

Margin 81 elite
72 pica

Practise keys learned

1 rug rugged hug hugged huge judge judged drudge drudged drug

2 drugged dredge dredged dredger edge edged egg egged judder

3 fur furred ruff ruffed err erred refer referred defer deferred

4 deed free freed her here herd herded fee hue hued heed heeded

5 judge judged hug hugged huge drug drugged dredge dredger egged

*Practise
finding the
home keys
without
looking*

First finger reach from home key "f" to bottom row key "v"

New key

6 fff vvv fff vvv fff vvv fff vvv fff vvv fff vvv fff vvv fff vv

7 fvf fvf fvf fvf fvf fvf fvf fvf fvf fvf fvf fvf fvf fvf fvf fv

8 fvv fvv fvv fvv fvv fvv fvv fvv fvv fvv fvv fvv fvv fvv fvv fv

9 fvfv fvfv fvfv fvfv fvfv fvfv fvfv fvfv fvfv fvfv fvfv fvfv fv

10 fvvf fvvf fvvf fvvf fvvf fvvf fvvf fvvf fvvf fvvf fvvf fvvf fv

11 fvfr fvfr fvfr fvfr fvfr fvfr fvfr fvfr fvfr fvfr fvfr fvfr fv

12 eve eve eve ever ever fever fever fever fevered fevered revere

13 veer veer veer veered veered veered reeve reeve reeve revered

*Tap the
keys
lightly*

Repeat keys learned

14 fur fur fur furred furred furred fee fee fee feed feed feed

15 defer defer defer deferred deferred deferred refer refer refer

16 referred referred referred feud feud feud feuded feuded feuded

17 her her her here here here herd herd herd herded herded herded

18 heed heed heed heeded heeded heeded hue hue hue hued hued hued

19 deed deed deed deer deer deer jeer jeer jeer jeered jeered

20 eve eve eve ever ever ever veer veer veer veered veered veered

21 rug rug rug rugged rugged rugged edge edge edge hedge hedge

22 hug huge huge fudge fudge fudge rudder rudder rudder urge urge

Wrists UP!

Elbows in

Practise using the hyphen and dash

Type one copy of the following sentences, correctly distinguishing between the hyphen and the dash. Use single line spacing for each numbered paragraph, with double between paragraphs. Type the numbers at the left hand margin, set your tabulator 2 spaces in from the margin for the start of paragraphs. Make your own line endings.

1. The first-class fare to Lowestoft by train was much too expensive — we all agreed to travel second-class.

2. Mid-December is not an ideal time to go on holiday, except to places such as North Africa or Australia, and this is the reason for lower tariffs in resorts in more northerly places — France, Holland, Belgium and Great Britain for example.

3. All compound numbers from 21 to 99 have a hyphen, when typed (or written) as words — twenty-one and ninety-nine are examples.

4. When dividing hyphenated words on the typewriter, at the right-hand margin the division should be made at the hyphen — co-operative, non-essential are examples of hyphenated words.

5. The self-satisfied look on her brother's face infuriated the girl — she left the room in silence.

6. Serbo-Croat is not a language known to most of us — can you speak it?

Keyboard diagram showing keys: e, r, u (top row); a, s, d, f, g, h, j, k, l, ; (home row highlighted); v, b, m (bottom row); SPACE BAR

A4 **Margin** 19 elite / 10 pica   **Margin** 81 elite / 72 pica

Practise keys learned

1   feed fed fee defer deferred refer referred feud feuded her

2   hue hued deer jeer jeered eve ever veer veered furred ruffed

First finger reach from home key "j" to bottom row key "m"

New key

3   jjj mmm jjj mmm jjj mmm jjj mmm jjj mmm jjj mmm jjj mmm jjj mm

4   jmj jmj jmj jmj jmj jmj jmj jmj jmj jmj jmj jmj jmj jmj jmj jm

5   jmm jmm jmm jmm jmm jmm jmm jmm jmm jmm jmm jmm jmm jmm jmm jm

6   jmjm jmjm jmjm jmjm jmjm jmjm jmjm jmjm jmjm jmjm jmjm jmjm jm

7   jmmj jmmj jmmj jmmj jmmj jmmj jmmj jmmj jmmj jmmj jmmj jmmj jm

8   jmju jmju jmju jmju jmju jmju jmju jmju jmju jmju jmju jmju jm

9   hem hem hem hemmed hemmed hemmed deem deem deem deemed deemed

10 germ germ germ gem gem gem gemmed gemmed gemmed mum mum mum

Practise finding the home keys without looking

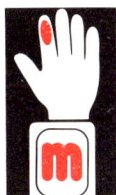

Repeat keys learned

11 fur furred ruff ruffed duff deed feed fed deer reed jeer veer

12 err erred due dude rude free freed refer referred defer feud

13 deferred her here herd herded hue hued heed heeded rug rugged

14 huge judge judged drudge drudged drug drugged edge edged edger

15 eve ever fever fevered revere revered veer veered reeve reeved

16 hem hemmed deem deemed germ gem gemmed mum hem deem germ gem

Keep your eyes on your book

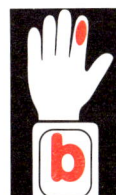

First finger reach from home key "f" to bottom row key "b"

New key

17 fff bbb fff bbb fff bbb fff bbb fff bbb fff bbb fff bbb fff bb

18 fbf fbf fbf fbf fbf fbf fbf fbf fbf fbf fbf fbf fbf fbf fbf fb

19 fvbf fvbf fvbf fvbf fvbf fvbf fvbf fvbf fvbf fvbf fvbf fvbf fb

20 frvb frvb frvb frvb frvb frvb frvb frvb frvb frvb frvb frvb fb

21 jmfvb jmfvb jmfvb jmfvb jmfvb jmfvb jmfvb jmfvb jmfvb jmfvb jb

Say the letters quietly to yourself as you type

20

Exercise 110

1 Type the following list of spellings, under the heading. Centre the list horizontally. Leave *at least one clear inch* before typing the heading.

WORDS FREQUENTLY SPELT WRONGLY

paid
recommend
fortunately
convenient
consequence
certainly
substitute
confident
professional
liaison
achieved
experience
disappointment
economics
field

2 Re-type the above list, putting the words into alphabetical order.

3 Type the following list, correcting it as you type.

DIFFICULT WORDS TO SPELL

achievment
foriegn
yeild
recieve
sensable
accesory
woolen
prefered
occured
apalling
neccessary
excitible
inevitible
proffession
dissipline
colledge

Check your list with your dictionary.

4 Re-type the above list, when you have corrected it, putting the words into alphabetical order.

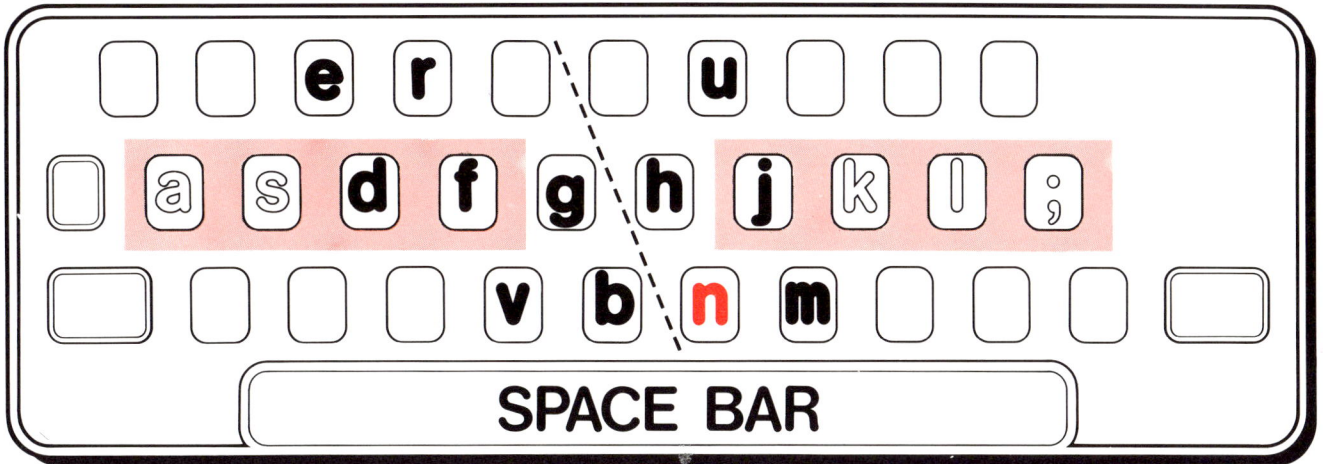

```
  e   r        u
a s d f g h j k l ;
      v b n m
```

SPACE BAR

A4

Margin 19 elite / 10 pica

Margin 81 elite / 72 pica

Practise keys learned

1 ebb ebb ebb ebbed ebbed ebbed bee bee bee bed bed bed bedded

2 bedded bedded beef beef beef beer beer beer rub rub rub rubbed

3 rubbed rubbed grub grub grub grubbed grubbed grubbed dub dub

4 furred feed free deed here judge judged ever veered hugged

5 hemmed refer referred defer deferred ruff ruffed jeered rude

Practise finding the home keys without looking

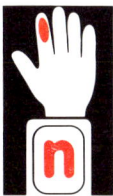

First finger reach from home key "j" to bottom row key "n"

n

New key

6 jjj nnn jjj nnn jjj nnn jjj nnn jjj nnn jjj nnn jjj nnn jjj nn

7 jnj jnj jnj jnj jnj jnj jnj jnj jnj jnj jnj jnj jnj jnj jnj jn

8 jnn jnn jnn jnn jnn jnn jnn jnn jnn jnn jnn jnn jnn jnn jnn jn

9 jnjn jnjn jnjn jnjn jnjn jnjn jnjn jnjn jnjn jnjn jnjn jnjn jn

10 jnnj jnnj jnnj jnnj jnnj jnnj jnnj jnnj jnnj jnnj jnnj jnnj jn

11 jnju jnju jnju jnju jnju jnju jnju jnju jnju jnju jnju jnju jn

12 been been been fern fern fern fun fun fun rub rub rub nub nub

13 nub nubbed nubbed nubbed never never never even even even even

14 evened evened evened run run run runner runner runner rung end

15 end end ended ended ended mend mend mend mended mended mended

16 fend fend fend fender fender fender bend bend bend bun bun bun

Return carriage smartly at the end of each line

Elbows in

Repeat keys learned

17 deed feed deer jeer err fur furred ruff ruffed due dude rude

18 her here herd herded hue hued heed heeded rug rugged hugged

19 huge judge judged drudge drudged drug drugged dredge dredged

20 dredger edge edged egg egged judder eve ever fever veer veered

21 hem hemmed deem deemed germ gem mum ebb ebbed bee bed bedded

22 been fern fun rub even run runner rung end mend fend fender

Wrists UP!

Exercise 109

Read through the following exercises, look up any words you think are wrongly spelt, and then re-type the exercises, correcting the spelling errors. There are *three* in each passage.

1   How should space be allocated between various departments and where should these be situated? For instance, perhaps a drawing office should be on the top floor to make the best use of daylight; should the male room also be on the top floor? Where should the cantene be? As bulk deliveries of food have to be maid to it, the obvious place would seem to be the ground floor, but this position may give difficulty in the dispersal of smells and heat.

2   When considering material for desks, would is often thought more suitable than metal, being lighter in wait, cheaper, quieter and warmer, also more easily repaired. For desk tops Formica is suitable for hard ware but where appearance is important, leather cloth is quite hard-wearing.

3   In the country, the post office is much more than a modern, competitive buisness. It has a social roll as well. Rural postmen collect outgoing mail, carry a range of stamps for all and can obtain postal orders for there regular customers. Many postmen collect pensions on behalf of the elderly and perform voluntary services like carrying prescriptions and small items of shopping for the housebound.

4   Most money passing over post office counters is that payed out or collected for goverment departments and local authorities. Without the income recived for this work, many offices would face closure - in the country as well as in many towns. A whole new range of services is being planned now that The Post Office is a separate organisation from British Telecom and country dwellers will be among the people who will benefit.

5   Some years ago, there was only The Post Office to deal with all aspects of communication, but nowadays we have Brittish Telecom as well. Some people may think we have benefitted from this change, but if you are writing a book about Office Practise, it is more difficult to collect information.

```
  e  r      u
a s d f g h j k l ;
    c v b n m
      SPACE BAR
```

Margin 19 elite
10 pica

Margin 81 elite
72 pica

Practise keys learned

1   freed freed grub grubbed dub dubbed fevered revere revered fur

2   feud feuded hue hued deer fed gemmed mummer veneer veneered

3   merge merged murmur murmured under render vend vended evened

Practise finding the home keys

Second finger reach from home key "d" to bottom row key "c"

New key

4   ddd ccc ddd ccc ddd ccc ddd ccc ddd ccc ddd ccc ddd ccc ddd cc

5   dcd dcd dcd dcd dcd dcd dcd dcd dcd dcd dcd dcd dcd dcd dcd dc

6   dcc dcc dcc dcc dcc dcc dcc dcc dcc dcc dcc dcc dcc dcc dcc dc

7   dcdc dcdc dcdc dcdc dcdc dcdc dcdc dcdc dcdc dcdc dcdc dcdc dc

8   dccd dccd dccd dccd dccd dccd dccd dccd dccd dccd dccd dccd dc

9   dcde dcde dcde dcde dcde dcde dcde dcde dcde dcde dcde dcde dc

10 cur cur cur cure cure cure cured cured cured recur recur recur

11 recurred recurred recurred curve curve curve curved curved

12 curved curd curd curd curb curb curb curbed curbed curbed cub

13 cub cub cube cube cube cubed cubed cubed church church church

Feet flat on floor

Return carriage without looking up

Repeat keys learned

14 fee feed fed free freed err erred refer defer herd herded rug

15 huge judge drudge egged eve ever veer veered revered hemmed

16 deem deemed germ gem mum mummer been even run runner end bun

17 fender bend ended cur curd curb curve cure cub cube cubed cud

18 recur recurred fence fenced hence dunce munch munched chum

19 much cuff cuffed beg begged rebuff rebuffed buff buffer buffed

20 muff muffed duffer church verger reference deference defence

21 bun burn under crude mud demure gummed hummed judge bung dumb

22 mug mugger mugged bend end ended mend mended creed crumb numb

Sharp brisk taps

FOR YOUR TYPING FOLDER 17

Follow previous instructions for typing these exercises (see page 77).

(see page 77)

A TYPIST'S REFERENCE BOOKS

1   A book that helps with difficult points of grammar is ....

2   A book that has words arranged in groups according to meaning is
     ....

3   Famous people still living are listed in ....

4   Famous people who are now dead are listed in ....

5   Explanations of how to write and speak to titled people are in
     ....

6   A large atlas contains maps, and also information about climate, products,
     population, terrain, rivers, oceans, lakes, ... and ....

7   A small encyclopaedia published annually is ....

8   .... Almanack is another general reference book published annually.

9   Everything in connection with postal services is explained in the
     ....

10   Everything a typist needs to know about work on the typewriter is contained in
     ....

SPOT THE SPELLING MISTAKES

There are *five* spelling mistakes in the following passage. Read it through first, then
type it with the corrections made, on A5 landscape paper with double line spacing.

Datapost provies a fast and reliable service for deliverying packets over-night
throughout Britian. The service now extends to many overseas countries. It can
be on a regular basis or as and when required. Datapost is increasingly popular
and has over 8000 customers. The range of material handled, from legal
documents to chemical samples, gets wider and wider. Their is a new "Datapak"
available which saves time and money on packing and transit charges.
International Datapost is growing all the time and now includes 15 countries
world-wide, with an "on-demand" service to 12 of these. Datapost is a Royal
Male service which has speed and reliability.

SPACE BAR

A4 **Margin** 19 elite / 10 pica   **Margin** 81 elite / 72 pica

Find home keys without looking

Practise keys learned

1 fee feed greed gruff cuff buff merge murmur render evened vend

2 recurred recurrence refer reference defer deference curve cube

3 hem deem runner fence dunce chum veneer veneered merger furred

Typing home key "k"

New key

4 kkk ddd kkk ddd kkk ddd kkk ddd kkk ddd kkk ddd kkk ddd kkk dd

5 dkd dkd dkd dkd dkd dkd dkd dkd dkd dkd dkd dkd dkd dkd dkd dk

6 dkk dkk dkk dkk dkk dkk dkk dkk dkk dkk dkk dkk dkk dkk dkk dk

7 dkdk dkdk dkdk dkdk dkdk dkdk dkdk dkdk dkdk dkdk dkdk dkdk dk

8 dkkd dkkd dkkd dkkd dkkd dkkd dkkd dkkd dkkd dkkd dkkd dkkd dk

9 kmdc kmdc kmdc kmdc kmdc kmdc kmdc kmdc kmdc kmdc kmdc kmdc km

10 eke eke eke eked eked eked meek meek meek deck deck deck check

11 check check checked cheek cheek cheek cheeked cheeked cheeked

12 keen keen keen keener keener keener neck neck neck bedeck

13 kerb kerb kerb knee knee knee creek creek creek creek creek

14 buck buck buck duck duck duck ducked ducked ducked chucked

Say each key quietly to yourself as you type it

Wrists UP!

Repeat keys learned

15 defer deferred fur furred refer reference referred need needed

16 her herd herded heed heeded hue hued jeer jeered eve ever even

17 hem hemmed deem deemed mum mummer ebb ebbed bed bedded beefed

18 rub rubbed grub grubbed been fern fun rub numb evened runner

19 end ended mend mended fend fender fended bend bender rung bun

20 cur cure cured recur recurred cube curb curbed church cuffed

21 beg begged rebuffed church reference deference defence dunce

22 eke meek check keen neck kerb knee creek bedeck buck ducked

Eyes on book

Back straight

23

A TYPIST'S REFERENCE BOOKS

The best possible dictionary must of course come first on the list of typist's reference books, followed by:

Roget's Thesaurus, which is a "treasury" of words, arranged in groups according to meaning, and is much more comprehensive than a dictionary.

Fowler's *Modern English Usage*, which helps with difficult points of grammar (eg whether to put in an apostrophe or not).

Who's Who gives information about famous people still living.

Who Was Who gives information about famous people who have died.

Black's *Titles and Forms of Address* explains how to write and speak to titled people.

A large atlas gives information about climate, products, population, terrain, rivers, oceans, lakes, boundaries and principal cities.

AA or *RAC Handbooks* contain useful maps, information about hotels, ferries, distances between cities, population.

Pears Cyclopaedia is a small, one-book encyclopaedia which is published annually and therefore nearly always more up-to-date than the larger multi-volumed encyclopaedias.

Whitaker's Almanack is another general reference book published annually.

The Post Office Guide gives information about everything in connection with postal services, and is issued (usually) every year by The Post Office.

The Typewriting Dictionary – this explains everything any typist can wish to know about layout, punctuation, paragraphing and correct ways of addressing letters and envelopes.

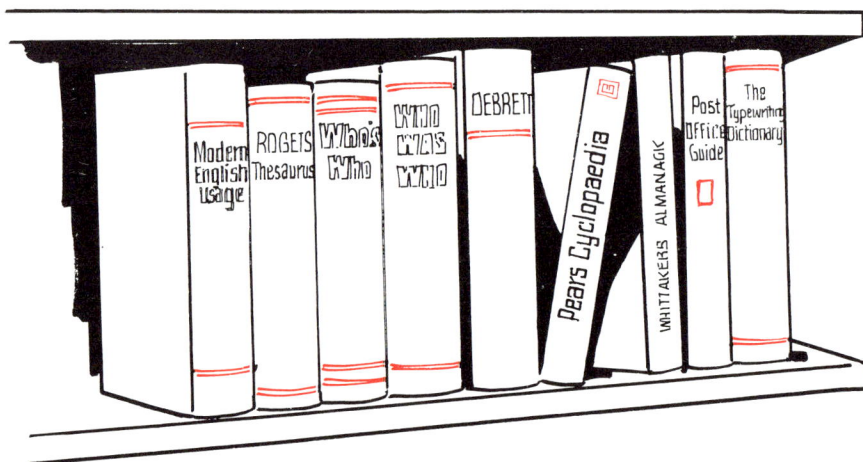

There are many, many more reference books available but the above 12 would enable typists in most jobs to cope with day-to-day queries and minor problems.

Keyboard diagram showing keys: e r u (top row), a s d f g h j k l ; (home row highlighted), c v b n m (bottom row), SPACE BAR

A4

Margin 19 elite
10 pica

Margin 81 elite
72 pica

Practise keys learned

1 deer free freer heed heeded jeered veered revered never even

2 rum dumb dumber green greener red redder fence fenced defence

3 reference church recurred beg begged check cheek cheeked creek

Find home keys without looking

Typing home key "s"

New key

4 ddd sss ddd sss ddd sss ddd sss ddd sss ddd sss ddd sss ddd ss

5 dsd dsd dsd dsd dsd dsd dsd dsd dsd dsd dsd dsd dsd dsd dsd ds

6 dss dss dss dss dss dss dss dss dss dss dss dss dss dss dss ds

7 dsds dsds dsds dsds dsds dsds dsds dsds dsds dsds dsds dsds ds

8 dssd dssd dssd dssd dssd dssd dssd dssd dssd dssd dssd dssd ds

9 dsde dsde dsde dsde dsde dsde dsde dsde dsde dsde dsde dsde ds

10 dress dress dress guess guess guess chess chess chess cheese

11 cheese cheese fuss fuss fuss fussed fussed fussed fuse fuse

12 fuse fused fused fused refused refused refused rush rush rush

13 desk desk desk desks desks desks musk musk musk cress cress

Eyes on book

Return carriage smartly

Repeat keys learned

14 furs feeds deeds reeds jeers errs ruffs dues frees herds hues

15 heeds rugs hugs judges drudges drugs dredges edges eggs sheds

16 eves fevers reveres veers hems germs deems gems ebbs bees beds

17 beers rubs grubs dubs ferns evens runs runners rungs ends buns

18 curs cures recurs curves curds curbs cubs cubes churches ekes

19 decks checks cheeks necks keen kerbs knees kedgeree bucks desk

20 rebuffs references dunces defences numbs numbers greens runner

21 sunk seek seeker check checked junk dusk bunk debunk bunked

22 musk duke dukes judges fudges duck deck buck bucks beck becks

Feet flat on floor

Back and arms straight

24

PREPARING FOR TYPEWRITING EXAMINATIONS

a) Arrive early in the typewriting room and practise a few alphabetical and figure drills from your typing textbook, to make sure your machine is in perfect working order. If it is not, report the fault to the teacher in charge of the examination (the invigilator) as soon as possible. Your typewriter should have been cleaned in readiness the day before, especially the typeface – clogged b's, c's, o's and p's could lose you marks.

b) Take with you hard and soft rubbers (the soft one for erasing on carbon copies), a pencil and whatever else you make corrections with. Intermediate and advanced typewriting examinations may require you to rule with a ballpoint, and for this purpose a fibre-tipped pen is the best – others collect "fluff" from the paper and make blobs, which look messy. For these later examinations a ruler will be needed, too.

c) Take with you backing sheets – A4 and A5 – new and uncreased, preferably on coloured paper (duplicating paper is useful) so that you do not get them mixed up with your typing paper.

d) In addition to the above, some paper tissues are useful, in case the room gets warm and your hands become sticky, leaving fingerprints on your worked exercises.

e) Take with you a card over which to erase, when there is a carbon copy in your typewriter. A postcard with a view on one side is ideal for this purpose. Small scraps of paper for rubbing out over *can* be left behind the top copy, and may cause a blank patch on your carbon copy!

f) Your typewriter ribbon should have been changed about a week before the typewriting examination, so that your typescript is not too dark and difficult to erase. If you think it is very faint, your invigilator will change it for you, but try to avoid this if at all possible. As long as your typing is readable, it will pass an examiner.

g) You will be asked to put away your typing textbook before the examination starts, but you MAY BE ALLOWED AN ENGLISH DICTIONARY so don't forget to bring this to the examination room with you. A dictionary helps to decipher writing or abbreviations you cannot read easily.

h) Most typewriting examination boards allow reading time before an examination actually starts, and, usually, candidates are permitted to make notes during this time, either on spare paper, or on the examination paper itself. Make sure you know what you are allowed to do in this reading time, and make the best use of it that you can. READ AND RE-READ all the instructions concerning the exercises slowly and calmly, so that you can understand them.

i) Once you have started typing, work steadily through until you have finished the last question. *Do not re-type any of the exercises until then.* Always remember that however badly you think you may have done one of the exercises, it is better than no exercise at all. Even a heading, or the first few words of a sentence may gain you one or two marks – which may mean the difference between pass and failure.

```
    e   r   t       u
  a   s   d   f   g   h   j   k   l   ;
        c   v   b   n   m
              SPACE BAR
```

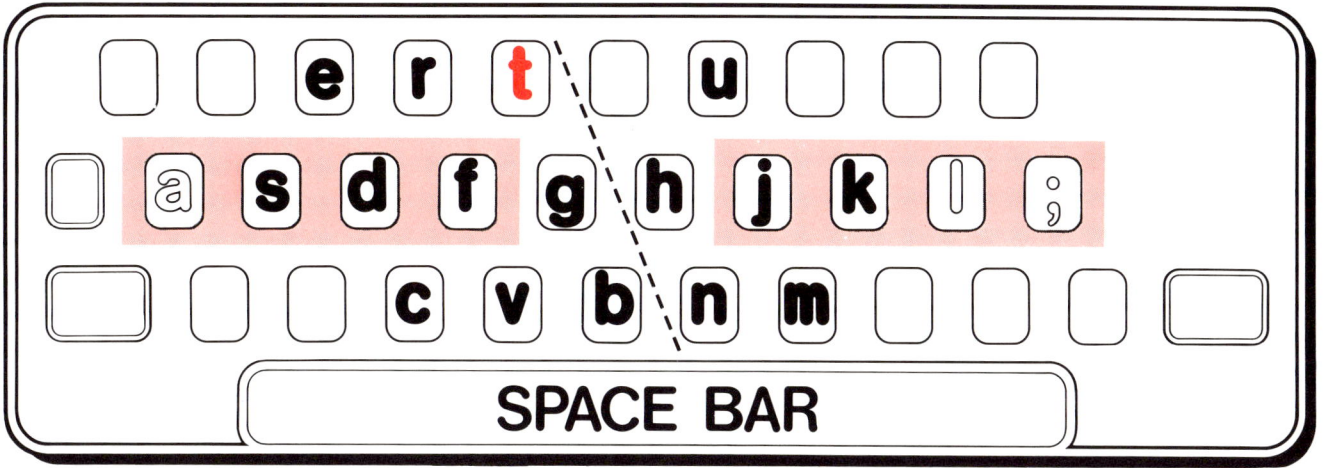

A4   **Margin** 19 elite / 10 pica   **Margin** 81 elite / 72 pica

Practise keys learned

1   cheeses fuses refuses refused rush rushes desk desks fuss musk

2   ducks bucks defers refers recurs veneers merges murmurs vends

Find home keys, without looking

First finger reach from home key "f" to top row key "t"

3   fff ttt fff ttt fff ttt fff ttt fff ttt fff ttt fff ttt fff tt

4   ftf ftf ftf ftf ftf ftf ftf ftf ftf ftf ftf ftf ftf ftf ftf ft

5   ftt ftt ftt ftt ftt ftt ftt ftt ftt ftt ftt ftt ftt ftt ftt ft

6   fhf fhf fhf fhf fhf fhf fhf fhf fhf fhf fhf fhf fhf fhf fhf fh

7   tht tht tht tht tht tht tht tht tht tht tht tht tht tht tht th

8   ftft ftft ftft ftft ftft ftft ftft ftft ftft ftft ftft ftft ft

9   ftfr ftfr ftfr ftfr ftfr ftfr ftfr ftfr ftfr ftfr ftfr ftfr ft

10 debt debt debt fret fret fret fretted fretted fretted let let

11 let letter letter letter jet jet jet jetter jetter jetter just

12 just just juts juts juts must must must muster muster muster

13 them them them then then then thence thence thence theme theme

14 tent tent tent tents tents tents tented tented tented tended

15 tended tender tender tender tenders tenders tenders jest jest

16 jest jests jests jests jester jester jester jesters jesters

17 jesters bet bet bet bets bets bets better better better best

18 best best nest nest nest vest vest vest crest crest crest

New key t

Wrists UP!

Fingers slightly curved

Repeat keys learned

19 feet jut duet meter metre drugget there the them these thus

20 event events bent refuses refused begged reference references

21 frees heeds jeers veers checks bedecks runners renders evens

Back straight

25

SECTION 6

Aiming for Accuracy

Keyboard diagram showing top row keys: e r t y u; home row: a s d f g h j k l ; ; bottom row: c v b n m; SPACE BAR

A4

Margin 19 elite / 10 pica

Margin 81 elite / 72 pica

Practise keys learned

1 tuft tufts tufted furs ruffs feeds jeers errs erred dues duet

2 duets hues herds heeds refers defers rugs hugs drugs edges

3 fever fevers fevered vent vents vented venture venturer verse

4 reverse reverses reversed stem stems stemmed three seven ten

5 seventeen teem teems tender tenders tendered tense tensed

6 tent tents tenure term terms terse theme then thence therms

7 net nets setter setters just must bet bets better best bested

Find home keys without looking

Return carriage smartly

First finger reach from home key "j" to top row key "y"

8 jjj yyy jjj yyy jjj yyy jjj yyy jjj yyy jjj yyy jjj yyy jjj yy

9 jyj jyj jyj jyj jyj jyj jyj jyj jyj jyj jyj jyj jyj jyj jy

10 jyy jyy jyy jyy jyy jyy jyy jyy jyy jyy jyy jyy jyy jyy jy

11 jyjy jyjy jyjy jyjy jyjy jyjy jyjy jyjy jyjy jyjy jyjy jy

12 jyyj jyyj jyyj jyyj jyyj jyyj jyyj jyyj jyyj jyyj jyyj jy

13 jyju jyju jyju jyju jyju jyju jyju jyju jyju jyju jyju jy

14 furry furry furry they they they ruby ruby ruby yet yet yet

15 jersey jersey jersey grey grey grey fussy fussy fussy dressy

16 dressy dressy fury fury fury yes yes yes merry merry merry key

17 key key keys keys keys keyed keyed keyed jury jury jury jetty

18 jetty jetty funny funny funny sunny sunny sunny nervy nervy

19 nervy ferry ferry ferry hurry hurry hurry duty duty duty duty

y New key

Say the letters quietly to yourself as you type

Repeat keys learned

20 urge urges urged urgent surge surges surged grey green red

21 redden redder cheese cheeses reeds reedy guess guesses guessed

22 guest guests church churches gruff gruffer grunt grunted grey

Remove paper from machine with the paper release lever

26

5   Make a copy of the form below and complete it with the details below. Use A5 landscape paper.

To: The Regional Director, Singapore Convention Bureau, SINGAPORE

Please send me information on:
Convention and conference facilities
Exhibitions
Accommodation
Sightseeing

Name _____

Title _____

Company/Association _____

Address _____

_____

Telephone No _____

Type of business/industry _____

Tick: exhibitions, accommodation and sightseeing.

Fill in Mrs Bradwell's name, address and telephone number. (Her title is "Mrs".)

Leave "Company/Association" blank.

For "Type of business/industry" type "Author of textbooks".

A4

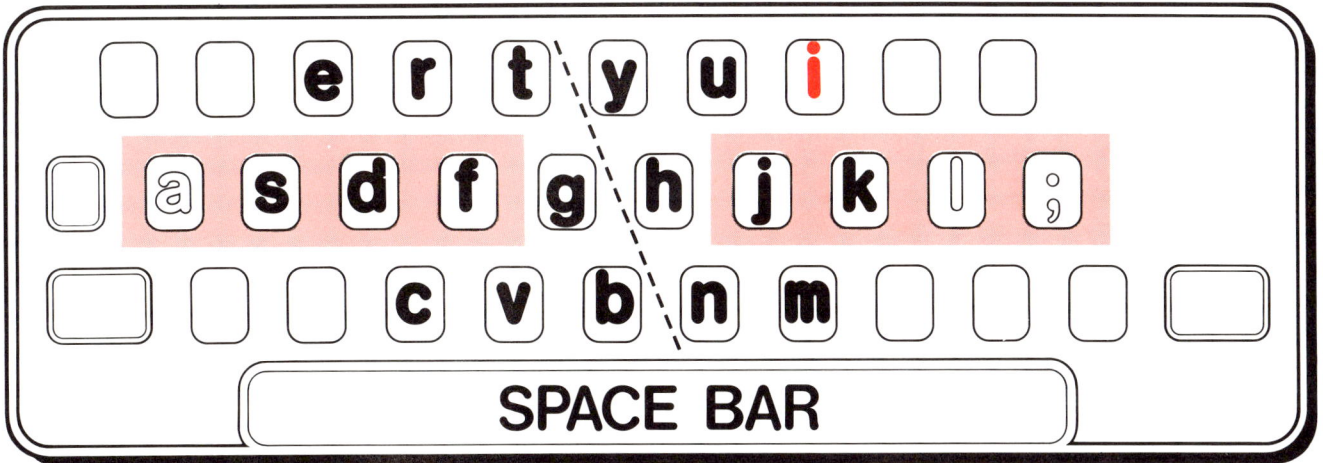

Margin 19 elite / 10 pica   **Margin** 81 elite / 72 pica

Practise keys learned

1   furry they yet yes jersey fussy dressy fury keyed funny ferry

2   hurry duty sunny merry seventeen tenders setters just must cub

Find home keys without looking

Second finger reach from home key "k" to top row key "i"

New key

3   kkk iii kkk iii kkk iii kkk iii kkk iii kkk iii kkk iii kkk ii

4   kik kik kik kik kik kik kik kik kik kik kik kik kik kik kik ki

5   kii kii kii kii kii kii kii kii kii kii kii kii kii kii kii ki

6   kiki kiki kiki kiki kiki kiki kiki kiki kiki kiki kiki kiki ki

7   kiik kiik kiik kiik kiik kiik kiik kiik kiik kiik kiik kiik ki

8   jki jki jki jki jki jki jki jki jki jki jki jki jki jki jki jk

9   his his his him him him this this this it it it its its its is

10   is is sit sit sit sits sits sits sitter sitter sitter sitters

11   sitters sitters suit suit suit suits suits suits suited suited

12   suited fine fine fine fines fines fines fined fined fined find

13   find find refine refine refine refines refines refines refiner

14   refiner refiner refinery refinery refinery infirm infirm

15   infirm inherit inherit inherit injure injure injure injury

16   injury injury injured injured injured ink ink ink inked inked

17   inked inked inky inky inky inset inset inset insert insert

18   insert inserts inserts inserts insect insect insect insect

Check position: wrists, arms, back, feet

Repeat keys learned

19   the desk is inky but he sits there with the guests in the firm

20   her green suit is very tidy but she refuses the bright dress

21   he fed the ducks but she tended the hens by the refinery

22   the seventeen runners ventured even further but never hurried

Keep your eyes on your book

27

3 Re-type the following page of manuscript, on A4 paper, with double line spacing.

LOOKING AFTER STATIONERY IN AN OFFICE → Centre

[Indented paragraph]

Stationery forms only a small part of the stock held in a firm, but it is becoming more and more expensive, and issues of stationery should be controlled carefully, for economy reasons. *[t/s]*

It is useful to have a list of all the items in the stationery *[outside of the]* cupboard attached to the door, and sent round to all staff *[stet]* likely to be ordering stationery, so that the requisition forms for ordering stationery can be completed from it.

Shelves in cupboards should be labelled. The cupboards must be kept locked, with keys in the possession of at least 2 people in case one *[stet]* is absent for any reason. Unlocked cupboards encourage the *[erase]* indiscriminate and haphazard issuing of stationery and also people to help themselves, with no records of who has taken which item.

Issuing of stationery must be carried out at certain times on pre-arranged days. No busy office worker can afford to be interrupted constantly and unexpectedly during a working day by requests for ballpoint pens or a typewriter ribbon. A notice stating times of issuing stationery should be *[t/s]* displayed clearly on the door of the stationery cupboard and could *[stet]* also be sent round with the list of stationery available.

4 Mrs Bradwell is planning a business trip to Singapore and wants 2 copies of the following information about flights, on A5 landscape paper.

[caps] Some of the Airlines to Singapore

Air India
Alitalia
British Airways
Burma Airways
Cathay Pacific
Czechoslovak
Bimein

Japan
KLM Royal Dutch
Lufthansa
Pan Am
Phillippines
Qantas
Royal Brunei

Sabena
Scandinavian
Singapore International
Thai Airways
[TWA] UTA French
Yugoslav

Keyboard diagram showing home row keys with SPACE BAR

A4 | **Margin** 19 elite / 10 pica | **Margin** 81 elite / 72 pica

Practise keys learned

1   her sister is in the nursery but she is very unfit

2   the seventeen bright dresses suit every buyer in the city

3   they think the figure three hundred is right

4   she met him by the trees in the summer time

5   his feet hurt but he did his best by resting by the fence

Practise finding home keys

Typing home key "l"

New key

6   sss lll sss lll sss lll sss lll sss lll sss lll sss lll sss ll

7   sls sls sls sls sls sls sls sls sls sls sls sls sls sls sls sl

8   sll sll sll sll sll sll sll sll sll sll sll sll sll sll sll sl

9   slsl slsl slsl slsl slsl slsl slsl slsl slsl slsl slsl slsl sl

10   slls slls slls slls slls slls slls slls slls slls slls slls sl

11   klsd klsd klsd klsd klsd klsd klsd klsd klsd klsd klsd kl

12   kill kill kill skill skill skill skills skills skills skilled

13   skilled skilled full full full fully fully fully fuller fuller

14   fuller fullest fullest fullest silly silly silly silliness

15   silliness silliness silkiness silkiness silkiness dull dull

16   dull duller duller duller dullest dullest dullest dulled dulls

17   dulls dulls till till till live live live lively lively lively

18   chill chill chill children children children keenly keenly

Say the letters quietly to yourself as you type

Eyes on book always

Repeat keys learned

19   the silly girl is in the tent by herself feeling thirsty

20   men skilled in engineering try every engine fully

21   the children ride by the bright river but they see very little

Return carriage smartly

2 Type the letter below, with one carbon copy and an envelope, to
Stanley Thornes (Publishers) Ltd   Educa House   Old Station Drive
Leckhampton Road   Cheltenham   Glos   GL53 0DN. The letter is to be
sent by recorded delivery. Today's date. A4 paper.

For the attention of Mr D Manley

Heading: Introduction to the Office   caps

I enclose the first 3 chapters of the above proposed book for your inspection and ~~evaluation~~ validate. Your comments together with those of your assessors will be of great interest.

NP/ [If you decide to publish my book, I would be prepared to send off the remaining chapters to you ~~by the~~ within six months.

As I mentioned to you on the telephone last wk, I also hv in mind an answer book and a supplementary exercise book, if you consider there is a market for them, but we can discuss these at a later date.

Yrs ffly

obviously

and I look forward to receiving them.

Encs

SPACE BAR

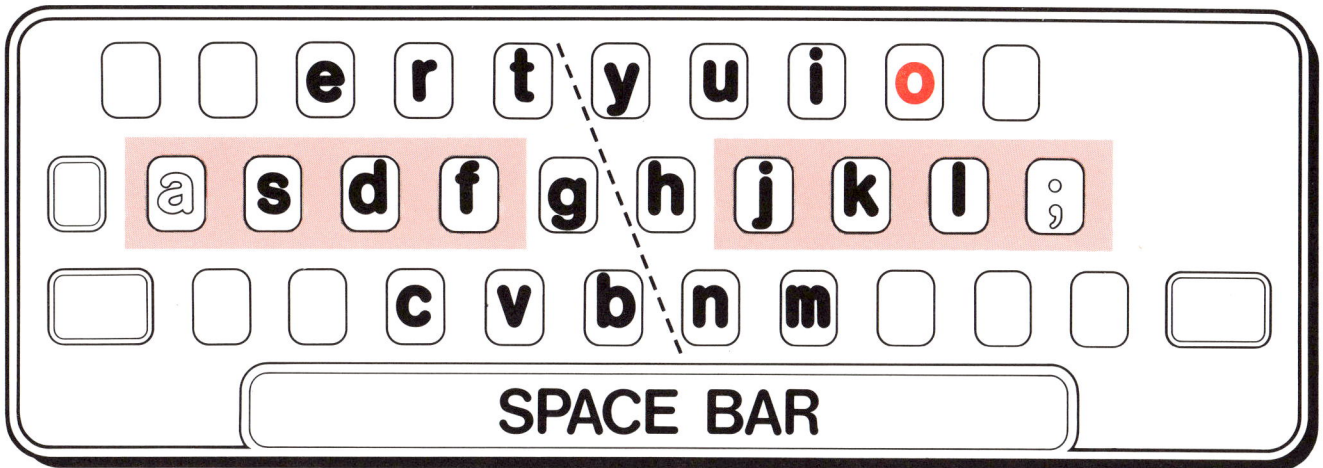

Margin 19 elite / 10 pica	**Margin** 81 elite / 72 pica

Practise keys learned

1   they fetched the turkeys by cycling three miles

2   there is little fuel in the bunkers but they still use diesel

3   three buyers like bright green in stylish dresses

Tap keys lightly

Third finger reach from home key "l" to top row key "o"

New key

4   lll ooo lll ooo lll ooo lll ooo lll ooo lll ooo lll ooo lll oo

5   lol lol lol lol lol lol lol lol lol lol lol lol lol lol lol lo

6   loo loo loo loo loo loo loo loo loo loo loo loo loo loo loo lo

7   lolo lolo lolo lolo lolo lolo lolo lolo lolo lolo lolo lolo lo

8   lool lool lool lool lool lool lool lool lool lool lool lool lo

9   solo solo solo solo solo solo solo solo solo solos solos solos

10 look look look looks looks looks looking looking looking

11 looked looked looked book book book books books books booked

12 booked booked tool tool tool tools tools tools stool stool

13 stool shoot shoot shoot shooting shooting shooting shout shout

14 roof roof roof roofed roofed roofed foot foot foot top top top

15 boy boy boy toy toy toy one one one four four four fourteen

Feet flat on floor

Fingers curved

Repeat keys learned

16 obvious serious trouble devious correct incorrect corrected

17 school collect collected collection collector common commoner

18 come go colour coloured colouring clock clocks clocked coded

19 it is obvious some children go to school for nothing but fun

20 his illness is not serious so he should recover soon

21 the collection of old clocks is mostly in the middle room

22 different colours form the very useful coding for documents

Wrists and arms straight

29

FINAL PROGRESS TEST

You help a writer of textbooks on office practice with re-typing some of her manuscripts and her business letters. Her name and address is Mrs Lorna Bradwell Cherrytrees   Victoria Avenue   Rushden   Northants   NN12 0NU. Her telephone number is: 73421.

1   Type the following A5 letter, with one carbon copy and an envelope, to The Manager   Barwest Bank PLC   High St   Rushden   Northants   NN14 3NU. The author's own address has to be typed at the top of the paper, followed by the reference (LB/your own initials), the date and the inside address.

Dear Sir   (Date for today)

I enclose a cheque for £150 which I would like paid

uc/ into my _investment_ _account_

NP No 7632218. [Could you please send me a statement of this account together

w ✓ (a statement of) my current a/c

No 89243710 — I do not seem to hv recd these for some months.

Yrs ffly

The keyboard diagram shows the home keys highlighted: **a s d f g** and **h j k l ;** with letters **e r t y u i o** on the top row, and **c v b n m ,** on the bottom row, plus the **SPACE BAR**.

A4   **Margin** 19 elite / 10 pica   **Margin** 81 elite / 72 pica

Practise keys learned

1   the boys left to go to the common for rugger or cricket

2   some girls like fussy dresses but most like bright colours

3   the routes to the church did not seem obvious to the boys

Second finger reach from home key "k" to bottom row key comma

4   kkk ,,, kkk ,,, kkk ,,, kkk ,,, kkk ,,, kkk ,,, kkk ,,, kkk ,,

5   k,k k,k k,k k,k k,k k,k k,k k,k k,k k,k k,k k,k k,k k,k k,k k,

New key ,

Leave ONE space after a comma, before typing the next word.

un, *NO SPACE before a comma*

6   book, tools, book the tools, the stool, they look, the fur,

7   the school, the boys, the clocks, the clocks tick every hour

8   hold the door for him to come through, for he is busy

9   your friend is coming to the house soon, so finish your food

10   it is right for them to give so much time here, not in school

11   the roof of the tool shed is off, so look out

12   his book is lost, but hers is on the desk, here

13   fourteen children should go, if they would like to

14   the flight is solo, so only the flier is there

Check: feet, wrists, arms, back

Repeat keys learned

15   our greetings were given to you by him, not her

16   they will be sitting together, on the bench

17   the girl injured her leg, but they took her home

Name : Mrs June Farmer
      20 The Riddings
      Ball Hill
      Coventry CV2 4RF

Tel. No. 419850

Date for today
Date of birth 24 August 1956
Nationality British
Typing speed 50 words a minute
Shorthand " 100 " " "

FOR YOUR TYPING FOLDER 16

Follow previous instructions for typing these exercises (see page 77).

HEADINGS ENCLOSED BY UNDERSCORE

1 With an "enclosed" heading, after the first line of underscore, turn up
.... before typing the heading.

2 Turn up .... before typing the second line of underscore, below the
heading.

3 Underscore should be started and finished over the .... and
.... letters of the heading.

TYPING ON LINES

1 When typing on lines, it is necessary to use the variable line spacer on the
typewriter so that letters with "tails" do not ....

2 When typing forms with dotted or continuous lines, leave .... space
after side headings before starting lines.

3 Always type forms in .... line spacing or .... line spacing.

4 Type lines slightly below side headings so that ....

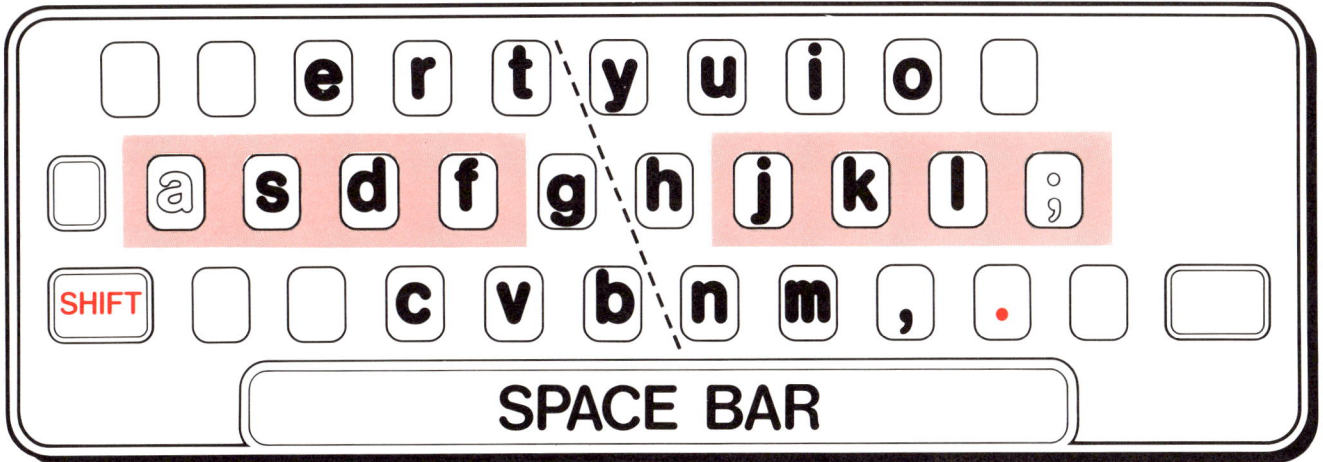

Margin 19 elite
10 pica

Margin 81 elite
72 pica

Practise keys learned

1 the stones rolled to the door, by the house

2 more children looked to see us, but the fog held

3 the luck of the lottery held, but the boys still lost

4 the business opened on time, so nothing could be done

New key

Third finger reach from home key "l" to bottom row key fullstop

5 lll ... lll ... lll ... lll ... lll ... lll ... lll ... lll ..

6 l.l l.l l.l l.l l.l l.l l.l l.l l.l l.l l.l l.l l.l l.l l.

7 l.. l.. l.. l.. l.. l.. l.. l.. l.. l.. l.. l.. l.. l.. l.

*Keep eyes
on copy
always*

Capital letters – left hand shift key

Use your LEFT little finger for the LEFT hand shift key to type capital letters on the
right hand side of the keyboard. Press the shift key FIRMLY and hold it down until
the letter is typed.

Leave TWO spaces after a fullstop at the end of a sentence.

New key

8 Jill is busy. Jill Hill is coming to the house soon.

9 Lily, hold the door for us. Lily Jolly likes bright colours.

10 Jim Hill likes cricket or rugger. Molly is his sister.

11 John Moon does not like school. Keith Mills loves his.

12 Look, the time on the clock over there is nine. Kim is here.

13 Jenny Jones is to run for the school. Lyn Kent is not.

14 Lucy Onions might come to the disco. Her sister should do.

15 Over there is the other tour. Let us join it for fun.

16 Your mother is coming to meet you. I hope mine is.

17 Nick Miller looks better. He is still not very fit, though.

*Tap keys
lightly*

Exercise 108

From the rough draft below, type a top and one carbon copy of the form with continuous lines; then complete the carbon copy from the details given on page 210.

Caps/ THE MIDLAND SECRETARIAL AGENCY

Frederick Rd

Edgbaston

Birmingham   B15   4NX

Sp caps/ APPLICATION FORM

Name _____

Address_____

_____

_____

Tel No_____ Date of birth_____

Nationality_____

Typing speed_____

Shorthand speed_____

Signature_____ Date_____

Keyboard diagram showing home row keys highlighted: a s d f g h j k l ; with e r t y u i o above, c v b n m , . below, SHIFT keys on both sides, and SPACE BAR.

Margin 19 elite / 10 pica   **Margin** 81 elite / 72 pica

A4

Practise keys learned

1 You ought to go to the meeting to be held here in the morning.

2 Joe took Jill to the circus in York, but she disliked it.

3 Young children often like circuses, so beg for visits.

4 Jill Jolly left her friends to go to see her mother in school.

Capital letters – right hand shift key

5 Ted. Fred. Green. Ted Green. Fred Green. Dick Grey.

6 Dick Green. Bob Dickson. Fred Dickson. Bob Coles.

7 Violet Smith. Fred Thomson. Dick Smith. Violet Brett.

8 Timothy Foster. Robert Foster. Robert Ellis. Bob Brett.

New key SHIFT

TWO spaces after a fullstop

Right and left hand shift keys

9 Jolly Ted Brett. Jill Green is coming. Joe Hill is here.

10 Ted Jolly is coming, too, but not by bus. He cycles to York.

11 Fred Smith goes to school in Bristol. His sister visits him.

12 Fur is cosy, but it is too hot for June. November is chilly.

13 Lily likes the cold, but Fred does not. It gives him coughs.

Keep eyes on copy always

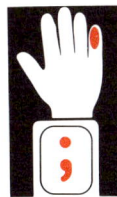

Typing home key "; " semi-colon

14 ;;; 111 ;;; 111 ;;; 111 ;;; 111 ;;; 111 ;;; 111 ;;; 111 ;;; 11

15 1;1 1;1 1;1 1;1 1;1 1;1 1;1 1;1 1;1 1;1 1;1 1;1 1;1 1;1 1;1 1;

New key ;

Return carriage smartly

Leave ONE SPACE after a semi-colon.

16 The fern is evergreen; it will look fresh even in December.

17 Send the letter soon; it needs to be received urgently.

18 The job should be yours; you must look tidy for your tests.

19 Fred is the cousin of Robert; they both like cycling to York.

Exercise 107

Type one copy of the form below on A5 landscape paper in double line spacing with margins on 1″ left and right. Leave 1″ minimum at the top.

BANKER'S ORDER

Account No   _____

To   _____

Address   _____

            _____

            _____

Date _____ Signature _____

Please pay to the account of the Friends of the Ashburton Museum, Barwest Bank PLC High Street Luton, the sum of _____ on _____ of this year and every succeeding year until further notice.

Special note:

    When breaking a line by a word (as above) leave **one space** before and after the word.

On the form you have prepared, type in the following details:

To Lloyds Bank PLC

High Street Bromswood Lanes T81 9B6

Date for today

Sign it yourself

The order is for £10 to be paid

on 1 January each year

Account No : 603273

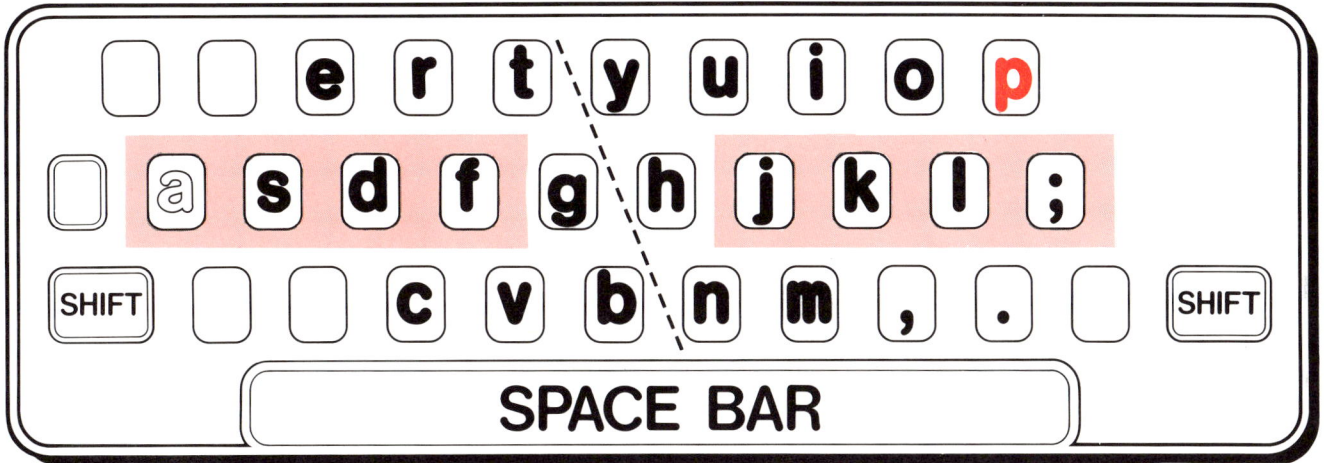

A4 | **Margin** 19 elite / 10 pica | **Margin** 81 elite / 72 pica

Practise keys learned

Single line spacing. Turn up *twice* between drills.

1   The school in York is for boys only, so Betty is entered for the school for girls in Chester.

2   In November or December, meetings held during the evenings should not be before seven.

3   The fogs in the cold months give some children chest illnesses but they no longer die from them.

4   Evergreen ferns thrive in good light; they must be given lots of moisture, too, during sunny months.

5   The girls going to the disco should be Sue, Molly, Eileen, Joy, Jill, but not June. She is still in Bournemouth.

Listen for the bell

Return carriage smartly

Fourth finger reach from home key semi-colon to top row key "p"

New key

6   ;;; ppp ;;; ppp ;;; ppp ;;; ppp ;;; ppp ;;; ppp ;;; ppp ;;; pp

7   ;p; ;p; ;p; ;p; ;p; ;p; ;p; ;p; ;p; ;p; ;p; ;p; ;p; ;p; ;p; ;p

8   ;pp ;pp ;pp ;pp ;pp ;pp ;pp ;pp ;pp ;pp ;pp ;pp ;pp ;pp ;pp ;p

9   ;p;p ;p;p ;p;p ;p;p ;p;p ;p;p ;p;p ;p;p ;p;p ;p;p ;p;p ;p;p ;p

10   ;pp; ;pp; ;pp; ;pp; ;pp; ;pp; ;pp; ;pp; ;pp; ;pp; ;pp; ;pp; ;p

11   l;p l;p l;p l;p l;p l;p l;p l;p l;p l;p l;p l;p l;p l;p l;p ;p

12   pool pool pool type type type typing typing typing typist

13   typist typist typists typists typists employ employ employ

14   employs employs employs employed employed employed employer

15   employer employer employee employee employee chop chop chop

16   choppy choppy choppy chopper chopper chopper chopped chopped

17   chopped ship ship ship ships ships ships shipped shipped

18   shipped skip skip skip skipper skipper skipper skipped skipped

19   skipped people people people telephone telephone telephone

ONE space after a semi-colon

Keep wrists UP!

33

TYPING A FORM WITH CONTINUOUS LINES

As when typing a form with dotted lines, move the platen slightly upwards before typing the underscore, so that when information is added by the typist, what is typed is in line with the headings.

Start typing lines 2 spaces from the side headings.

Exercise 106

Type a top and carbon copy of the form below on A5 portrait paper. Double line spacing. Margins 1″ left and right. Type heading not less than 1″ from top of paper.

STATEMENT OF PRIVATE TELEPHONE CALLS

Name   _____

Department _____

Extension   _____

Amount   _____

Date   _____

Take the forms out of your typewriter and complete the carbon copy with the following details:

Name: Michael Johnson.   Department: Sales (Export).   Extension No 137.   Amount owing: £3.20.   Date 1 December 198-.

Start typing the information where the lines start.

SPACE BAR

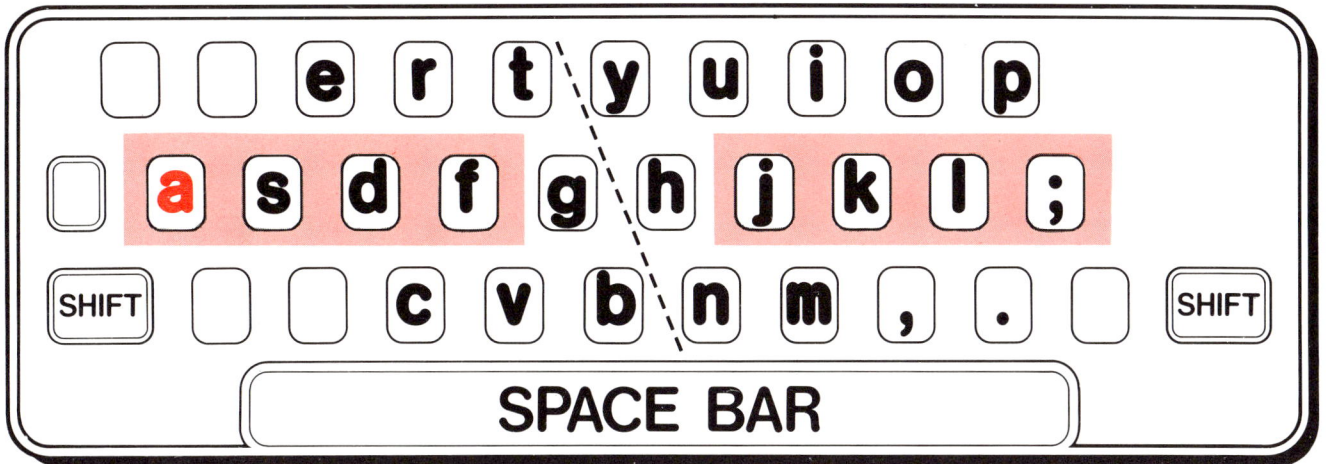

Margin 19 elite / 10 pica

Margin 81 elite / 72 pica

Practise keys learned

Single line spacing. Turn up twice between drills.

1   The typing pool does not employ the number of girls it once
    did; modern technology is reducing the number of jobs for
    copy typists.

Feet flat!

2   The crossing could be choppy; if the ship does go, the
    skipper recommends booking one of the berths. This helps you
    to sleep for most of the crossing.

3   The firm in the city employing the most people is one of the
    biggest, but even they could soon be chopping the number of
    their personnel if the recession continues.

4   The skill needed by everyone using teleprinters or computers
    is typing.

Tap keys lightly

Typing home key ''a''

New key

5   sss aaa sss aaa sss aaa sss aaa sss aaa sss aaa sss aaa sss aa

6   sas sas sas sas sas sas sas sas sas sas sas sas sas sas sas sa

7   ;aa ;aa ;aa ;aa ;aa ;aa ;aa ;aa ;aa ;aa ;aa ;aa ;aa ;aa ;aa ;a

8   sasa sasa sasa sasa sasa sasa sasa sasa sasa sasa sasa sasa sa

9   saas saas saas saas saas saas saas saas saas saas saas saas sa

10 ;a;p ;a;p ;a;p ;a;p ;a;p ;a;p ;a;p ;a;p ;a;p ;a;p ;a;p ;a;p ;a

Keep eyes on book ALWAYS!

11 all all all tall tall tall call call call lass lass lass and

12 and and has has has had had had ask ask ask asked asked asked

13 asks asks asks tasks tasks tasks make make make makes makes

14 makes made made made camp camp camp camps camps camps camper

15 camper camper camped camped camped late late late later later

34

Warm-up drill

1   Doing a job with zeal means doing it with enthusiasm, but something more than zeal may be needed - skill, expertise and experience, too - before real success can be achieved. This will not come quickly.

Revise typing measurements

2   The size of the pedestal desk that you ordered has now been changed to 145 cm (4' 9") instead of 137 cm (4' 6"). We hope this will be acceptable.

3   Card index boxes 127 mm x 76 mm (5" x 3") are now available in 6 colours - as well as the original mottled brown.

4   Manilla envelopes 90 mm x 140 mm (3½" x 5½") are at present out of stock. We hope to have fresh supplies in about 2 weeks.

5   The heavy-duty carpet, in dark green, 2 m wide, is still £5.50 per metre.

TYPING ON CONTINUOUS LINES

Instead of dotted lines, forms are sometimes typed with lines by underscore – a continuous line. Again, it is necessary to ensure that the "tails" of letters do not touch the line when completing these forms on a typewriter:

<u>Typing on a continuous line</u>   Right

Typing on a continuous line   Wrong

Typing on a continuous line   Wrong

Practise typing on a continuous line

With shift lock depressed, type a continuous line from margin to margin (margins on ½") on A5 portrait paper.

The underscore is a special repeater key on electric typewriters.

Take the paper out of the machine, re-insert it and type on the name of your school or college. Remember to make sure that the "tails" of letters clear the line, but are not too far above. Use your variable line spacer for this very fine adjustment.

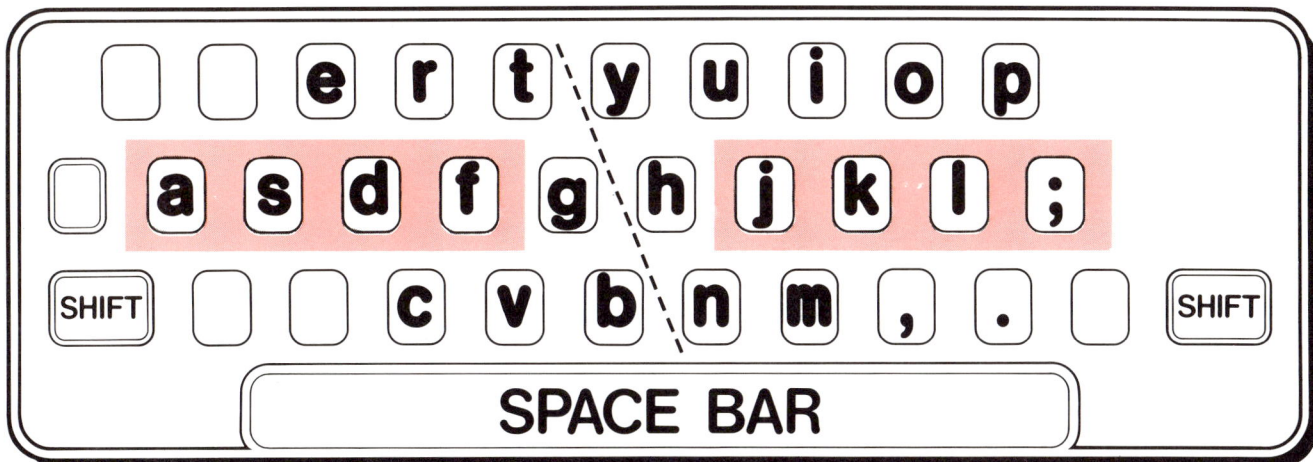

A4   **Margin** 19 elite / 10 pica   **Margin** 81 elite / 72 pica

Practise keys learned

1   Ted and Alan took Alice and Amanda to pay for the tea. All
    four of them had eaten very little, so the bill came to less
    than they thought.

2   The tents at the large camp site looked pleasant and roomy,
    but Tessa and Sarah did not stay. They had ideas about
    camping at the coast, near a beach, from Monday to Friday.
    Later, the party sailed for an island near to the French
    mainland. They all had plans to reach Paris by river.

Wrists and arms straight

TWO SPACES after a fullstop

Revise keys "g" and "h"

3   He had eggs; she had a gashed leg; lasses sell glasses.

4   He has a keg; Ada has some ale; she leads the goat to grass.

5   George goes to the game; Geoff guesses his team may lose.

Feet flat on floor

Revise home keys "f" and "j"

6   Freda and Jack took a train to the seaside, but the journey
    had to be broken because of fog. They came back to their home
    just in time to be faced by a fire in a house not far off.

Return carriage smartly

Revise home keys "d" and "k"

7   Dad likes pork, but Katy has fads and dislikes underdone meat.

8   She eats salads and asks for fruit, too. David likes cakes.

Listen for the bell

Revise home keys "s" and "l"

9   Pay the lass as she leaves the school or else she may sell it.

10 Sales of small items take place often on market stalls.

35

An alternative way to fill in a form on the typewriter is to start all the information at the same point, as in the example below.

Exercise 104

Type a top and one carbon.

```
JOGGING FOR HEALTH

A group will meet twice weekly to jog approximately
3 miles (morning or evening - to be decided).  If
you would like to join us, please complete the form
below and hand it (or post it) to:

Mrs Gill Bates
Archery Farm
Winyates
Bromswood
Lancs
T45 8BC


Name          Miss Janice Jefferies
          ...........................................
Address       49 Coppice Road
          ...........................................
              Bromswood
..................................................
              Lancs
..................................................
              T67 9BC
..................................................
Telephone No 293567
          ...........................................
Date          20 November 198-
          ...........................................
```

Exercise 105

Type a top and one carbon of the form above (typing headings only), take them out of your machine, and then, on the carbon copy only, fill in the details. Use double line spacing and set margins (for the form only) on 1″ left and right. Start typing about 1″ from the top of the paper.

Re-set your margin two spaces from the "o" in "No", for typing the details on the form.

SPACE BAR

A4

Margin 19 elite
10 pica

Margin 81 elite
72 pica

Revise home keys "a" and semi-colon

1 Take the plates to the tray and hand it to Ada as she passes.

2 Half an apple a day is good for teeth; a complete apple is better.

3 The dearest furs are the most attractive; it is not easy to make a choice.

Hold shift key down with little finger until letter has been typed

Third finger reach from home key "s" to top row key "w"

New key

4 sss www sss www sss www sss www sss www sss www sss www sss ww

5 sws sws sws sws sws sws sws sws sws sws sws sws sws sws sws sw

6 sww sww sww sww sww sww sww sww sww sww sww sww sww sww sww sw

7 swsw swsw swsw swsw swsw swsw swsw swsw swsw swsw swsw swsw sw

8 swws swws swws swws swws swws swws swws swws swws swws swws sw

9 swlo swlo swlo swlo swlo swlo swlo swlo swlo swlo swlo swlo sw

10 sweet sweet sweet sweets sweets sweets sweeter sweeter sweeter

11 sweeten sweeten sweeten write write write writer writer writer

12 writers writers writers week week week weeks weeks weeks weak

13 weak weak weaker weaker weaker weaken weaken weaken weakens

14 weakens weakens weakened weakened weakened awake awake awake

15 while while while when when when walk walk walk walks walks

16 walks walker walker walker where where where were were were

Keep eyes on copy ALWAYS!

Repeat keys learned

17 Sweep the camp site and make the place look tidy after we all leave; all hands to this task will make it easier.

18 We will all walk to the sweet shop while you are away in the town; we know where to find cheap sweets as well as good ones.

ONE SPACE after a semi-colon

Exercise 102

Complete the carbon copy of the form you have typed in Exercise 101 with the details on the form in the example below.

```
WOODPECKER RAMBLING CLUB


Membership Form

Name Miss Margaret Joanne Dixon
.............................................

Address Hillview
.............................................

57 Bath Street
.............................................

Ilkeston
.............................................

Derbyshire      DE6 7DB
.............................................

Telephone No 71854
.............................................

Date 14 November 198-
.............................................
```

Exercise 103

Type the following form on A5 landscape paper. Use dotted lines. Then complete it on your typewriter, for yourself.

Favourite Discs

Name :- - - - - - .   Age - - -

School - - - - - · - — - - - - ..

First choice - - - - — - - ..

Second choice - - - - — - .

Third choice - - - - - - - ..

Date - - - - - - -

Practise keys learned

1   Write the letter when you have time; we will wait for you.

2   It may take weeks to receive a reply; we wish it would not.

3   Walter, Anna, Poppy and Molly all took a coach for Manchester and planned to stay with an aunt there; the aunt was waiting for the little party when the coach arrived at the coach station. It was late because of bad weather and foggy roads.

Return carriage smartly – DON'T LOOK UP!

Third finger reach from home key "s" to bottom row key "x"

New key

4   sss xxx sss xxx sss xxx sss xxx sss xxx sss xxx sss xxx sss xx

5   sxs sxs sxs sxs sxs sxs sxs sxs sxs sxs sxs sxs sxs sxs sxs sx

6   sxx sxx sxx sxx sxx sxx sxx sxx sxx sxx sxx sxx sxx sxx sxx sx

7   sxsx sxsx sxsx sxsx sxsx sxsx sxsx sxsx sxsx sxsx sxsx sxsx sx

8   sxxs sxxs sxxs sxxs sxxs sxxs sxxs sxxs sxxs sxxs sxxs sxxs sx

9   sxsw sxsw sxsw sxsw sxsw sxsw sxsw sxsw sxsw sxsw sxsw sxsw sx

10   exit exit exit tax tax tax taxi taxi taxi taxed taxed taxed

11   mix mix mix mixed mixed mixed mixer mixer mixer extra extra

12   extra expect expect expect expected expected expected exercise

13   exercise exercise exercises exercises exercises exercised

14   exercised exercised exact exact exact exactly exactly exactly

Wrists UP!

Repeat keys learned

15   The taxi will wait by the exit at the back of the hotel, exactly where it is expected by the porter.

16   Do all the exercises every week; this is the way to attain extra skill.

17   John and Alexis are good mixers, but their friends Wendy and Max are not; they prefer to avoid parties and social events.

TYPING A FORM WITH DOTTED LINES

Special notes:

When typing forms with dotted lines, leave **one space** after typed headings, before the dotted line starts.

Always switch to double or 1½ line spacing, otherwise there will not be sufficient room to type in the information on the dotted lines.

Move the platen slightly upwards (using variable line spacer) so that the dotted line is a little below the heading.

The fullstop is one of the special repeater keys on an electric typewriter.

Exercise 101

Use A5 portrait paper for the form below, with both margins on 1″. Double line spacing. Leave at least one clear inch at the top. Type a top and one carbon.

```
WOODPECKER RAMBLING CLUB


Membership Form

Name
       ...............................................
Address
          ............................................

       ...............................................

       ...............................................

       ...............................................
Telephone No
                .......................................
Date
       ...............................................
```

Filling in a form with dotted lines on the typewriter

Start typing on dotted lines over the **first** dot.

Using your variable line spacer, find the correct position for typing so that letters with tails – "j's", "p's", "q's", "y's", for example – do not touch the dots. This takes a little practice. Do not type so far above that there is a great deal of space below. All that is necessary is to clear the dots, as in the example on the next page.

The reason for typing dotted lines slightly below the headings at the side is so that the typing on the dotted lines can be exactly aligned with the headings.

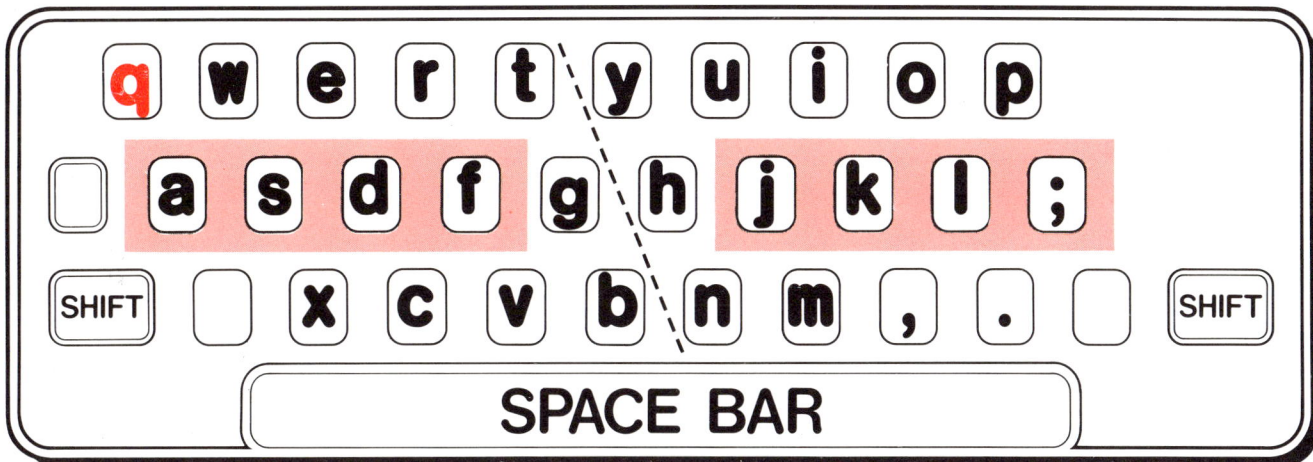

Margin 19 elite 10 pica   Margin 81 elite 72 pica

Practise keys learned

1 Winnie Watts went by taxi to the West End of London to see the shops last Wednesday. The extra cost of the taxi was worth it; Winnie was able to avoid the rush hour crowds.

2 The exact number of people expected to arrive at the meeting was not known, but about sixteen hundred was estimated.

3 While we were exercising in the garden, there were six boxes of mixed groceries delivered.

TWO SPACES after a fullstop

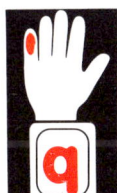

Fourth finger reach from home key "a" to top row key "q"

New key

4 aaa qqq aaa qqq aaa qqq aaa qqq aaa qqq aaa qqq aaa qqq aaa qq

5 aqu aqu aqu aqu aqu aqu aqu aqu aqu aqu aqu aqu aqu aqu aq

6 qua qua qua qua qua qua qua qua qua qua qua qua qua qua qu

7 equal equal equal quite quite quite quiet quiet quiet quietly

8 quietly quietly quieter quieter quieter quit quit quit quits

9 quits quits quick quick quick quicker quicker quicker quickly

10 quickly quickly require require require enquire enquire

11 enquire queen queen queen queenly queenly queenly quack quack

12 quack quacked quacked quacked quacker quacker quacker quacker

Return fingers to home keys

Repeat keys learned

13 We may enquire about the dates of the holidays tomorrow, as the Personnel Department should know by then. We all plan to go to Spain or Italy, to a quiet place, and we should go early in the summer, as July or August would be too hot. We hope to be able to go in May. We shall pay equal shares of the cost and shall require someone to look after our savings.

Back straight

Warm-up drill

1 It was an amazing occurrence, and had it been featured as the plot of a novel or play, would have been considered far-fetched. Life is often stranger than fiction, however, and the little crowd which quickly gathered in the road were forced to believe the evidence of their eyes.

Words that are often spelt wrongly

2 received receipt reference necessary unnecessary occasion separate

3 occur occurred prefer preferred liaison difference differed

4 defer deferred speak speech relief belief relevance language

5 gauge buoyant position possession decision partition seize cease

TYPING ON DOTTED LINES

When typing on dotted lines (for example, when completing a form on the type-writer) it is necessary to start typing slightly above the line, so that letters with "tails" – j, p, q, y – do not have the tails touching the dots:

Typing on a dotted line ....   (Type dots to the centre of the page and type the words above.)

Use your variable line spacer, and move the alignment scale above the dots. This takes a little practice.

Practise typing on a dotted line

Type a dotted line from margin to margin on some spare practice paper, remove it from your machine, and replace it, aligning as mentioned above. Type your name on the dotted line. Check that "tails" (if any) are not touching the line, but your name should not be so far above the dotted line that there is too much space:

Typing on a dotted line
....   Typing too far above dotted line

Typing.on.a.dotted.line   Typing too near to dotted line

Exercise 100

Starting on the 7th line from the top edge, type four dotted lines across A5 portrait paper, in double line spacing. Type your name, address and date on these lines, aligning carefully as before. Set margins on ½" left and right. Start typing your name and address over the first dot on each line.

SPACE BAR

A4

Margin 19 elite
10 pica

Margin 81 elite
72 pica

Practise keys learned

1 The ducks on the lake quacked as they quickly swam to the
bread which we had thrown on to the water for them. It was
quite late in the evening when we left and there was a long
queue for the coach. We felt quite tired when we arrived
home.

*Final
letter
key*

Fourth finger reach from home key "a" to bottom row key "z"

New key

2 aaa zzz aaa zzz aaa zzz aaa zzz aaa zzz aaa zzz aaa zzz aaa zz

3 aza aza aza aza aza aza aza aza aza aza aza aza aza aza aza az

4 azz azz azz azz azz azz azz azz azz azz azz azz azz azz azz az

5 azaz azaz azaz azaz azaz azaz azaz azaz azaz azaz azaz azaz az

6 azaq azaq azaq azaq azaq azaq azaq azaq azaq azaq azaq azaq az

7 zoo zoo zoo zeal zeal zeal zebra zebra zebra glaze glaze glaze

8 glazed glazed glazed zest zest zest dozen dozen dozen dazzle

9 dazzle dazzle ooze ooze ooze zoom zoom zoom zero zero zero

10 maze maze maze amazed amazed amazed amazing amazing amazing

*Eyes
on copy
ALWAYS!*

Repeat keys learned

11 There are one dozen zebras at the zoo. We were amazed to see
them, and their zest for living.

12 For protection from zero temperatures, the houses had
specially glazed windows.

13 The headlights of the car dazzled us and our driver almost
skidded on the muddy ooze of the country lane.

14 The party soon lost its way in the maze and had to signal for
help. The lazy members of the party turned back and left the
others to puzzle their way out.

*Remove
paper from
machine
using the
paper
release
lever*

Exercise 98

Type a copy of the index below on A5 landscape paper, centring vertically and horizontally. This is an example of where 5 spaces could be left between the columns instead of 3, to make more effective use of the space available. Single line spacing.

THE DAILY TIMES CLASSIFIED INDEX

Appointments	54, 66, 67, 68, 69, 70
Education (Posts and Courses)	70
Business to Business	71
Entertainments	35, 36, 37, 41
UK Holidays	28
Overseas Travel	27, 28, 30, 40, 42
House and Garden	39
Motors	56, 58, 60, 62, 64, 65
Personal	51
Property	46, 47, 48, 49, 50, 51
Shopping by Post	40

Exercise 99

Type a copy of the timetable below on A5 landscape paper, with enclosed heading, centring vertically and horizontally. Use double line spacing.

BRITISH AIRWAYS SHUTTLE WEEKDAYS

Heathrow	Glasgow
0715	0715
0815	0815
1015	1015
1215	1215
1415	1415
1615	1615
1815	1815
2015	2015

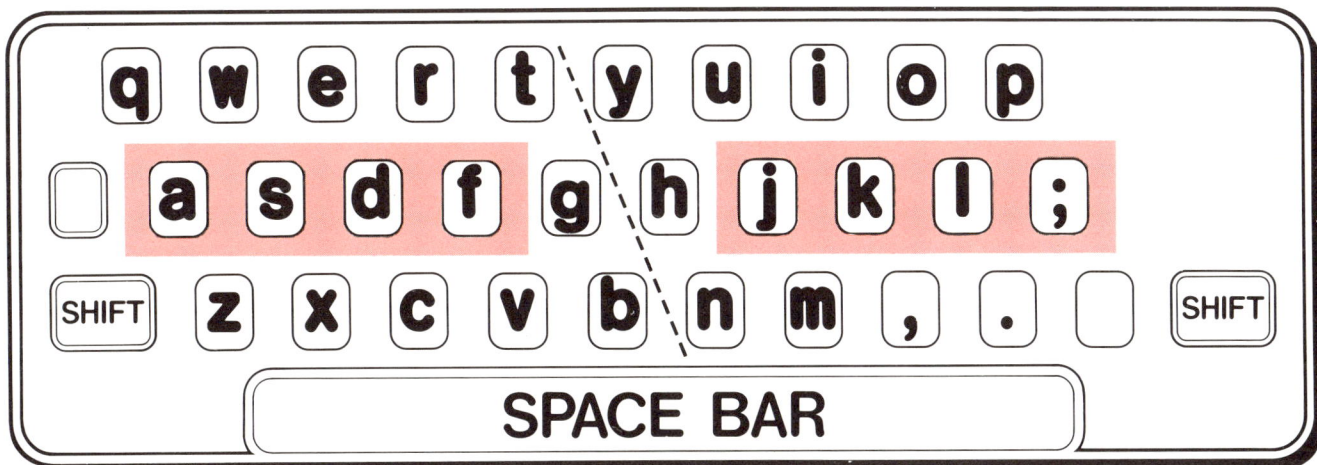

The keyboard diagram shows keys: q w e r t y u i o p / a s d f g h j k l ; / SHIFT z x c v b n m , . SHIFT / SPACE BAR

A4 **Margin** 81 elite / 72 pica   **Margin** 19 elite / 10 pica

Practise keys learned

1   Take the new girl to see the birds at the zoo. She should enjoy the extra treat and quickly see all the caged animals as well. Every creature in the zoo may not be contented but they are all fed well and kept healthy.

Return fingers to home keys

Revise keys learned

a	2	as and any all ask apple alas art artful arm armed army
b	3	bet better bud budded boot boat boater bubble bubbling
c	4	cut cutter cutting cost costing cup cope coping coped
d	5	date dated doubt doubter doubtful dun debt debit debtor
e	6	err erred erring earn earned earning each even evening
f	7	fun funny fill filled feel felt field fit fitter fitting
g	8	get give given gift goes gate gated goat got great grate
h	9	have had hope hoped hoping hunt hunted hunter hunting hill
i	10	ink inky inked inn inns injure injured injuring inspect
j	11	just justly jokes joker jive jeer jeered jeering jilt jilted
k	12	keep kick kicked knot knotted kind kindly kinder kneel knelt
l	13	lock locked like liked lose loose line luck lucky luckier
m	14	me met meet must most main mainly might mightier mite mine
n	15	nun nine none nunnery neat neatly neater note noted nothing
o	16	one own oval over out outside often open off order out outside
p	17	pea peep peeping people proof prove proved prop proper propped
q	18	quiz quizzed quit quite quiet quick quicken quickly question
r	19	rate rates rating rise rising rose roll roller rolled run ran

Check posture

Eyes on book

Return carriage smartly

40

Warm-up drill

1   Lazing on a beach during a holiday is delightful while the sun shines, but other interests are essential to prevent boredom quickly setting in, when clouds gather and the prospect of deepening a tan disappears.

Shift key drill

2   The most commonly used letter in the English language is E, followed by T, A, O, I, N and S. After S come H, R, D, L, C, U, M, W, F, G, Y, P, B, V, K, J. The three least frequently used letters are X, Q and Z.

COLUMNS WITH HEADINGS ENCLOSED BY UNDERSCORE

To give greater prominence to a heading over a column, it can be typed between two lines of underscore, as in the examples below:

DISCOUNT VOUCHERS

CUSTOMER REGISTRATION CARD

MAILING LIST

TOTAL COST

Special notes:

Turn up **twice** after underscore before typing heading.

Turn up **once** after heading before typing final underscore, because underscore takes up very little space.

Start and finish underscore under first and last letters of heading.

Exercise 97

Type a copy of the above headings on A5 landscape paper. Leave 6 clear line spaces between each heading. Left hand margin on 1½″. Right hand margin will not be needed.

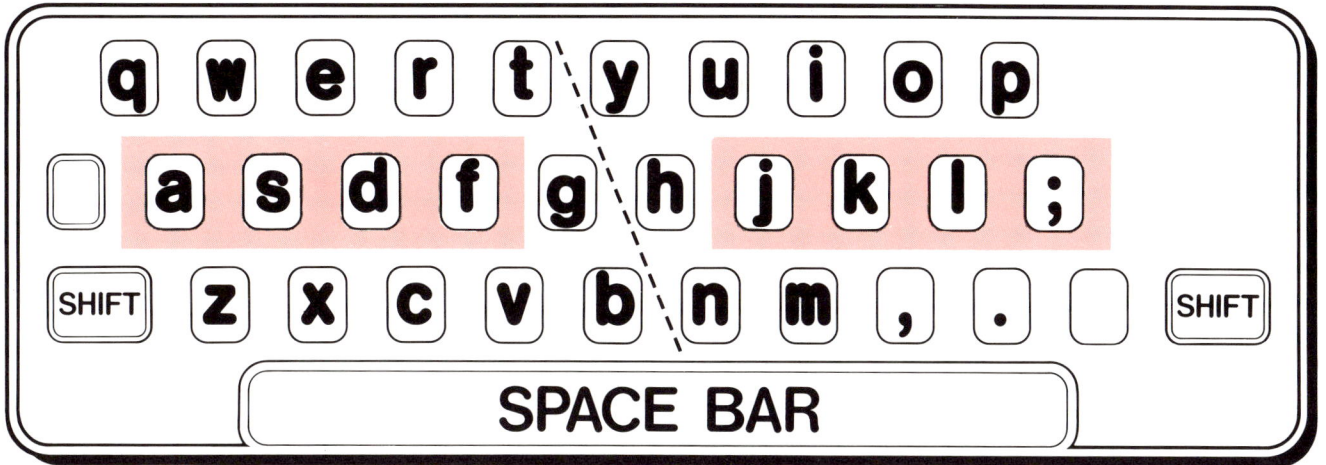

q w e r t y u i o p
a s d f g h j k l ;
SHIFT z x c v b n m , . SHIFT
SPACE BAR

A4 **Margin** 19 elite / 10 pica   **Margin** 81 elite / 72 pica

Practise keys learned

1   The new member of the office staff was quite early, even with flexible working hours operating. She learned with joy that she could leave early and get home before six to Zinnia Lodge.

TAP keys lightly

Revise keys learned

s 2   save saved safe said say sole sigh sell seller selling sent

t 3   talk talker talked test tested testing tint tinting torn torch

u 4   urn urge urgent union undo untidy unequal uncle under unite

v 5   vase veer vivid vividly very velvet veto vex vicar view vocal

w 6   wake waken weak weakling wick worn worry worried work workers

x 7   extra excel excellent exclude exclusion fix fixture excess

y 8   yard yeast you your yourself young yet yolk yes yell yellow

z 9   zoo zeal zealous zebra zero zinc zip zone zoom zest zodiac

Wrists UP!

Repeat keys learned

10   Quickly brown the fudge, as before, and just add extra pieces of mint over a high heat for a waxy appearance.

Feet flat on floor

11   Ada, Zoe and Ben came to the dance forgetting that they had instructed Karen, Vera and Joy to meet them quite near to the exit of the lido swimming pool.

12   The quest for zinc started about the middle of June. Great hopes and keen expectations have been aroused, with many folk awaiting the outcome.

Say the letters to yourself as you type

13   The quizmaster joked and laughed with the excited contestants before they appeared on television.

41

2 Type the following memo with 2 carbon copies, to Miss I Greenacre   Local Deliveries Manager, from Mr F Lock   Security Transport Manager. Date for 18 October 198-. Mark one carbon copy "For the attention of Mr T Evans   Manager". Heading: "Schedule for 25 October 198-".

Below is the schedule for 25 October. Mr G Dodd's removal, Lamb's Furniture Co, the Belvedere Bookshop and Barwest Bank are local, so will be your especial responsibility, as usual, with final arrangements left to you:

Firm	From	To	Time
Barwest Bank PLC	Leighton Buzzard	Milton Keynes	0900
Lamb's Furniture Co Ltd	Luton	Leighton Buzzard	1000
Brickfield Building Society	Leighton Buzzard	Newcastle upon Tyne	1430
Mr G Dodds	Leighton Buzzard	Milton Keynes	1500
Belvedere Bookshop	Leighton Buzzard	Brackley	1600

3 Type the following letter to Andrew Appleby & Co Ltd   Arrow Works   Cobnall Road   Redditch   Worcs   B93 5QN. The letter is for the attention of Mr Charles Vernon   Purchasing Officer. Take one carbon copy. Type an envelope. Heading: "Spare Parts for SP94 Vans". The letter will be signed by Mr Lock. Date for 17 Oct 198-.

Dear Sirs

[As give below] the info you requested today during our tel conversation [regarding the above] will be sent to you during the course of this week.

Yours ffly

4 Typist Re-type the notice below, on A5 with each centred, please, except where indicated:

WTC TRANSPORT CO LTD
Grovebury Road
Leighton Buzzard
Beds
LU7 8SL
leave blocked

Tel (0525) 555568

N O W   O F F E R   T H E   F O L L O W I N G   S E R V I C E S :

Household removals

Security in transit of cash and other valuables

Parcel delivery - guaranteed 24-hour service

Storage under controlled conditions of furniture etc
leave 4 lines clear
Terms reasonable - telephone above number for quotations

A4

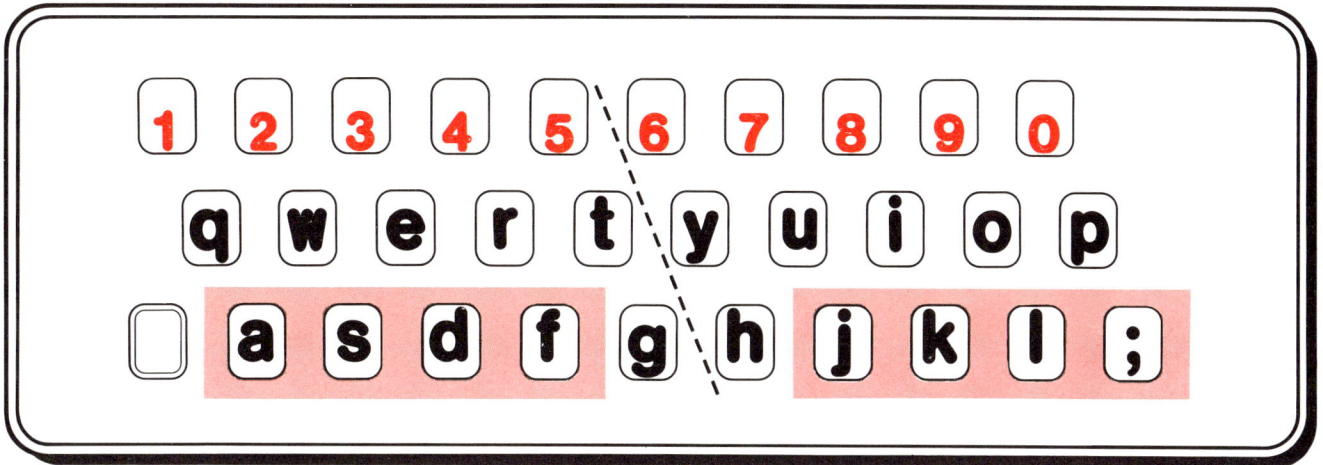

Margin 19 elite / 10 pica   **Margin** 81 elite / 72 pica

Practise keys learned

1   Joy quickly packed sixteen dozen jugs of liquid malt in her new boxes; the van came to collect them very early.

2   In the jazz shop we sell albums by Queen, Roxy Music and David Bowie.

Typing figures

Find the home keys in the usual way. From the home keys, find the third row of keys; check from your typewriter keyboard – your fingers should rest on (left hand) 4, 3, 2, 1 and (right hand) 7, 8, 9, 0. Your two first fingers are also used to type (left hand) 5 and (right hand) 6. Practise finding the figure row. Using the third row of keys as a base, type the following drills.

1-5 New keys   **6-0** New keys

3   r4rtr5 r4rtr5 r4rtr5 r4rtr5 r4rtr5 r4rtr5 r4rtr5 r4rtr5 r4rtr5

4   u7uyu6 u7uyu6 u7uyu6 u7uyu6 u7uyu6 u7uyu6 u7uyu6 u7uyu6 u7uyu6

5   e3i8 e3i8 e3i8 e3i8 e3i8 e3i8 e3i8 e3i8 e3i8 e3i8 e3i8 e3i8

6   w2o9 w2o9 w2o9 w2o9 w2o9 w2o9 w2o9 w2o9 w2o9 w2o9 w2o9 w2o9

7   q1p0 q1p0 q1p0 q1p0 q1p0 q1p0 q1p0 q1p0 q1p0 q1p0 q1p0 q1p0

8   Ted sold 123 pairs of shoes in March, but only 120 in April.

9   We shall order 890 copies of the books and hope to sell 800.

10   They took with them 54 loaves, 67 cakes and 38 tins of fruit.

11   The date today is 29 March; tomorrow will be 30 March.

12   The correct way to type the date is 29 March 1985.

13   Mary is aged 18, Tom is 19, Sally is 20 and Mandy is just 21.

14   The firm plan to sell 1008 cartons of tinned vegetables.

15   The total of 28, 49, 56, 47 and 84 is 264.

16   The firm sent me 12 blue hats; this was wrong as I ordered 14.

17   The trip across Canada took several weeks; it was 3000 miles.

PROGRESS TEST 6

You work for WTC Transport Co Ltd   Grovebury Road   Leighton Buzzard
Beds   LU7 8SL, phone (0525) 555568, as assistant secretary to Mr F Lock
Security Transport Manager. The following would be some of your jobs.

1   Type a copy of the following letter with one carbon copy and an envelope. Address
the letter to Mrs AA Maxwell   34 Milcote Close   Abbeydale   Leighton Buzzard
Beds   LU9 5SL. Date the letter 17 October 198-. It will be signed by Mr F Lock
Security Transport Manager.

Dear Mrs Maxwell

I am writing to confirm our telephone conversation of yesterday, when I promised to let you have our earliest available dates for the removal of yr household effects fr yr present address (above) to 9 Yeovil Rd Taunton. [Taunton]

The dates are as follows:

Typist – days + months in full, please.

Day	Date	Time of Departure
Mon	1 Nov	1500 hours
Tues	2 Nov	1400 "
Thus	4 Nov	0900 "
Fri	5 Nov	1200 "
Wed	3 Nov	1100 "

Leave ditto marks please

In order to make a firm booking for one of these dates, it will be necessary for you to let me know the date preferred by return of post, or by telephone if that will be quicker.

Yrs sincerely

198

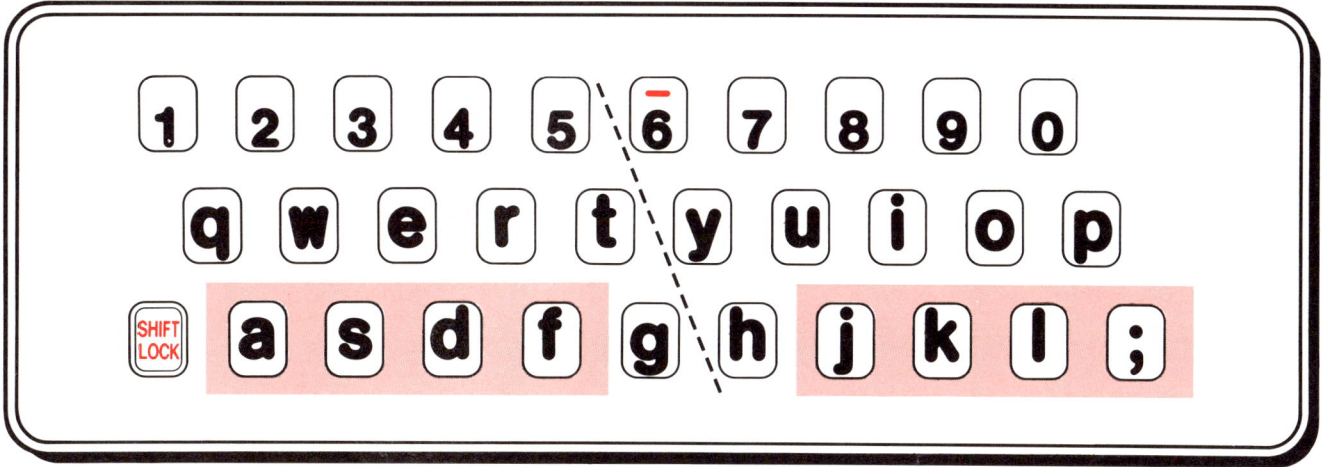

A4   **Margin**   19 elite   10 pica   **Margin**   81 elite   72 pica

Practise keys learned

1   Jo moved 6 dozen quires of grey paper last night, packed into 45 boxes. The van collecting them was FAB 987X. Until the delivery, the printing department was almost out of paper. There are 24 sheets of paper in a quire.

Underscoring

Right hand. First finger reach from "u" to figure 6 with left hand shift key held down. This will give you a line which is continuous if you repeatedly tap the figure 6. This line is used for underscoring headings or words requiring emphasis. The shift lock should be used if a long continuous line is to be typed. DO NOT use the carriage return lever before underscoring. Return the carriage back to the beginning of the word or sentence without leaving any line spaces beneath.

2   Important meeting tonight at 2100

3   Do come. The train leaves at 0800 hours. Mary and Jeffrey are NOT coming. We shall be a party of 4 only. This will make it much easier to plan trips.

New key   *New key*

Final punctuation is NOT underscored.

4   The name of the writer is CAROLINE THOMAS. She is famous for her historical novels about the TUDOR PERIOD. Her latest book is entitled THE EARL OF LEICESTER. It is very readable.

5   I can count on you absolutely to meet me in town on Friday 23 April at 1400. It is very important and I must be able to rely upon you completely. DO NOT LET ME DOWN, PLEASE.

43

FOR YOUR TYPING FOLDER 15

Follow previous instructions for typing these exercises (see page 77).

TYPING COLUMNS

1 To centre columns horizontally, the longest line in each column is added together plus ....

2 This total is deducted from ....

3 The remainder is then divided by 2, which gives the number of spaces available for ....

4 When working out tab sets, add the left hand margin to the total of letters in the longest line of the first column plus .... This gives the first tab set.

5 For the next tab set, add the first longest line to the number of spaces between the columns and then add on ....

6 To check that your calculations are accurate, the last tab set plus the longest line in the column should equal ....

7 Before starting to type columns, all previous tab sets should be cleared, the left hand margin should be re-set, the right hand margin moved out of the way and the paper guide set on ....

8 Columns are typed .... the page, with the tabulator stopping precisely at each column.

9 When there are headings over columns, they may be wider than the column, and must therefore be calculated as the .... line, otherwise the headings will overlap.

ERRORS – CAUSE AND CURE

If this is where you make mistakes	Practise these drills
Third row (q w e r t / p o i u y)	Page 59
Middle row (home keys) (a s d f g / ; l k j h)	Page 59
Bottom row (z x c v b / . , m n)	Page 59
Numbers – do they slow you down?	Pages 79, 100, 111
Capital letters – do they fly up into the air?	Pages 31, 32, 87
Spacing between words – do you miss these?	Pages 65, 173
Margin warning bell – do you ignore it and forget to return your carriage after the end of the word?	Type warm-up drills with margins on 2″
Carriage return – are you too slow?	Page 81
Words with double letters – do they slow you down?	Pages 79, 141
When you are trying to type quickly, do you make many, many mistakes?	Page 158
When you are trying to type accurately, do you slow down?	Pages 65, 173, 224
Do you make many mistakes in any sort of practice?	Pages 133, 151

CORRECTING ERRORS

Correcting errors is an important part of every typist's job – no typist, however expert and accurate, types completely without mistakes – and learning how to put them right is part of learning to type.

Correction methods

Eraser shields

Eraser shields made out of clear (or coloured) plastic are available with different sized spaces in them which can be placed over the letters – or words – to be corrected. This avoids erasing (or using correcting fluid on) letters that are correct.

In the example below, two of the headings are wider than the column beneath, and therefore have to be counted as the longest line.

INCENTIVE GIFTS PRICE LIST SEPTEMBER 198-

Catalogue No	Description	Retail Price
		£
T 50	Notepad	2.17
T100	Telephone Index	2.70
T200	Executive Set	3.60
T450	Clip Tidy	7.39
T700	Memo Board	0.64
T950	Telematic	2.83

Your plan for the above will look like this:

The total number of typing spaces is: 12 + 15 + 12 =   39
On to 39 is added 6 (2 × 3 = spaces between columns) 6
                                                      ___
                                                      45

Space must be allowed for headings, if they are wider than the columns, when working out margins and tab sets, otherwise they will overlap the next column.

Exercise 95

Centre the above columns horizontally and vertically on A5 landscape paper.

Exercise 96

Centre the columns below horizontally and vertically on A5 landscape paper.

PAPER FASTENING ACCESSORIES

Clips	Pins	Bulldog Clips
Paper fasteners	Drawing pins	Magnetic
Paper binders	Draughtmen's pins	Plastic
Windmill clips	Coloured drawing pins	Board
Star clips	Map pins	Foldback
Mitre clips	Plated pins	Contemporary
Giant clips	Thumb tacks	Traditional

Eraser

Although this method may take a little longer than the other four, it is still the most effective, especially on a manual typewriter, and it is essential to practise it so that it is carried out quickly and effectively:

a) Move the carriage all the way to the left or right, using the margin release, so that eraser dust will not fall into the type basket.

b) Do not turn paper up (or down) unless there is a carbon copy (see page 85) – this will avoid any possibility of the paper slipping.

c) Erase lightly in one direction, brushing rubber dust on to the desk (an eraser shaped like a pencil with a brush at the opposite end is ideal).

d) Carbon copies should be erased separately with soft pencil rubber.

e) Re-type (if you are doubtful of the position of the typing point, switch the machine to "stencil" – see page 6 – and tap lightly to check first).

Correction paper

This is a small, rectangular piece of paper, one side of which is covered with chalk. When the chalky side of the paper is struck by the typewriter key, a layer of chalk is deposited on the paper, covering any print directly under it. Correction paper is quick and easy to use, but remember that **the correction may not be permanent** – the chalky deposit can flake off, exposing the error underneath it.

Correction fluid

There are two types – water based and spirit based. The spirit-based fluid dries very quickly (10 to 20 seconds).
Hints for using correction fluid:

a) Open the bottle and wipe the brush on the inside of the bottle opening to remove any surplus fluid.

b) With the **tip** of the brush **dot** the fluid over the mistake. **Do not paint out whole phrases**. Too much fluid is very noticeable.

c) Allow the fluid to dry thoroughly before you re-type the correct letter.

Correction fluids may be obtained to match almost any colour of typing paper.

Type-over ribbons

These can be fitted to manual typewriters (see page 6).

Lift-off ribbons

Lift-off ribbons can be used on all self-correcting typewriters (electric and electronic) that have provision for fitting the tapes, but they are suitable only for correcting errors made with carbon ribbons. The correction is only made, obviously, on the TOP copy – the carbon copy has still to be dealt with by using correction fluid before typing in the correction.

Warm-up drill

1   Mary zealously re-organised all the files in the cabinet while her boss was absent, but quite soon discovered that because he hadn't been told of the new system, it was no advantage to him on his return.

Concentration drill

2   Budapest Buenos Aires Belgrade Bombay Brisbane Brussels Berlin

3   Cairo Calcutta Cape Town Chicago Copenhagen Gibraltar Helsinki

4   Adelaide Amsterdam Ankara Athens

COLUMNS WITH HEADINGS

Blocked headings

In the example below, the heading over each column starts in the same place as the column. These are "blocked" headings.

TIME BELOW IS AT 1200 UK TIME

Place	Time		Place	Time	
Adelaide	9.30	pm	Budapest	1.00	pm
Amsterdam	1.00	pm	Buenos Aires	9.00	am
Ankara	2.00	pm	Cairo	2.00	pm
Athens	2.00	pm	Calcutta	5.30	pm
Belgrade	1.00	pm	Cape Town	2.00	pm
Berlin	1.00	pm	Chicago	6.00	am
Bombay	5.30	pm	Copenhagen	1.00	pm
Brisbane	10.00	pm	Gibraltar	1.00	pm
Brussels	1.00	pm	Helsinki	2.00	pm

Your rough plan for the above example should look like this:

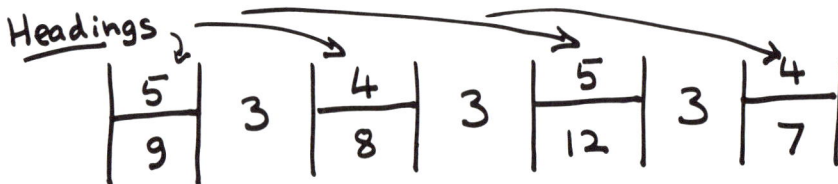

The figures over the "boxes" represent the headings that must be added to the plan.

Exercise 94

Centre the above columns horizontally and vertically on A5 landscape paper.

It is much easier to put mistakes right while the paper is still in the typewriter. **Always read through (proof read) your typing carefully before taking it out of the machine.** However, when an error *is* noticed afterwards, the following procedure should be carried out to make sure the word to be corrected is re-aligned:

a) Switch the machine to "stencil" (see page 6). This will enable you to check that your work is in the right position without making an obvious mark on the paper.

b) Ensure exact alignment by using the alignment scale and variable line space.

c) Bring the typing point exactly over a thin letter (eg i or l).

d) Move to the error, check gently; if the position is right, switch back to the normal typing position of the ribbon, and re-type (not too heavily).

e) Any carbon copy will have to be corrected similarly, and separately. It is never possible to re-align top copy and carbon copy together.

f) If the correction is nearer to the bottom of the typing paper than the top, turn the paper back instead of turning on, so that the error lies on the "erasure table" (see page 10). The paper is less likely to slip.

Practise correcting errors

1   **Type a row of ten a's spacing twice between each. Turn up twice. Type a row of ten c's. Return to the first line. Erase each a and re-type with the first ten letters of the alphabet.**

   Return to the second line. Erase each of the ten c's. Re-type with the first ten letters of the alphabet.

2   **Type the words listed below. Correct the mistakes that are underlined with the letter in brackets at the right hand side. Correct each mistake as it is made.**

opron	wrsh	stind	(a)
glend	vand	frook	(b)
rat	pooket	eook	(c)
cog	wort	eiition	(d)
iasy	dot	dask	(e)
gat	dew	orten	(f)
huard	fitht	hihh	(g)
le	faitj	rigots	(h)
o	tn	lettle	(i)
lury	tar	puice	(j)
tind	bool	cooo	(k)
jive	hauv	abbe	(l)
ne	exao	tine	(m)

Exercise 93

Centre the columns below vertically and horizontally on A5 landscape paper. Single line spacing.

TELEPHONE ALPHABET

A for Andrew	J for Jack	S for Sugar
B for Benjamin	K for King	T for Tommy
C for Charlie	L for Lucy	U for Uncle
D for David	M for Mary	V for Victory
E for Edward	N for Nellie	W for William
F for Frederick	O for Oliver	X for Xmas
G for George	P for Peter	Y for Yellow
H for Harry	Q for Queenie	Z for Zebra
I for Isaac	R for Robert	

Your plan for the 3 columns in Exercise 93 should be like this:

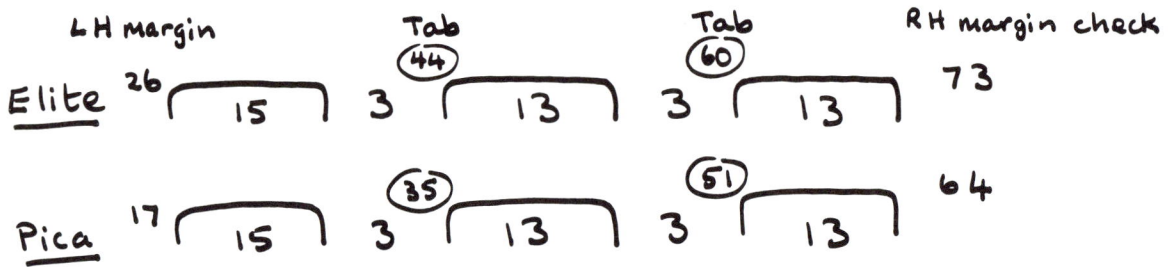

Start typing on line 12 or 13 (there is an odd number left after deducting 12 typing lines from 35 on A5 landscape paper).

Special note:

Using the tabulator on a typewriter: Columns are typed **across the page**, using the tabulator to stop at each column, because there is less chance of missing an item in a column. **Do not type down the page.**

194

SECTION 3

Becoming a Proficient Typist

Columns are normally centred horizontally and vertically (from top to bottom of the paper).

Exercise 92

Type the columns below on A5 landscape paper, centring horizontally and vertically.

There are 3 columns in this exercise. Working out the tab stops is the same as in the previous exercises, remembering *two* sets of 3 spaces each have to be added to the total number of spaces in the longest line in each column. Single line spacing.

FAMOUS ROSES

Ballerina	Precious Platinum	Albertine
Blessings	Prima Ballerina	Altissimo
Chinatown	Princess Michiko	Casino
Fragrant Cloud	Peer Gynt	Compassion
Glenfiddich	Silver Jubilee	Danse du Feu
Iceberg	Super Star	Dublin Bay
Just Joey	Troika	Elegance
Mischief	Wendy Cussons	Ena Harkness
Pascala	Whisky Mac	Excelsa
Peace	Yesterday	Golden Showers

Lines down on A5 landscape paper – 35. Spaces across 100 elite, 82 pica.

Elite

Tab (41)   Tab (61)   RH margin check
75

24 [14] 3 [17] 3 [14] 75

Total : 51

Deduct from 100
              51

Divide by 2   2) 49
                 24
                 25

Margins: 24 Left
          75 Right

Pica

Tab (32)   Tab (52)   RH margin check
66

15 [14] 3 [17] 3 [14] 66

Total : 51

Deduct from 82
             51

Divide by 2   2) 31
                 15
                 16

Margins: 15 Left
          66 Right

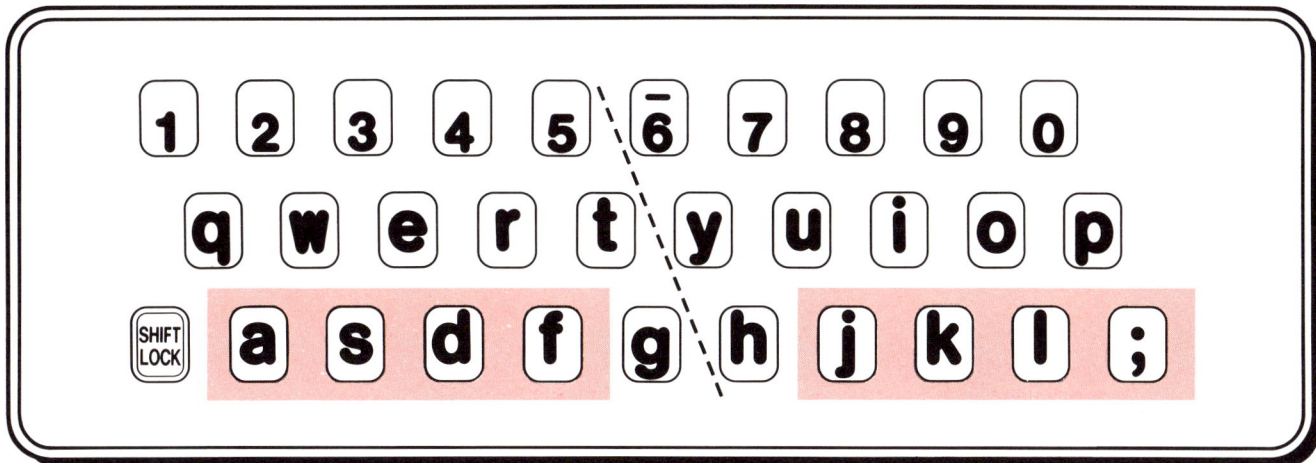

Practise keys learned

Please let each committee member have 20 tickets. This should
speed up sales. It is amazing how quickly even the largest
number of tickets may be disposed of if all members share the
selling. I believe 120 tickets have been printed and they are
numbered so that an exact record of sales is kept.

Using the backspacer

New key

Find the backspacer key on your typewriter (its position varies from machine to machine); depress it with either your left or your right fourth finger, from home key "a" or home key "semi-colon". The backspacer takes your carriage back one space and is very useful when centring headings on your paper.

CENTRING HEADINGS

Your typing paper (A4 size) has 100 typing spaces from right to left if your type-writer has *elite* pitch, and 82 spaces if your typewriter has *pica* pitch. *Pitch* means the size of your typeface – elite typewriters print 12 letters to an inch; pica typewriters print 10 letters to an inch.

The centre of your typing paper (A4) is:

elite: 50 on the scale

pica: 41 on the scale

Tap your space bar until the *typing point* on your typewriter is exactly under either 50 or 41 on the scale above it. Your typing point is where the typeface strikes the paper (see page 10).

From this centre point you can now calculate the position on the scale to start typing a heading so that it is in the centre of your A4 paper, by using the backspacer. Check that the paper guide is on zero.

Before setting tabs, check that your calculations are right, by deducting the figure you made a note of (elite 40, pica 31) from 100 or 82, ie elite 60, pica 51.

Now add tab set to number in second box as below:

These two sets of figures should agree. If they do not, go back and check your additions from the beginning.

Before starting to type columns

Clear all previous tab sets – some machines have a special control for this or, alternatively, you can depress tab clear and tab bar together, which clears all tab stops simultaneously.

Re-set the left hand margin to correspond with that worked out on the plan.

Move the right hand margin to the end of the platen.

Check that your paper guide is on zero. This is **most important**, as if the paper guide has been moved out of position, it will make the final placement of the columns incorrect, in spite of all the careful calculations you have just made.

Insert the paper with the left hand edge as close as possible to the paper guide.

Exercise 90

Type the columns on page 190 under the main heading, on A4 paper, following the plan on page 191.

Exercise 91

Following the instructions for Exercise 90, type the columns below, centring horizontally across A4 paper. Single line spacing.

SOME POPULAR NAMES FOR BOYS

Leave 2
clear lines
after main
heading

Alan	Edward
Alec	Eric
Anthony	Ian
Brian	John
Colin	Keith
David	William

How to centre the title of this book:

TYPING SKILLS

a) Check that your paper guide (see page 10) is on zero.

b) Check that the left hand edge of your typing paper is against the angle of the paper guide.

c) Move the typing point (by holding the carriage release lever) until it is at 50 (or 41).

d) Count the number of letters in the title of this book and add on the space between the two words (13).

e) Divide this total by 2 to give 6 (ignore the odd number).

f) You are now ready to backspace 6 times from your typing point (or central point).

g) When you have finished backspacing, set the shift lock and type the heading.

If you have carried out these seven steps correctly, the heading will be (almost) in the centre of your paper (you will be one space out).

Headings do not have fullstops at the end.

Centre your own name, in capitals, in the same way.

Centre the name of your town or city, as above.

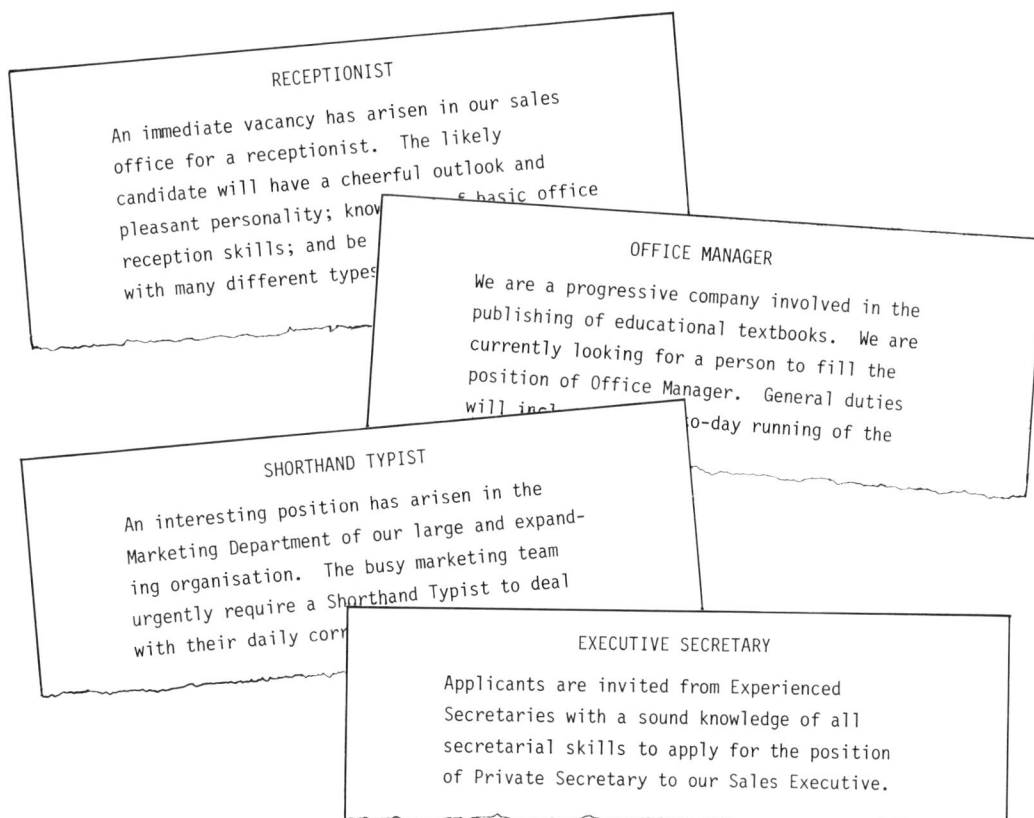

RECEPTIONIST

An immediate vacancy has arisen in our sales office for a receptionist. The likely candidate will have a cheerful outlook and pleasant personality; know ...f basic office reception skills; and be ... with many different types ...

OFFICE MANAGER

We are a progressive company involved in the publishing of educational textbooks. We are currently looking for a person to fill the position of Office Manager. General duties will incl ... ...o-day running of the

SHORTHAND TYPIST

An interesting position has arisen in the Marketing Department of our large and expand- ing organisation. The busy marketing team urgently require a Shorthand Typist to deal with their daily cor...

EXECUTIVE SECRETARY

Applicants are invited from Experienced Secretaries with a sound knowledge of all secretarial skills to apply for the position of Private Secretary to our Sales Executive.

To centre columns horizontally across A4 paper

To centre the columns at the foot of page 190:

Count up longest word in each column: $9 + 8 = 17$

Add on 3 spaces for distance between columns: 3

Total number of spaces required: 20

It helps to avoid making mistakes with this arithmetic if a simple plan is made on a piece of scrap paper, as below:

Each "box" represents a column.

Deduct total of spaces from spaces across A4 paper:

	elite 100	pica 82
	20	20
	80	62
Divide the remainder by 2:	40	31

This is the number of spaces you have remaining for your left and right hand margins. The right hand margin will not be needed, but the figure is useful as a check that your calculations are correct later on, so make a note of it.

Add 40 (31) to your simple plan:

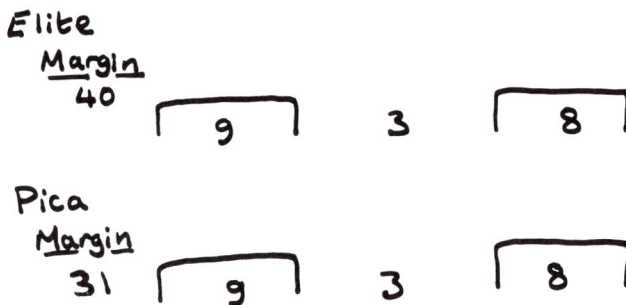

Tab sets

To work out where to set tabs, add up:

elite $40 + 9 + 3 = 52$ tab set

pica $31 + 9 + 3 = 43$ tab set

These tab sets will stop your typewriter where the second column starts.

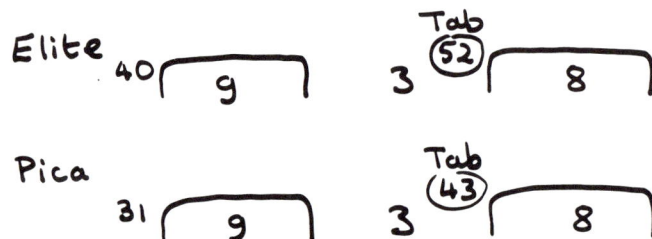

THE TABULATOR

The tabulator (whose position varies on different makes of typewriter) has three keys – one to set the tabulator, known as *tab stop*, one to clear the tab stop, known as *tab clear*, and the tabulator itself, which moves the carriage along to the various tab stops. Some typewriters have a device which *clears all the stops* at once. With the help of your teacher, locate the tab stop, tab clear and tabulator, and then clear all the tab stops, by depressing tab clear and tab bar or key together. To re-set tab stops, move your typing point until it is opposite the number on the scale where you want your first stop, and press your tab stop.

New keys

Using the tabulator for centring headings

Clear the right and left hand margins by moving them as far as they will go to left and right.

Clear the tab stops.

Move your typing point to the centre of the paper and set your tab stop on 50 or 41. After each heading (or line) is centred, press your tab bar or key. Your typing point will then automatically return to the centre ready for the centring of the next line.

Using your backspacer and tabulator, centre the following headings.

Check first: paper guide and left hand edge of paper.

There are 500 sheets of paper in a ream

Punctuation is never underscored

PITCH MEANS THE SIZE OF THE TYPEFACE

The most usual pitches are elite and pica

THERE ARE MANY OTHER SIZES OF PITCH

REVISION OF TYPING LISTS

Lists are not centred vertically – all that is necessary is to turn up 7 from the top of A4 paper and type the heading.

The longest line should be centred horizontally, the left hand margin re-set and the right hand margin pushed to the end of the platen – it will not be needed.

Exercise 89

Type a copy of the following on A4 paper.

<u>MERCHANT SHIPS</u>

Turn up 3 after main heading

Alvega
Atlantic Causeway
BP Avon
Corona
Dart
Elk
Esk
Fornello
Port Toronto
Iris
Ivy
Lygaon
Nordic Ferry
Pict
Queen Elizabeth II
Saxonia
Tay
Test
Uganda
Wye
Yorkshireman

TYPING COLUMNS

There is a saving of paper if a list is divided up into columns typed across the page:

<u>SOME POPULAR NAMES FOR GIRLS</u>

Alison	Fiona
Angela	Gillian
Claire	Jane
Christine	Kate
Deborah	Margaret
Eleanor	Patricia

UPPER CASE AND LOWER CASE LETTERS

Capitals typed on a typewriter are also known as *upper case*. This means that to type them you have to use the shift key and/or shift lock.

Small letters typed on a typewriter (without the shift key) are also known as *lower case*. Upper case and lower case are sometimes shortened to *uc and lc* as an instruction to the typist.

In the headings above, which you have just centred, there are five different ways of varying them:

Lower case without underscore	Lower case without underscore
Lower case and underscored	<u>Lower case and underscored</u>
Upper case without underscore	UPPER CASE WITHOUT UNDERSCORE
Upper case and underscored	<u>UPPER CASE AND UNDERSCORED</u>
Initial capital and lower case	Initial Capital and Lower Case

The sixth way to vary a heading, and for special emphasis, is to type it in

S P A C E D   C A P I T A L S

Capitals without spaces are "closed capitals".

When typing in spaced capitals:

type the letter, then tap the space bar once. Between each word, tap the space bar *three* times. This separates words clearly from each other.

T H E L M A   J   F O S T E R

L A N S D O W N E   S T R E E T

W O R C E S T E R   T E C H N I C A L   C O L L E G E

Practise typing in spaced capitals and centre as headings:

Your own name

The name of your street

The name of your school (or college)

An abbreviation for "capital letters" is *caps*; this is an alternative instruction to *uc* for the typist.

An instruction to a typist to type a heading in spaced capitals is often given as *sp caps*.

Abbreviations for "underscore" are *us*, or a line underneath the letter or word.

Warm-up drill

The fancy dress was quaint, but the girl who planned to wear it was vexed by the
fact that it was shabby and the colours were faded. She gazed at the costume
for a long time before finally deciding to take it back and look for another.

Exercise 87

Type a copy of the following paragraphs

a)   as they are

b)   with all 3 paragraphs indented

c)   with all 3 paragraphs blocked

d)   with all 3 paragraphs hanging

A hanging paragraph is typed with the first line starting at the left hand
    margin and the second and all other lines starting two spaces in. Hanging
    paragraphs are used mainly for sub-paragraphs. To avoid typing any line but
    the first at the left hand margin, this should be re-set and the backspace key
    and margin release used for the first line of each paragraph.

       Indented paragraphs can be typed in single or double line spacing. The
    first line starts half an inch in from the left hand margin and it saves time to
    set the tab at this point.

Fully blocked paragraphs are quicker to type, as every line, including the first
one, starts at the left hand margin. When typing blocked paragraphs with double
line spacing, an extra line must be left between the paragraphs to make it quite
clear where a new paragraph begins.

Exercise 88

**Type a copy of the following on A5 paper, with a carbon copy, using double line
spacing and blocked paragraphs.**

sp caps   POSTNOTES

Postnotes are on sale at all post offices & are notepaper,
envelope and stamp all-in-one - so attractive and cheaper in a
pack of five. Think of the saving in time & trouble - just
write yr ltr, send it down & add the address (to anywhere
in the UK) & post it.

NP/

Top quality paper, first-class postage pd up to 60g. On
sale @ 21p each or a pack of five for only £1.00.

189

Practise keys learned

1 Put every box on the table; there is plenty of room.

2 The coats and hats have furred edges; they will be too hot.

3 The judge is over sixty; he is a very wise and learned man.

4 She keeps extra packets of exercise paper in the next office.

5 As it is lined paper, she uses it for Petty Cash and Postage.

Exercise 1

Centre the following headings in spaced capitals (sp caps).

H O M E   K E Y S   (total letters and spaces: 17)

T A B U L A T O R   B A R   (total letters and spaces: 26)

C E N T R I N G   H E A D I N G S

P A R T S   O F   T H E   T Y P E W R I T E R

Exercise 2

Repeat the above headings as indicated below.

1 In closed capitals (upper case).
2 In closed capitals and underscored.
3 In lower case.
4 In lower case and underscored.

Exercise 3

Centre the following headings in lower case and underscored.

Typewriter Accessories

Computers and Calculators

Post Office Services

Mail Room Equipment

The Post Office Guide

3 Type the following letter to Office Equipment Supply Co Ltd   Knightley Road
Bromswood   Lancs   T45 7BC. It will be signed by the Sales Manager,
Mr S Mostyn. Take one carbon copy and type an envelope. Date for today.
Mark the letter for the attention of Mr F Rogers   Chief Buyer.

Heading   <u>Telephone Indexes</u> Accessories   stet /

We are now in a position to supply a variety of the above (and prices) of which details are given ~~below~~ in the attached catalogue. Delivery in most cases is ex stock. A (of 10%) <u>discount is allowed</u> for orders over £100.

4 Re-type the following price list, with one carbon copy, on A5 portrait paper. Type
on the carbon copy: For the attention of the Branch Manager, Glasgow.

DESK LAMPS — NEW PRICES FOR 198-

99 Anglepoise — now £17.00 ~~£15.00~~ each

20 — Matt Black/Silver
21 — Nugget Brown and Mushroom
22 — White and Matt Black
23 — Fern and Cypress Green

90 Anglepoise — now £22.50 ~~£21.00~~ each

01 — Black
02 — White
04 — Fern Green
06 — Red
15 — Mushroom
17 — Brown
19 — Cypress Green

4-33 Anglepoise — now £43.00 ~~£41.00~~ each

01 — Black
02 — White
06 — Red

Architect Lamps 85A — now £12.30 ~~£11.50~~ each

White
Black
Red
Orange
Grey

A4

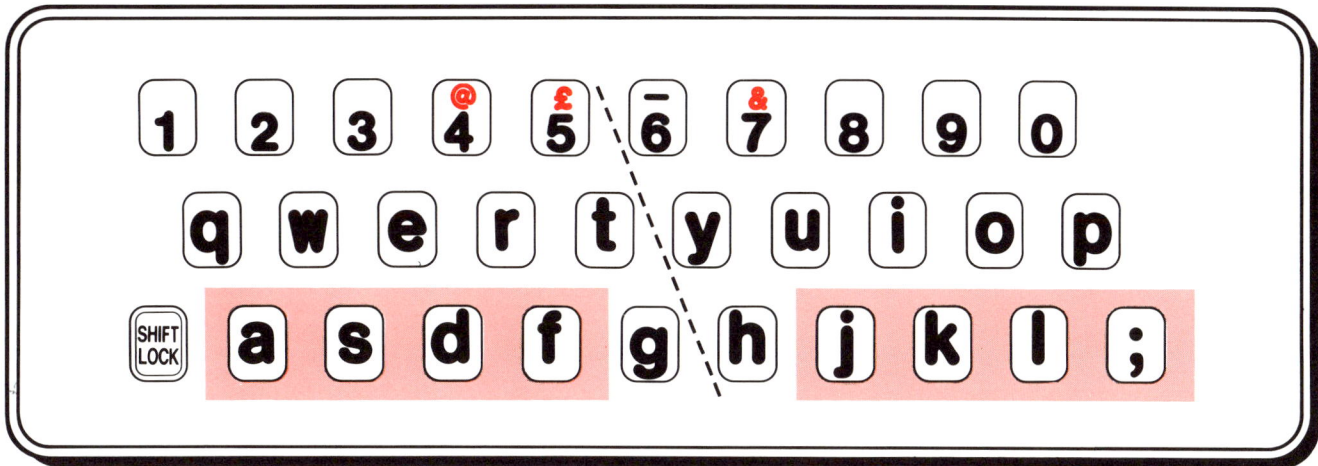

Margin 19 elite / 10 pica

Margin 81 elite / 72 pica

Practise keys learned

1 The size of the boxes made the porter stagger under their weight and caused him to jolt the kindly friend who quickly stopped to help.

New key £

Left hand first finger reach from ''r'' to figure 5 with right hand shift key held down. This will give you the £ sign. Do not leave a space between the £ sign and the number.

2 r5£ r5£ r5£ r5£ r5£ r5£ r5£ r5£ r5£ r5£ r5£ r5£ r5£ r5£ r5£

3 The price of the typewriter ribbons is £5 for a box of 6.

4 The 55 reams of typewriting paper are £165, or £3 per ream.

5 There was a discount for ordering goods costing more than £50.

New key @

Left hand first finger reach from ''r'' to figure 4 with right hand shift key held down. This will give you the @ sign.

6 r@4 r@4 r@4 r@4 r@4 r@4 r@4 r@4 r@4 r@4 r@4 r@4 r@4 r@4 r@4

This sign is an abbreviation for the words ''at the price of'' and is used on commercial documents such as invoices.

7 The price is 12 pairs @ £3 per pair less discount.

8 Please send 2 @ £15 each to my new address.

9 The order stated 190 @ £8 each, but I have received only 90.

Check: hands, wrists, feet, back!

New key &

Right hand first finger reach from ''u'' to figure 7 with left hand shift key held down. This will give you the & sign.

10 u&7 u&7 u&7 u&7 u&7 u&7 u&7 u&7 u&7 u&7 u&7 u&7 u&7 u&7 u&7

This sign is an abbreviation for the word ''and''; it is used *only* as follows:

When typing Mr & Mrs on letters, envelopes and invitations

When typing addresses: 78 & 79 Main Street

When typing registered names of firms: Messrs Jones & Brown Ltd.

The correct name for ''&'' is ''ampersand''.

PROGRESS TEST 5

You work in the Sales Department of Shaw & Short Ltd   Wholesalers
Whitaker Street   Manchester   M96 8TB.

Part of your job consists of typing invoices. In addition, you bring price lists up-to-date, ready for re-printing, and help with typing letters and memos. A typical morning's work might include the following jobs:

1   An invoice. The customer is John Parsons & Co Ltd   23 Bull Market   Huddersfield
West Yorkshire   HD4 2BQ. Take 3 carbon copies. Type an envelope.

```
The invoice No is 4527 dated 29 September 198-      VAT Reg No is 11558924

Cat No  FA 7942
Qty  10
Description  First Aid Kits 1-5 employees
Unit price  £7.35
Total cost
VAT
Total amount including VAT

Cat No  FA 7922
Qty  15
Description  First Aid Kits 51-100 employees (wall mounted)
Unit price  £35.48
Total cost
VAT
Total amount including VAT

Cat No  FA 7945
Qty  11
Description  First Aid Kits 101-150 employees (wall mounted)
Unit Price  £40.49
Total cost
VAT
Total amount including VAT

Invoice total                          Terms nett
```

Work out the missing figures, including the final total, for the invoice.

Mark one of the carbon copies "For the attention of the Dispatch Department" and one of the other carbon copies "For the attention of the Accounts Department".

2   Type a memo (no carbon copy) from Mrs M Dawkes   Sales Department to
Mrs G Lee   Personnel Department. Date for 29/9. Use your own initials for the typist's part of the reference. Heading: First Aid Kits.

```
You asked me recently about First Aid Kits for your department and
                           may                     There are now
stet/ mentioned that you might need some extra ones. We now have all sizes in

stock so if you could let me know how many you think you may need, I

will see that they are supplied to you without delay.  They range in

size from 1-5 employees to 101-150 employees, so it will be up to you to

decide how many you can conveniently site in each office.
```

Practise keys learned

Please deliver to our address at 7 & 8 Lilac Avenue, two boxes

of carbon paper A4 size, @ £6 per box; the boxes should be

addressed to Mr & Mrs J K Vernon and marked <u>URGENT</u>.

The ampersand (&) is an abbreviation for the word "and", but should be used only in the three instances given on the previous page. If it is used anywhere else, it is incorrect.

In Exercise 4, below, there are *two* instances of the ampersand being used incorrectly. Type the exercise, substituting the word "and" for the ampersand where you think it has been used wrongly.

Exercise 4

Use double-line spacing. This means setting your line space selector on 2, which will leave one clear line space between lines of typing.

Messrs Wilson & Co is situated at 77 & 79 Parkside, Upper

Colville, Leicester. Prices are reasonable, & the latest

price list will remain almost completely unchanged, except

where it has not been possible to maintain prices at their

present level. Prices include VAT, & this makes it easy

for buyers to estimate the total amount of their orders.

Fractions

Most typewriters have special keys for some of the more commonly used fractions. All typewriters have a key for the fraction "½". Locate the "½" on your typewriter and locate the other fraction keys, too. They will all be typed from the home key "semi-colon" with the right little finger, but some of them may be typed with the shift key too.

Percentage sign

On most typewriters, this is typed with the left shift key over the "½" fraction. Use your right little finger.
NO SPACE is left between the figure and the percentage sign.

Practise typing fractions and percentage sign

1 Terms are usually stated on invoices and often are 2½% for
payment within 30 days.

2 Another cash discount offered may be 3¾% for payment within
30 days.

3 House agents charge between 1¼% and 1¾% commission on their
sales.

TYPING LETTERS WITH INSET MONEY COLUMNS

Exercise 86

Type the following letter on Office Equipment Supply Co Ltd A4 letterheading (or on A4 bond) with one carbon copy and an envelope. Date for 2 March 198-. The letter will be signed by K Benson   Sales Manager. Use your own initials on the reference.

```
        St Paul's Printing & Label Co Ltd
        127 Mount Pleasant
        Bromswood
        Lancs        T45 5PY


        For the attention of Mr F Preece  Manager


        Dear Sirs

        I give below prices for the items of stationery mentioned by you on
        the telephone today.  Delivery can be ex stock, and we shall be
        pleased to dispatch immediately on receipt of your order:
```

Turn up 2

```
        1 card index cabinet catalogue No 531  @  £16.95  VAT  £2.54
        4 sellotape dispensers     "       "  0705 @  £12.17  VAT  £7.30
        2 autofiles                "       "  644  @  £ 4.50  VAT  £1.35
```

Turn up 2

Keep @ signs under each other

Use double quotation marks for "ditto". Type ditto marks under the centre of the word

```
        I look forward to hearing further from you.

        Yours faithfully
        OFFICE EQUIPMENT SUPPLY CO LTD




        K Benson
        Sales Manager
```

Special note:

Letters giving prices are often sent by firms instead of using quotation forms.

The invoice for the above goods, which were subsequently ordered by St Paul's Printing & Label Co, is on page 181.

An exception to the rule that sentences do not start with figures is made in the letter above. This is because the letter is in effect a quotation and the second paragraph deals almost entirely with figures.

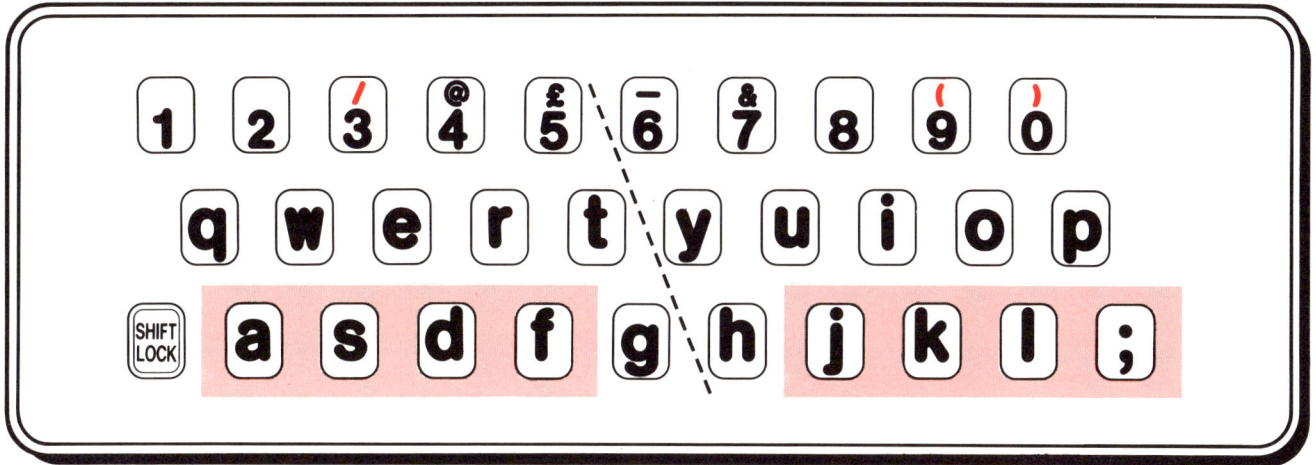

| A4 | **Margin** | 19 elite
10 pica | **Margin** | 81 elite
72 pica |

Practise keys learned

1   The lively, grey poodle just danced over to greet the lazy, brown fox.

2   soap make fish dish dock flap town turn maps city clam duty coal such wish kept vial cowl melt name shape right blame chair wield icicle got for box nap nor duels foe eye hem bid

New key

Left hand second finger reach from "e" to figure 3 with right hand shift key held down. This will give you the oblique / sign.

3   e3/ e3/ e3/ e3/ e3/ e3/ e3/ e3/ e3/ e3/ e3/ e3/ e3/ e3/ e3/

The oblique sign is used:

    For typing fractions not provided on the typewriter: 7/10   3/5

    For telephone numbers with more than one line: 5334/5

    For addresses (instead of the ampersand): 23/24 High St

    In place of the word "or": we shall ask him/her to go too.

There is *no space* before or after the oblique sign.

4   Please telephone Messrs Watkins & Sons Ltd; their number is Birmingham 59764/5/6.

5   He gave the address as 57/58 Clarendon Road, but it was wrong.

6   The tour is planned for men/women aged between 25 and 35.

7   If you add together 7/10, 3/5 and 11/20, the total is 1 17/20.

New keys

Right hand third finger reach from "o" to figure 9 with left hand shift key held down. This will give you the left hand bracket.

8   o9(o9(o9(o9(o9(o9(o9(o9(o9(o9(o9(o9(o9(o9(o9(

Right hand fourth finger reach from "p" to figure 0 with left hand shift key held down. This will give you the right hand bracket.

9   p0) p0) p0) p0) p0) p0) p0) p0) p0) p0) p0) p0) p0) p0) p0)

There is no space after a left hand bracket and no space before a right hand bracket.

4/5

Warm-up drill

1   The boy ate his supper without any of the jam that he loved, because he was too
lazy to get up from the table and fetch the jar from the cupboard; he expected
to have everything put in front of him and was quickly annoyed when it was not.

Practise word division at line endings

Type in a hyphen where the following words could be divided at the ends of lines.
Some should NOT be divided.

2   envelope letter personal registered urgent typed indicated

3   special labels valuable Elizabeth jugs greenish requested

4   quietly gems cupboard children endeavoured puzzle dozen

5   time difficult teach matter solemn seized please gardener

Preparation for accuracy/speed practice

Type each line 3 times.

ordinary ordinary ordinary ordinary ordinary ordinary ordinary ordinary ordinary
business business business business business business business business business
receives receives receives receives receives receives receives receives receives
receipt receipt receipt receipt receipt receipt receipt receipt receipt receipt
Similarly Similarly Similarly Similarly Similarly Similarly Similarly Similarly
necessary necessary necessary necessary necessary necessary necessary necessary

Accuracy/speed practice

BUYING AND SELLING

	Words
An example of an ordinary, everyday business transaction is when a	13
customer goes into a shop, chooses what he or she wants to buy, pays for	28
it (perhaps receives a receipt) and is given change. The exchange of	42
goods for money forms a part of everyone's life – the shopkeeper makes a	57
small profit on each transaction, which helps to pay the rent of the	71
shop, lighting, heating and the wages of any assistants employed.	84
Similarly, all firms, large or small, make their profit by selling goods	99
or providing services for which people are prepared to pay.	111
Employees of firms do not go "shopping" for anything they want to buy on	127
behalf of the firm. Instead, they write to the suppliers of these goods	141
asking for details – price, delivery date, catalogues or leaflets giving	156
any other information necessary.	163

1 **2** **3** **4** **5** **6** **7** **8** **9** **0**
q **w** **e** **r** **t** **y** **u** **i** **o** **p**
SHIFT LOCK **a** **s** **d** **f** **g** **h** **j** **k** **l** **;**

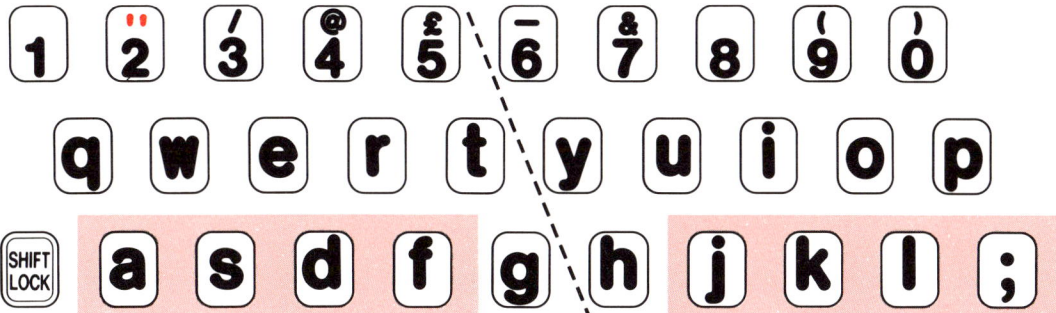

A4 **Margin** 19 elite / 10 pica   **Margin** 81 elite / 72 pica

Practise keys learned

1   Mrs Karen Parkinson (our new Personnel Manager) lives in York.

2   Mr and Mrs Forbes will be coming to see us early (about 1600).

3   Please deliver five crates @ £2 per crate (delivery extra).

4   Our new telephone number is Cardiff 656788/9 (two lines).

5   The parcel must go by EXPRESSPOST (it is an urgent delivery).

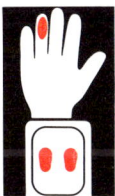

Left hand third finger reach from ''w'' to figure 2 with right hand shift key held down. This will give you double quotation marks ".

New key

6   w2" w2" w2" w2" w2" w2" w2" w2" w2" w2" w2" w2" w2" w2" w2"

Double quotation marks are used for:

Indicating speech: "I will come," said the girl.

Titles of books, newspapers: "The Daily Mail."

Inches, in measurement: There are 36″ in a yard.

Seconds, in time: 60″ were allowed for the sprint.

7   The customer said, "I would like to try on a pair of shoes."

8   "Double quotation marks," said Mrs Hamilton to her pupils, "are easy to understand if you remember that they are used to enclose words exactly as they have been spoken."

9   The publisher said to his secretary "Would you please send a letter to the ESC Board asking them for their 1985 Guide to their examinations, as I seem to have mislaid mine."

There is no space after quotation marks used before speech and no space before quotation marks at the END of speech.

Practise the hyphen and the dash

Type the sentences below. In 1–5 there are errors in the spacing. Correct these where you think they are wrong.

1 Typists should have well – cared for hands, as they are very conspicuous.

2 A mid – morning break is always welcomed by all types of worker-manual and sedentary.

3 The mother – of – pearl brooch was very much admired, but considered old-fashioned by some of the buyers.

4 Today, the long-awaited birthday is the 18th-once it was the 21st that was the all-important event.

5 The pupils – and there were over 50 of them in the classroom – listened with great attention to the remarks of their teacher. Their co – operation had been requested beforehand.

6 The salary offered was far more than the girl had expected – over £4000 a year.

7 The crowd of young people were amused by the staid newcomer and called him a " stick -in -the -mud ".

8 It was pitch -dark in the cellar – much too gloomy to find the old chairs they were looking for.

9 The two-year -old horses had been taken from their stables into the fields every day – but now this routine was stopped because of the groom's absence.

10 A little -used car may be almost as expensive to buy as a new one – and may not be as dependable.

A4

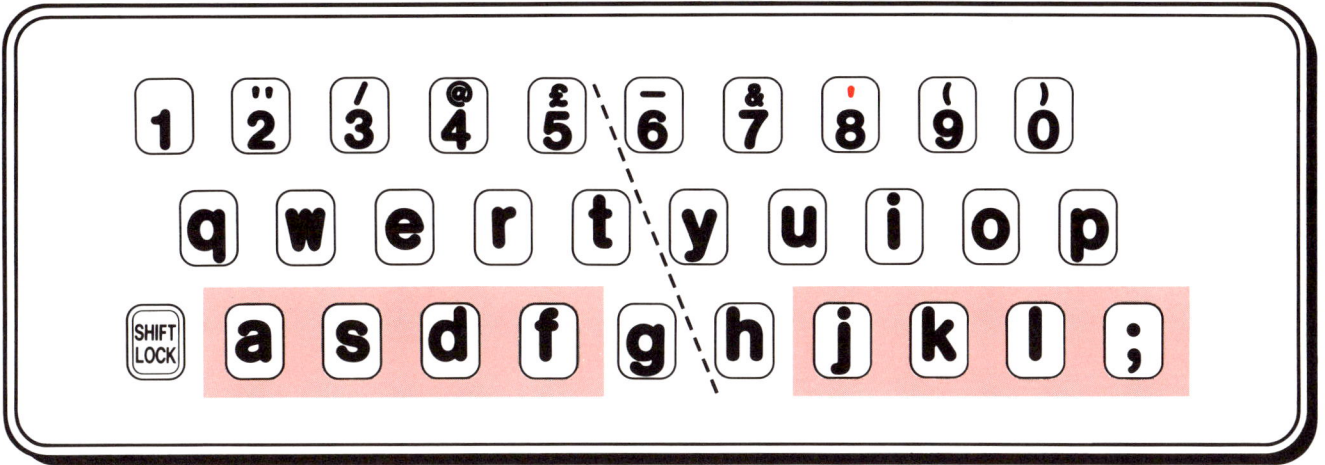

Margin 19 elite
10 pica

Margin 81 elite
72 pica

Right hand second finger reach from "i" to figure 8 with left hand shift key held down. This will give you an apostrophe ´.

New key

1 i8' i8' i8' i8' i8' i8' i8' i8' i8' i8' i8' i8' i8' i8' i8'

An apostrophe is used for:

Indicating possession: Tom's hat; the cat's paw

A letter omitted: can't; weren't; couldn't

Feet, in measurement: 5' 9" wide

Minutes, in time: 3' 55" (3 minutes 55 seconds) were allowed for the mile race.

Practise keys learned

2 The Chief Buyer said, "There will be a vacancy soon for a
junior secretary in my assistant's office. Advertise it first
around the firm and then in the "Evening Post" and also in the
"Chronicle" if there's nobody interested."

3 "It's high time to close the shop," the manager said, at the
end of the first day's sales.

4 "We start early in the morning (and afternoon too)," the young
man said, as he prepared to leave the office at the end of the
day's work.

5 The car is old, but its engine is still good and it's a
bargain for £250/£260.

3 The customer for this invoice is The Midland Secretarial Agency
Frederick Road Edgbaston Birmingham B15 4NX Invoice No 6702
Invoice date 30 April 198-   Order No   5678/5 dated 2 April 198-

Catalogue No   481B
Qty 1
Description Pedestal desk 137 cm x 100 cm (4' 6" x 3' 3")
Unit price £65
Total cost £65.00
VAT £9.75
Total amount including VAT £74.75

Catalogue No   497C
Qty 30
Description Card index boxes 127 mm x 76 mm (5" x 3")
Unit price £2.54
Total cost £76.20
VAT £11.43
Total amount including VAT £87.63

Invoice total £162.38   Terms nett

4 The customer for this invoice is Lamb's Furniture Co Ltd
35 Old Bedford Road Luton Beds LU2 7HQ   Invoice No 8553
Invoice date 28 May 198-   Order No 744 dated 31 April 198-

Catalogue No 500A
Qty 5
Description Glass-topped coffee tables 457 mm x 914 mm (1' 6" x 3')
Unit price £22.30
Total cost £111.50
VAT £16.73
Total amount including VAT £128.23

Catalogue No 701T
Qty 2
Description Dark mahogany TV cabinets 660 mm x 457 mm (2' 2" x 1' 6")
Unit price £95.00
Total cost £190.00
VAT £28.50
Total amount including VAT £218.50

Invoice total £346.73   Terms nett

Repeat keys learned

1   Extreme heat and cold affect everyone, and the Earth has zones
    which vary from tropical to arctic, but by wearing suitable
    clothing, people are able to live and enjoy leisure in most
    places, even though they may not quite like the climate.

2   Refer to chapters 12, 13, 14, 15 and 16, as well as page 351.

3   The lease has 997 years to run and will be for sale for £3000.

4   We shall require 24 boxes @ £3 per box (plus carriage and
    packing) by Thursday, 9 May 198-, at the latest. Please mark
    the consignment URGENT.

5   "Please move your bicycle," said the traffic warden, "as it is
    taking up space reserved for cars."

6   It's high time to start work when the clock strikes 9; its
    face is easy for everyone to see.

7   "The Daily Shout" is a newspaper which presents information in
    the form of pictures, rather than print.

8   The caller gave his telephone number as 8857/562 but when the
    operator dialled this number, all she heard was the "number
    unobtainable" tone.

9   The price of the fur coat was reduced in the summer sales to
    £250 and queues of people formed before 0900, eagerly hoping
    to be able to buy it.

10 For fractions not on your typewriter, use the oblique stroke.
    Examples are 9/10, 3/8 and 4/5.

11 The speaker said, "I have come here to talk to you seriously
    and I hope you'll all listen carefully."

Exercise 85

Type and rule up 5 invoice forms (as on page 175) omitting the numbers, and changing the name under "Bought of" to: Shaw & Short Ltd   Wholesalers Whitaker Street   Manchester   M96 8TB. VAT Reg No 11558924.

1 The customer for this invoice is GPR Developments Ltd 78 East Square Chelmsford Essex CM1 1JN   Invoice No 6332 Date 2 May 198- Order No 567 dated 2 April 198-

```
Catalogue No   22A
Qty  10 m
Description  Heavy-duty rubber-backed carpet, dark brown, 2 m wide
Unit price  £5.50 per metre
Total cost  £55.00
VAT  £8.25
Total amount including VAT  £63.25


Catalogue No   94B
Qty  25 m
Description  As above but 1 m wide
Unit price  £2.25 per metre
Total cost  £56.25
VAT  £8.44
Total amount including VAT  £64.69


Invoice total  £127.94                    Terms nett
```

2 The customer for this invoice is A L Carter and Company Limited Trentham Trading Estate High St Kirkcaldy Fife KY1 1LR   Invoice No 6541 Order No 3441 dated 2 February 198-   Invoice date 28 February 198-

```
Catalogue No   351/4
Qty  10 boxes
Description  Manilla envelopes 90 mm x 140 mm (3½" x 5½")
Unit price  £2.50 per box
Total cost  £25.00
VAT  £3.75
Total amount including VAT  £28.75


Catalogue No   351/5
Qty  5 boxes
Description  Manilla envelopes 120 mm x 235 mm (4¾" x 9¼")
Unit price  £3.25 per box
Total cost  £16.25
VAT  £2.44
Total amount including VAT  £18.69


Invoice total  £47.44                    Terms nett
```

Revise top row keys

ty   **1**   The party was held at the Country Club, and plenty of guests stayed until very late; Katy, Lotty and Marty all left early.

ru   **2**   The rough ruts in the road gather rain and mud in winter; in summer, the ruts are dusty and hard.

ei   **3**   Friends and neighbours will all receive notices inviting them to a discussion about the new Community Centre to be built on Dee Field; it is felt by some that it is not essential.

wo   **4**   The money was still owing when the shop closed, so Will wrote to Walter Brown to say he wanted the debt repaid at once, but Will knows how long Walter Brown took to repay his last debt.

qp   **5**   Quite peaceful people may sometimes be annoyed by questions which they feel are phrased impertinently. Plain speaking quickly helps people to understand but politeness is required.

Revise middle row keys (including the home keys)

es   **6**   The seaside is the place to see seals; they play on the warm sands and are amiable animals.

as   **7**   The addresses of the lasses are useful; we write to them and also to their dads.

af   **8**   The falls are an amazing sight, and all tourists have visits arranged as part of their planned programmes.

ad   **9**   The lady with the dark hair and frilly dress won first prize for dancing; she was rather attractive and had a good partner.

Revise bottom row keys

bn   **10**   Brian has been to Burma but Norman has not. Brian and Norman are friends now but did not know each other before last November.

vm   **11**   Vera may have to come home tomorrow, and her mother will visit her at home.

c   **12**   Charles can choose the car when his cousin comes to Carlisle.

x   **13**   Extra boxes of the exact design required are to be expedited to Hexham and Exeter next Friday.

z   **14**   The lazy guide lost his job at the zoo through lack of zeal.

INVOICES WITH TOTALS

When there is more than one item on an invoice, they have to be totalled up.

```
I N V O I C E                                    No 980301

                              Bought of:

St Paul's Printing & Label Co Ltd
127 Mount Pleasant            Office Equipment Supply Co Ltd
Bromswood                     Knightley Road
Lancs        T45 5PY          BROMSWOOD
                              Lancs       T45 7BC


Order No 73/992 Dated 13 March 198-

        Date   30 March 198-


Terms Nett                           VAT Reg No 63328819
```

Cat No	Qty	Description	Unit Price	TOTAL COST	VAT @ 15%	Total Amount inc VAT
			£	£	£	£
531	1	Card index cabinet	16.95	16.95	2.54	19.49
0705	4	Sellotape dispensers	12.17	48.68	7.30	55.98
644	2	Autofiles	4.50	9.00	1.35	10.35
						£85.82
		E & OE				

Note:

Items on invoices are typed in single line spacing, with double between items.

Turn up 2 after the line enclosing the headings before typing the £ signs. Turn up one after the £ sign, in the usual way.

Type the £ sign immediately before the figures in the total.

Practise keys learned

1   The dazzling red flowers growing in the park proved to be
quite a major attraction to the crowds strolling around on a
sunny day in June. Because of the unusual heat haze, the red
flowers were wilting by the end of the afternoon.

**Hold down the left hand shift key and type home key for semi-colon.
This will give you a colon.**

New key

2   ;:

The colon is used to show that some details follow, in the form of a list, or
further information. **Leave one space after a colon.**

3   The following typists from the Typing Pool will be on holiday
in June: Elizabeth Tonks, Phillippa Kent and Sarah Soames.

4   We shall need more furniture in the new reception area:
6 chairs, 2 low tables and a writing desk with chair.

5   These are the dates of the next 3 committee meetings: 24 May,
26 June and 28 July.

6   Miss Ribbon announced the examination results to the typing
class: Debbie Taplight had 79 marks; Jane Plodder had 52;
Kathy Quiver had only 36 marks.

Exercise 5

Centre the following headings, following the instructions in brackets.

1   Mr & Mrs Grant of "Parkside" 21 Hilltop, Bath   (lc and us)

2   Members 50p   (sp caps)

3   For Sale: typewriter, manual, good condition   (caps and us)

4   Lost: fountain pen possibly in canteen   (uc)

5   Bargain sale on Monday 5 May   (sp caps)

6   Caravan Club's Members Only   (caps and us)

7   Dogs not admitted   (sp caps)

8   Holiday Rota Office Staff   (caps)

9   Sales Figures for August   (lc and us)

10   Men's suits specially reduced   (caps)

Warm-up drill

The lazy brown fox quickly raced over to goggle at the white poodle.

Preparation for accuracy/speed practice

Type each line 3 times.

exploration exploration exploration exploration exploration exploration
development development development development development development
indications indications indications indications indications indications
prospects prospects prospects prospects prospects prospects prospects prospects
international international international international international
licensing licensing licensing licensing licensing licensing licensing licensing
barrels barrels barrels barrels barrels barrels barrels barrels barrels barrels
equivalent equivalent equivalent equivalent equivalent equivalent equivalent
tonnes tonnes tonnes tonnes tonnes tonnes tonnes tonnes tonnes tonnes tonnes
producers producers producers producers producers producers producers producers

Accuracy/speed practice

NORTH SEA OIL AND GAS EXPLORATION

	Words
In November, 1982, North Sea oil and gas exploration reached a	13
new milestone with the completion of the two thousandth well,	25
18 years after the first was drilled. The Energy Minister	38
made a statement in London to the effect that development had	51
passed an important stage in the North Sea success story, just	64
when there were new indications of brighter future prospects.	76
The Energy Minister stated that the North Sea discovery ratio was	90
extremely high by international standards. One in 12 wells	103
drilled had found oil or gas. Exploration activity continued to	116
rise, with 97 wells started in 1982 compared with 54 in 1980 and	129
73 in 1981. There were promising results from the seventh round	142
of offshore licensing.	147
Total production is running at over 2 million barrels a day,	159
equivalent to 100 million tonnes a year, making Britain one of	172
the top 6 producers in the non-Communist world.	182

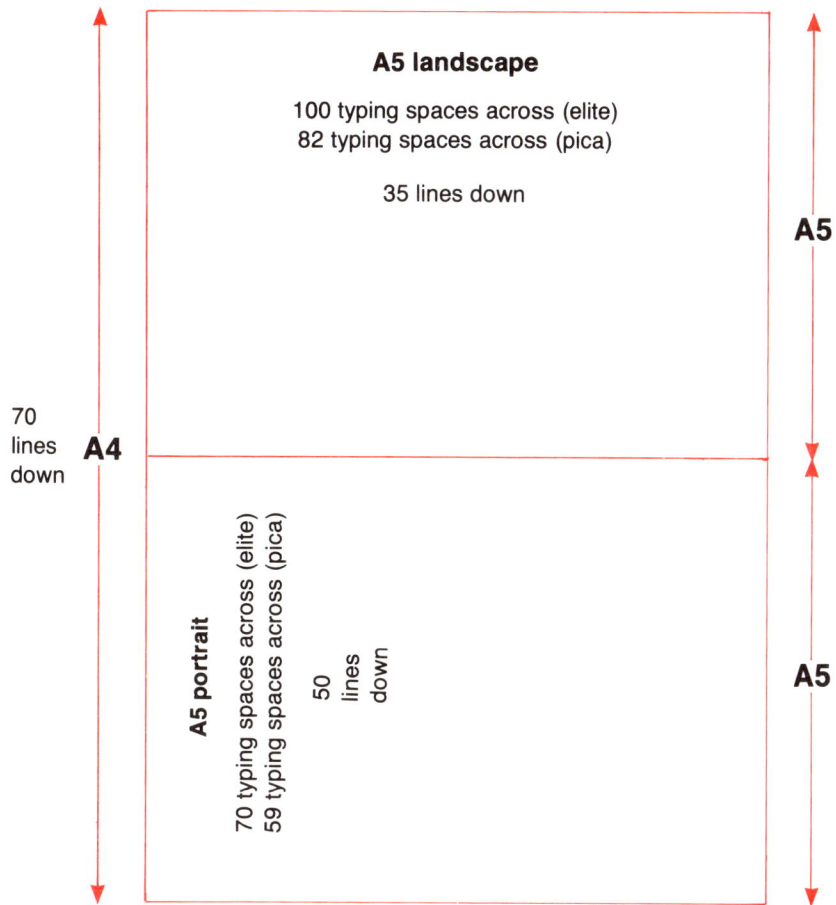

A5 landscape

100 typing spaces across (elite)
82 typing spaces across (pica)

35 lines down

A5

70
lines
down

A4

A5 portrait

70 typing spaces across (elite)
59 typing spaces across (pica)

50
lines
down

A5

Paper sizes

A5 paper is half the size of A4.

A5 paper may be used either with the short edge inserted into the typewriter (this is called PORTRAIT) or with the long edge inserted into the typewriter (this is called LANDSCAPE).

FOR YOUR TYPING FOLDER 14

Follow previous instructions for typing these exercises (see page 77).

INVOICES

1   Another name for an invoice is a ....

2   An invoice is numbered, dated, quotes the customer's order number and sets out
     the ....

3   Invoices are typed with .... copies.

4   Frequently, invoices are interleaved with .... carbon or ....
     is used. Both save the typist the job of inserting carbons.

5   Often, copies of carbons are different .... for ....
     identification.

6   "E & OE" typed on invoices means ....

7   This protects a firm if a typist makes a ....

8   To save the typist's time when typing invoices, NCR is often used, or
     .... carbon, which is already interleaved in sets and is ....
     after typing the invoice.

9   "Terms 2½% 30 days" means that if customers pay within .... they are
     allowed to deduct .... of the price from the invoice.

10   This is known as a "cash discount" and is an encouragement to customers
     to pay ....

TYPING MONEY IN COLUMNS

1   When typing money in columns, units must be under .... and tens under
     ....

2   The £ sign must be typed over the .... figure in the pounds column.

3   The decimal point between pounds and pence is always immediately under the
     ....

4   The total of a money column must be centred between the horizontal lines. To
     do this, underscore last line in column without ...., turn up
     .... to type total, then turn up .... for double underscore.

CENTRING VERTICALLY

Centring vertically means centring typing from top to bottom of the paper.

It is essential to make a rough plan on scrap paper before starting to type a vertical display, because accuracy is based on the number of typing lines added to the number of line spaces left between them.

A plan for the following:

T Y P I N G   S K I L L S

by

THELMA J FOSTER

would look like this:

Rough Plan

Back sp 12 or 13 ———— Sp caps ————	1 typing line
(turn up 3) x x x / x x x	2 line spaces
Back sp 1 ____lc____	1 typing line
(turn up 3) x x x / x x x	2 line spaces
Back sp 7 ———— caps ————	1 typing line
	7 Total lines and spaces

35 minus 7 = 28   (7 is total of lines and spaces)

Half of 28 = 14

14 + 1 for first typing line = 15

Turn up <u>15</u> single line spaces from top edge of A5 landscape

Finally, clear all tab stops, re-set tab stop for centre, and check that your paper guide is on zero and the left hand edge of your paper rests against the angle of the paper guide.

Then, with line spacing on single, turn up 15 line spaces, and you are ready to type the display above.

As a check, when you have taken your typing out of your machine, fold your paper from side to side – the fold should fall between the b and the y of "by".

TYPING MONEY IN COLUMNS

When typing money in columns, keep units under units and tens under tens.

```
  £
99.65
 9.01
50.00
 1.16
33.54
```

Type the £ sign over the first figure in the pounds column (turn up one).

The decimal point between pounds and pence is always immediately under the one above.

Similarly, type hundreds under hundreds:

```
  £
150.50
100.54
 33.98
  2.45
143.22
 54.99
```

Type the above examples for practise.

Typing totals of money columns

```
   £           Turn up 1
 75.90
 80.13
 12.00
 19.88         Underscore last figures in column WITHOUT turning up

187.91         Turn up 2 for total
               Turn up ONE. For double underscore, use interliner
               lever (see page 10) and move platen very
               slightly – less than a half line space –  and
               underscore again
```

Note:

£ sign is over the first figure, which happens to be in the total in this example.

Underscore for total is always extended on the left to include the £ sign.

Type the above example for practice. Try to keep your double underscore as close together as you can without the lines actually touching – it takes patience and care!

Exercise 84

Total the two columns at the top of the page and type them correctly.

Exercise 6

Type the display on the previous page on A5 portrait paper.

Make a rough plan exactly as for the landscape display, except that the lines down the page will be 50 and the spaces across 70 (elite) or 59 (pica).

Exercise 7

Type the following display on A5 portrait paper.

S T A T I O N E R Y   I S S U E S

only

on

WEDNESDAYS AND THURSDAYS

B E T W E E N

1000 HOURS AND 1100 HOURS

Exercise 8

Type Exercise 7 on A5 landscape paper.

Vertical centring

Line spacing may be varied *but* must always be noted on the rough plan or your display will not be centred vertically. This is the main cause of inaccuracies.

Exercise 9

Type the following display on A5 landscape paper, starting a new line after each oblique stroke, and choosing your own line spacing. Oblique strokes indicate line endings. DO NOT TYPE THEM.

GREENCROFT CLUB MEETING/Wednesday 14 April/at/1800/in/
GREENCROFT VILLAGE HALL

Exercise 10

Repeat Exercise 9 on A5 portrait paper.

Exercise 83

Rule up 5 invoice forms, tracing in vertical lines and typing headings as on page 175, using carbon paper for copies.

Complete them with the following details:

1 Invoice No 906888   A L Carter & Company Limited
   Trentham Trading Estate High St Kirkcaldy Fife KY1 1LR
   Order No 11289 dated 10 January 198-
   Invoice date 14 January 198-
   Terms nett
   Cat No P 66 Qty 1 Description Vending machine Unit price £485
   Total cost £485 VAT @ 15% £72.75 Total amount including VAT £557.75

2 Invoice No 907001 Lamb's Furniture Co Ltd 35 Old Bedford Road
   Luton Beds LU2 7HQ
   Order No 87751 dated 15 January 198-
   Invoice date 17 January 198-
   Terms nett
   Cat No 213 Qty 2 Description Typist's desks Unit price £60
   Total cost £120 VAT @ 15% £18 Total amount including VAT £138

3 Invoice No 979542 The Midland Secretarial Agency
   Frederick Road Edgbaston Birmingham B15 4NX
   Order No 925 dated 20 January 198-
   Invoice date 1 February 198-
   Terms nett
   Cat No AT 102-32 Qty 20 Description Ribbon cassettes all black
   Unit price £1.10 Total cost £22 VAT @ 15% £3.30 Total amount
   including VAT £25.30

4 Invoice No 981666 GPR Developments Ltd 78 East Square Chelmsford
   Essex CM1 1JN
   Order No 50987 dated 27 January 198-
   Invoice date 3 February 198-
   Terms nett
   Cat No 210 Qty 2 Description Electric staplers Unit price £62.50
   Total cost £125 VAT @ 15% £18.75 Total amount including VAT £143.75

The word "nett", meaning "not subject to deduction", may also be spelt "net".

Practise keys learned

1 Quickly type the letter, please, so that it may catch an early post, but take extra care with it, as it is amazingly easy to overlook an error when in a hurry. Despatch the letter by Friday, at the latest, and get it to The Post Office yourself; do not trust it to the office junior.

b

2 babble bobble hobby Bobbie cabbie hobble gobble nobble wobble

cobble cobbler rubbish rubber rubbed rubbing rubble robber

n

3 begin beginning beginner penny runner funny funnily sunny

kennel planned planner planning announce keenness dinner

thin thinner thinned tin tinny tinned granny grand personnel

m

4 grim grimmer swim swimming rum rummy gum gummed sum summer

summery summit comma mummy mummer drummer comment commentary

immediate immediately committee communicate stem stemmed

c

5 accede accedes acceded access accessory accession succeed

succession accuracy accurate accord accordance according

x

6 extra extreme exactly exacting excel excellent excelling fix

fixing fixture fixed wax waxed waxing expect expectation

expend expenditure expand expansion expert experience

z

7 puzzle puzzling puzzled dazzle dazzled dazzling dazzler

drizzle drizzling buzz buzzing buzzed buzzer dizzy fizzy

jazz jazzy fuzz fuzzy whizz whizzed whizzing daze laze zeal

Typing the question mark

?

New key

Locate the question mark on your typewriter – the position varies from machine to machine. It will be an upper case key, and quite probably typed with your right fourth finger from home key semi-colon.

The question mark is used in place of a fullstop at the end of a sentence, so there are **two spaces** after a question mark. There is **no space** between the preceding word and the question mark.

8 Shall we go now? What time is it? How are you? Have you

seen him? How long shall we have to wait for the train?

Shall we all go together to the Skating Rink, or on our own?

I N V O I C E   No 906323

Bought of:

Shaw & Short Ltd
Wholesalers   Office Equipment Supply Co Ltd
Whitaker St   Knightley Road
MANCHESTER   BROMSWOOD
M96 8TB   Lancs   T45 7BC

Order No 526 Dated 12 December 198-

Date 13 December 198-

Terms 2½% 30 days   VAT Reg No 63328819

Cat No	Qty	Description	Unit Price	TOTAL COST	VAT @ 15%	Total Amount inc VAT
HG 732 -89	1	Addressing machine	£190	£190	£28.50	£218.50
		E & OE				

The abbreviation "E & OE" means "errors and omissions excepted", ie if a typist makes a mistake when typing the price, it does not bind the seller. (In this case, the typist could have typed £19.00, which would have made a great deal of difference.)

"Terms 2½% 30 days" means that if the customers (Shaw & Short Ltd) pay for the addressing machine within 30 days, they are allowed to deduct 2½% of the price from the invoice. It is known as a "cash discount" and is an encouragement to customers to pay promptly.

Practise keys learned

1 Which is more important, speed or accuracy? Which comes first
when learning to type? It is more important to be accurate,
and speed will build up slowly but steadily with regular
practice. Correcting errors takes longer than the original
piece of typing, in many cases, so slowing down, with fewer
errors, makes good sense.

Accuracy drills – "short" to "longer"

a 2 a as ask all and are army aroma auntie arrive artist attract

b 3 be bed but bill bench built building backward businesslike

c 4 can act cash actor court caught caution charming chairman

d 5 do did does add dyed dried need ended ending needing needless

e 6 eat end ease trees wheel equips equipped exchanged exercises

f 7 of if off offer offered feeler duffle muffled fluffed fielding

g 8 go age aged agent gauge magic toggle glitter language governed

h 9 he him hop hope hoped hash hashed school hopeful honorary

i 10 in inn ink into impart impress included incurred increased

j 11 jet jot jotted joy jeer jeered enjoy injure injury jockey

k 12 key kit kid kind know sink click knock kennel kitchen knitting

l 13 lad all fall hall allow allowed swallow villainous millionaire

m 14 am ram mud mark marked mouse rummy merger merchant improvement

n 15 an no and any not once only nanny nature negative unnecessary

o 16 on one over tool obey noon order orchard ordinary original

p 17 up pup pip pipe piper supple dapple superb planned platform

q 18 quit quite quiet equal equate quarto quenched question equator

r 19 row roe road rower arrow borrow referred preferred preference

s 20 is sit sits miss misses fusses dismiss dismisses mistresses

t 21 at for sat sit that sitter hatter chatter shatter regretted

u 22 but undo under summer thunder numbered undertake underground

v 23 eve ever event nerve nervous violence violently involuntary

w 24 we owe away water weight weather whipping whitening wholesome

x 25 axe oxen exert exact extort extract extensive extraordinary

y 26 you yield your young youth yardage yawning youngster youthful

z 27 zoo zeal laze haze ozone azure amaze amazing waltzing organize

INVOICES

An invoice is a "bill". It is numbered, dated, quotes the customer's order number and sets out the full price. A great deal of the typing on an invoice, therefore, consists of figures, and it is most important that they are accurate.

Invoices are typed with many copies (sometimes up to 8 or 9) and NCR (see page 88) is used by many firms to save the typist the time and trouble of inserting and taking out carbons. An alternative to NCR is "one-time" carbon, which is already interleaved in the invoice "sets" and is discarded after typing the invoices. It still has to be removed by the typist, so only half of the job of using carbons is done for her.

Often, copies of invoices are different colours for easy identification.

Make one copy of the following invoice by tracing lightly over the vertical lines and typing in the headings.

I N V O I C E   No

                         Bought of:

                         Office Equipment Supply Co Ltd
                         Knightley Road
                         BROMSWOOD
                         Lancs   T45 7BC

          Date

Terms   VAT Reg No 63328819

Cat No	Qty	Description	Unit Price	TOTAL COST	VAT @ 15%	Total Amount inc VAT
		E & OE				

TYPING FOR SPEED

Either   type as far as you can in one minute

Or   type the whole passage as fast as you can without making numerous errors and check how long it took you to complete it.

A watch with a seconds hand is necessary for "timings", or, better still, a stop watch.

Keep a record in your typing folder of speed per minute, number of errors and date achieved.

A reasonable level of accuracy is one error per minute – more errors than this and you should slow down, after drilling corrections.

Always start a speed passage rather more slowly than you would normally type and build up your speed gradually – this way you will not make a lot of mistakes in the first two or three lines and lose your confidence.

Type the passage on the following page at your normal typing speed, concentrating on accuracy. If you make a mistake, leave it, and when you have finished the passage, practise each correction by typing one line of each. If you have no errors, practise any words over which you thought you hesitated, or which slowed you down.

The figures at the right hand side of the passage are NOT to be typed. In accuracy/speed practices, "standard" words are counted, not the actual words in each line. A "standard" word consists of five strokes. A stroke is a letter, space between words, use of tabulator for a new paragraph, or carriage return. A capital letter is counted as two strokes.

REVIEW OF WORDS AND FIGURES

General rule:

    use words **always** at the beginning of a sentence and for the figure "one"
    in sentences
    otherwise, use figures (see page 100 for details).

Exercise 81

There is an error in each of the following sentences, where figures are used instead of words, or vice versa. Type a corrected copy of each sentence.

1   2 or three people left the audience before the speaker had finished.

2   It was 1 day last autumn that we started planning our summer holidays.

3   The train was timetabled to leave the station at ten am.

4   The total cost of the dress, shoes and handbag came to twenty-four pounds.

5   The invoice was numbered one hundred and thirty and was dated 9 March 198-.

6   The address is: twenty-nine Grove Road Brighton Sussex BN4 8HF

Exercise 82

Type the following on A5 landscape paper, in double line spacing with indented paragraphs. Centre the heading.

NEW CATALOGUE

Our new catalogue has arrived from the printers + is full of ~~new~~ ideas, ? for gifts + for the home. Why not call one day + see for yourself? We are open from 9 am to 6 pm each

NP/ day except Sunday. [Ninety per cent of our callers are back again, which speaks for itself!

Preparation for accuracy/speed practice

Type each of the following lines 3 times. The words in them are taken from the accuracy/speed passage which follows. A4 paper. Margins both 1″.

certificate certificate certificate certificate certificate certificate

examination examination examination examination examination examination

information information information information information information

quantities quantities quantities quantities quantities quantities quantities

several several several several several several several several several

possible possible possible possible possible possible possible possible

complete complete complete complete complete complete complete complete

Accuracy/speed practice

A4 paper. Margins both 1″.
Type the heading before you start the passage. Double line spacing.

REASONS FOR FILING   Words

Filing means putting away papers so that they can be found when they are   14

wanted. Everyone has papers of some sort: a birth certificate, a school   29

report, examination certificates. These papers have to be kept because   44

of the information on them, which may be needed at a later date. Firms   58

keep papers for the same reason, and they have large quantities of   72

papers, because of the records stored on them. Filing should be done   86

every day if possible (several times a day, in fact) so that the files   101

are always complete.   105

Warm-up drill

1 The monotonous buzzing of the bees was an indication that they were soon to be
on the move, so the beekeeper donned his veiled hat and gloves and prepared to
cope with a quick swarming on to nearby trees.

Alternate-hand words

2 lap lame paid bid and dog rut may pen land wick fog tot the

3 then them sit did melt lay throb ivory blend tug urns vial

4 icicle quench lair whale aid jay coal dish eight fight coal

Preparation for accuracy/speed practice

Type each line 3 times.

unsuspecting unsuspecting unsuspecting unsuspecting unsuspecting unsuspecting

pensioner pensioner pensioner pensioner pensioner pensioner pensioner pensioner

total total total total total total total total total total total total total

disappoint disappoint disappoint disappoint disappoint disappoint disappoint

cigarettes cigarettes cigarettes cigarettes cigarettes cigarettes cigarettes

litre litre litre litre litre litre litre litre litre litre litre litre litre

recipient recipient recipient recipient recipient recipient recipient recipient

Accuracy/speed practice

VAT ON PRESENTS

	Words
Even the most modest present coming from overseas is subject to	13
Customs duty, and many unsuspecting people have to find several	26
pounds before they are able to receive their presents. For	38
instance, an old age pensioner had to pay duty and VAT on a safety	52
razor and blades sent from America. The total amount due was £3.43.	66
VAT comes into force on parcels from abroad valued at more than £40	80
from the EEC countries and £20 from other countries. Up to 50	94
cigarettes, a quarter bottle of spirits and a litre of wine are	106
allowed through the post without tax.	114
But most people forget that VAT is added to the value of the gift	128
plus its Customs duty. A £50 camera coming from America would have	144
Customs duty added of £7.50 and a further 15 per cent VAT of £8.62	158
so the recipient would have to pay a total of £16.12 for the so-	171
called gift, an arrangement which must disappoint a great many	184
people.	186

VERTICAL DISPLAY

It is often left to the typist to decide how to type a notice – using spaced capitals, closed capitals with or without underscore, or lower case, also with or without underscore. Display the following, using suitable line spacing and varying the headings:

Exercise 11

On A5 landscape paper.

Sale
of Office Equipment:
Addressing Machines
Franking Machines
Postal Scales
on Monday 20 October 198-
at 1400 in Town Hall
Bromswood

Exercise 12

On A5 portrait paper.

Quiz team to meet here on Friday, 13 April 198- at 1430 for match against Blackhill Comprehensive. Bring packed tea.
Gloria Greymatter
Freda Frump
Belinda Brain
Polly Prattle (travelling reserve)

TYPING THE TIME

There are three ways of typing the time:

a) Using am and pm (*ante meridiem* and *post meridiem* meaning before noon and after noon) with figures:

    10 am   5 pm   7.30 pm   11.15 pm

There is **no space** between am or pm, but one space between figures and am or pm. The fullstop in the figures separates hours from minutes.

b) Using o'clock, with which words or figures can be used:

    nine o'clock   12 o'clock   6 o'clock   10 o'clock

c) Using the 24-hour system, consisting wholly of figures:

    0001 hours (this is one minute after midnight)   0900 (9 am)   1200 hours (noon)   1500 (3 pm)   1700 hours (5 pm)   2200 hours (10 pm)   Midnight is always represented by the word, "midnight".

The 24-hour system is used extensively on the Continent, by airlines and the services, because it eliminates the possibility of an error between morning and afternoon.

The 24-hour system is typed without any fullstops between the figures, and the word "hours" may be abbreviated to "hrs" or typed in full.

Exercise 80

Re-type the following, using the 24-hour system:

Mrs Thomas is arriving at 9.30 am, followed by Mr Lyneham at 11 am and Miss Frankley at noon. The meeting will take place after lunch, at 2.30 pm in the Conference Hall. Tea will be at 3.30 pm and the concluding speeches will finish at approximately 5.15 pm.

FOR YOUR TYPING FOLDER 13

Follow previous instructions for typing these exercises (see page 77).

TYPING THE TIME

1   Before am and pm always use ....

2   There is .... space between am and pm.

3   There is .... space between figures and am or pm.

4   With o'clock, words or .... can be used.

5   The 24-hour system consists of ....

6   There are no .... between the figures and the word "hours" in the 24-hour system.

7   The 24-hour system is used by airlines and the services because it ....

8   The word "hours" may be abbreviated to .... or typed ....

In addition to deciding on lines, line spacing and types of heading, the typist is often left to decide on the size of paper that is most suitable for the display. In the following exercise, after you have made your rough plan, decide whether A5 landscape or A5 portrait paper would display the notice more effectively.

Exercise 13

A sponsored swim will be held in the Bromswood Swimming Baths on Sunday 8 June 198- starting at 0800 hours. Proceeds in aid of the mentally handicapped. Details from Debbie Sanders Personnel Department Ext 85.

Blocked vertical display

Blocking (also called "fully blocked" display) is a quicker way to display notices vertically and horizontally. Each line starts in the same place. The notice from page 63 will therefore look like the one below:

```
S T A T I O N E R Y   I S S U E S


only


on


WEDNESDAYS AND THURSDAYS

BETWEEN

1000 HOURS AND 1100 HOURS
```

This is a quicker method because it avoids having to centre each line separately.

Making a plan for blocked display

Count the letters and spaces **in the longest line** and deduct this from the maximum number of spaces across (this will depend on whether you are using A5 portrait or A5 landscape paper). Divide the remainder by 2. Set the left hand margin accordingly. The right hand margin should be moved to the end of the carriage – it will not be needed.

In the above example, the longest line is the first (number of letters and spaces 33). From 100 (or 70 if you are using A5 portrait paper) you will have 67 (or 37) with elite pitch. With pica you will have 49 or 26. Divide this by 2 (ignoring any odd number) and set your left hand margin:

   A5 landscape = left hand margin 33 elite, 24 pica

   A5 portrait   = left hand margin 18 elite, 13 pica

Each line then starts at the left hand margin.

Warm-up drill

1   You cannot hope to type accurately and quickly if you are sitting badly; slumping is uncomfortable and slows you down. It is vital to sit with your back supported and straight.

Practise hyphens and dashes

2   We worked out a route for the journey - it was not an easy task - and also calculated the mileage. Bourton-on-the-Water sounded a delightful and interesting place to visit but we decided it was too far for a one-day ride. We must take it easily - for the first few days - or our holiday might turn into an endurance test.

Preparation for accuracy/speed practice

Type each line 3 times.

Marketing Marketing Marketing Marketing Marketing Marketing Marketing Marketing
presents presents presents presents presents presents presents presents presents
estimated estimated estimated estimated estimated estimated estimated estimated
protection protection protection protection protection protection protection
address address address address address address address address address address
postage-paid postage-paid postage-paid postage-paid postage-paid postage-paid

Accuracy/speed practice

Post-A-Book

	Words
The Book Marketing Council discovered that the British spend	13
£120 million a year on books as presents and decided that they	26
might spend more if it were made simpler. The Post Office	38
agreed and estimated that they could increase book sales by	50
£4 million in 1982.	54
With the Post-A-Book scheme, it is possible to choose a book,	68
and take it to the sales counter of the bookshop where the	79
special postage-paid packs are sold. They come in three sizes,	92
are padded for protection, and contain a card for you to write	105
your special message on. Then you simply complete the address	118
panel on the envelope and pop the book and card into it.	129
There's no need for stamps, string or paper and The Post Office	143
dispatch it first-class, so that it should arrive next day.	155
The cost of postage varies with the size of the postage-paid	167
pack, and the cost of the whole thing is less than sending a	180
book in the normal way.	184

Exercise 14

Display the following in *blocked* style on A5 portrait or landscape paper. Choose your own line endings, line spacing and types of headings.

```
Greencroft Sports Club Badminton Championships on Wednesday 14 April 198-
at 1900 hours
```

Exercise 15

Repeat Exercise 14 on either A5 portrait or landscape paper (whichever you did not choose before).

TYPING MENUS

Menus are the one example of vertical and horizontal display. They can either be centred or fully blocked. Below is an example of a menu centred vertically and horizontally:

```
                    M E N U

                     Soup
                  Grapefruit
               Prawn Cocktail
                    Melon

                    *****

                 Roast Turkey
                 Roast Beef
                 Fillet Steak
                 Grilled Trout

                    *****

              Jacket Potatoes
                    Peas
                  Sprouts
                  Carrots

                    *****

                 Ice Cream
                   Trifle
              Fresh Fruit Salad

                    *****

                   Coffee

                    *****
```

Turn up 3 after "MENU"

Single line spacing for each course

Turn up 2 before and after asterisks

Exercise 16

Type the above menu on A5 portrait paper, centring each line.
Make a rough plan first, ALLOWING ONE CLEAR LINE SPACE BEFORE AND AFTER the five asterisks.

FOR YOUR TYPING FOLDER 12

Follow previous instructions for typing these exercises (see page 77).

TYPING WEIGHTS AND MEASUREMENTS

1 When typing metric units or their abbreviations, the same symbol is used whether singular or plural, without the addition of ....

2 There is no fullstop after the ....

3 There is always a space left between figures and ....

4 The abbreviation for kilometre is ....

5 The abbreviation for gram is ....

6 The abbreviation for millimetre is ....

7 The abbreviation for centimetre is ....

8 Litre is .... abbreviated except by ....

9 Yards, feet and inches can be abbreviated to ....

10 There is .... space between abbreviations and figures.

11 Alternatively, the .... apostrophe can be used for .... and the .... apostrophe for ....

12 There is no similar sign for ....

13 The .... is used for the multiplication sign, with .... space before and .... space after.

14 Pounds and ounces are abbreviated to .... and ....

15 The letter "s" is .... added for plural.

METRIC CONVERSION TABLE

Length		Mass	
1 in = 25.44 mm		1 lb = 0.454 kg	
1 ft = 304.8 mm		1 cwt = 50.80 kg	
1 yd = 0.914 m		1 ton = 1.016 tonnes	
1 mile = 1.609 km		1 kg = 2.205 lb	
1 m = 3.281 ft			

Temperature

$0{}^\circ C = 32{}^\circ F$ (freezing)
$10{}^\circ C = 50{}^\circ F$ (rather cold)
$20{}^\circ C = 68{}^\circ F$ (quite warm)
$30{}^\circ C = 86{}^\circ F$ (very hot)

Area

$1\ ft^2 = 0.093\ m^2$
$1\ yd^2 = 0.836\ m^2$
$1\ mile^2 = 2.590\ km^2$
$1\ m^2 = 10.746\ ft^2 = 1.916\ yd^2$

Volume

1 gal = 4.546 ℓ
1 ℓ = 0.220 gal

A fully blocked menu

A fully blocked menu has its longest line centred on the paper. Count letters and spaces in longest line, deduct from 100 or 82, divide remainder by 2, and re-set left hand margin (the right hand margin will not be needed).

Centre the menu vertically, too.

```
M E N U


Hors d'oeuvre
Tomato Soup
Whitebait

*****

Chicken Casserole
Braised Steak and Kidneys
Veal and Ham Pie

*****

Apple Tart and Cream
Strawberries and Cream
Ice Cream

*****

Coffee

*****
```

Exercise 17

Type the above menu on A5 portrait paper, starting each line at your left hand margin.

Exercise 78

1 The size of A4 paper is 210 mm x 297 mm (8¼" x 11¾").

2 The size of A5 paper is (portrait) 143 mm x 210 mm (5 7/8" x 8¼").

(NOTE: When there is no fraction on your typewriter, use figures and sloping (oblique) stroke with no spacing in between, as above.)

3 Half of A5 is called A6. The size of this is 105 mm x 148 mm (4 1/8" x 5 7/8").

4 Post Office Preferred sizes of envelopes (POP) are within the range 90 mm x 140 mm (3½" x 5½") and 120 mm x 235 mm (4¾" x 9¼").

5 The order for the carpet was for a square 15' x 15' but was incorrectly delivered as 15' 6" x 15' 6".

Imperial weights

Pounds and ounces are abbreviated to: lb   and   oz

No "s" is added for the plurals.

Leave one space between figures and abbreviations.

Exercise 79

1 The shopping list included 5 lb potatoes, 2 lb tomatoes and 4 oz tea.

2 There are 16 oz in one lb.

3 There are 14 lb in one stone.

4 There are approximately 28 g in one oz.

5 There are 112 lb in one hundredweight (cwt).

Menus are sometimes typed on A4 paper, if they are exceptionally long, ie if typing lines and spaces amount to around 40 or more.

Exercise 18

Type this menu on A4 paper, centring vertically, and centring *each line* horizontally.

M E N U

Seafood Cocktail
Soup of the Day
Smoked Mackerel
Smoked Salmon
Melon
Grapefruit

*****

Steak and Kidney Pudding
Mixed Grill
Veal Cutlets
Roast English Lamb
Roast Scotch Beef
Roast Pheasant
Grilled Plaice
Cold Ham
Cold Turkey

*****

Roast Potatoes
Boiled Potatoes
Creamed Potatoes
Peas
Carrots
Cauliflower
Green Salad

*****

Cheese and Biscuits

*****

Coffee

*****

Exercise 19

Repeat the above menu in fully blocked style.

TYPING WEIGHTS AND MEASUREMENTS

Metric units

Metric units and their abbreviations in most common use are:

metre	m
kilometre	km
centimetre	cm
millimetre	mm
litre	this is not abbreviated, except by handwritten ℓ with a loop
gram	g
kilogram	kg

The letter "s" is not added for the plurals: 5 cm   9 km   8 m

There is always a space left between the figure and the symbol.
There is no fullstop after the symbol.

Type the following for practice

Wool is often sold in grams - 50 g balls, 25 g balls, or 20 g balls.

The equivalent of one inch is 25 mm.

One yard equals 39 cm.

The equivalent of 8 km is 5 miles.

The item on the invoice which was omitted was: 10 m @ £2.54 per m.

It is 50 km to the city centre according to the signpost, but the map gives 51 km as the correct distance.

We agreed that 4 litres of water would be sufficient for the day.

The notice in the greengrocer's shop had been changed overnight from 10p per kg to 20p per kg, which was considered a rather large increase.

Imperial measurements

Yards, feet and inches can be abbreviated to:

  yd   ft   in   (no "s" is added for the plurals)

The size of the room is 5 yd 2 ft 7 in × 4 yd 2 ft 6 in

Leave one space between abbreviations and figures.

Alternatively, use the single apostrophe for feet and the double apostrophe for inches (there is no similar sign that can be used to abbreviate yards):

The desk measured 4′ 6″ × 3′ 3″ and the table was 2′ × 1′ 3″

No space between figures and signs but space between signs and "x" used for multiplication sign.

TYPING A LIST

Lists are always blocked, with the longest line centred horizontally. The heading may be centred over the page, or blocked with the list.

Centring vertically is not essential. Leave at least a clear inch at the top of the paper by turning up 7, or more if wished (this will depend on the number of items in the list).

Exercise 20

Type the following list on A5 paper.

<u>STATIONERY</u>   (centre)

```
        staplers and staples
        perforators
        adhesive tape
        paper clips
        pins
        rubber bands
        bulldog clips
        treasury tags
        folders
        labels
        rubber thimbles
        string
        brown paper
        rubber stamps and pads
        wire baskets
        typing paper
        letterheading
        memoranda
        envelopes
        carbon paper
        typewriter ribbons
        duplicating paper
        duplicating ink
        ink stencils
```

Exercise 21

Re-type the list in Exercise 20 in alphabetical order.

Block the heading.

SECTION 5

Specialised Typing

Practise keys learned

Quickly take the short cut by the junction and avoid the
longer route which will go past a dozen busy factories.
Take extra care when crossing as heavy lorries constantly
come unexpectedly out of the warehouses.

Preparation for accuracy/speed practice
Type each line 3 times.

applications applications applications applications applications applications
interview interview interview interview interview interview interview interview
advertisement advertisement advertisement advertisement advertisement
especially especially especially especially especially especially especially
information information information information information information
requested requested requested requested requested requested requested requested

Accuracy/speed practice

	Words
Many applications for jobs do not result in an interview. One of the	14
reasons is that the applicant has not read the advertisement properly	28
and has applied for a job for which she is totally unsuitable. Points	42
to check especially are: age, experience, skills needed. The other main	57
reason for no interview following a letter of application is that the	71
letter was badly spelt and untidily written and set out or did not	85
supply the information requested.	92

TYPING THE EXCLAMATION MARK

! *New key*

You may have an exclamation mark as an upper case key on your typewriter. If you haven't, you can make one by typing an apostrophe, backspacing once, typing a fullstop. This is known as a combination character (one made up from two characters on your typewriter).

Type a line of exclamation marks for practice.

Leave two spaces after an exclamation mark, as it is used instead of a fullstop at the end of a sentence. There is **no space** before an exclamation mark.

Practise typing the exclamation mark

Mind the step! He shouted, "Help! Help!" Beware of the dog!
Fire! Fire! Please leave at once! From a long way off we
could hear the cry, "Coming!" FINAL SALE REDUCTIONS TODAY!

3 Then, Mrs Maxwell has asked you to re-type the following notice with each line centred. No copy is needed. Use A5 landscape paper.

```
S A L E   O F   S E C O N D S

The usual quarterly sale of seconds will be held ~~on~~ next:

WEDNESDAY

THURSDAY

FRIDAY

5, 6 and 7 July

in the

CANTEEN

~~between~~
```
stet/ ~~from~~ 5 pm to 6 pm

O/ The usual staff discount of 20% will apply. ~~PLUS an additional discount of 15% making a total in all of 35%.~~

uc/ Staff are limited to total purchases of £50 (after discount) on any
us/ one day.

4 Finally, the Sales Manager has asked if you would type a short personal letter for him to his son. Mr Benson's home address is: The Larches   78 Downland Road Bromswood   Lancs   T44 5BJ
Type an envelope for this letter to: Master W Benson   Ingram House Greencoats School   Willerby   Hull   North Humberside   HU10 6EW
No carbon copy is needed. Use plain A5 portrait paper. Date for today.

Dear Bill

Thank you very much f yr ltr & the gd news abt the cricket match last Saturday. What a splendid score you made — I'm sure yr place in
NP/ the team is now quite safe [I shall be up to see you on Sunday as usual — abt 12 — & we will go to the White Hart for lunch. Bring Peter Long if his parents are not coming
[Lots of love

TYPING THE HYPHEN

New key

Locate the hyphen key on your typewriter – on many machines it is the lower case key below the question mark.

The hyphen is used for:

> dividing two parts of a compound word: second-hand   first-class
> co-operative

> dividing a word at the right hand margin when there is insufficient space to complete it.

There is no space before or after a hyphen.

Type a line of hyphens:

Now go back without turning up and type a line of underscore.

A line made by typing hyphens is a broken line.

A line made by the underscore gives a continuous line.

Practise typing the hyphen

1   The list is up-to-date and the first interview will start
mid-morning.

2   The uniform looked so old-fashioned, the staff refused to wear
it until it had been re-designed.

3   We shall not be leaving for thirty-six hours, and by that time
the cross-channel ferry service will be operating normally.

WORD DIVISION

Until now, you have typed the lines from this book exactly as they were printed, starting a new line when it was printed on the page. From this point you will be making your own line endings and setting your own margins.

On A4 paper:

> the **left hand** margin must never be less than 1″

> the **right hand** margin must never be wider than the left.

The right hand margin should be kept as even as possible, but it cannot be exactly level, and to avoid large "gaps" or words jutting out into the right hand margin, it is necessary occasionally to divide words at the line end by using a hyphen. **The hyphen is never typed on the left when dividing a word.**

The warning bell (usually about 5 or 6 spaces from the margin setting) is to tell the typist to come to a decision about whether the word can be finished, whether a space should be left and the word continued on the next line, or whether a word should be divided.

PROGRESS TEST 4

You work for Office Equipment Supply Co Ltd in the Sales Department. The Sales Manager is Mr K Benson and, as part of your duties in the Sales Department, you help Mr Benson's secretary when she is busy.

1 Mr Benson's secretary (Mrs Lynne Maxwell) has asked you to type a memo (with one carbon copy) to the Head Receptionist, Miss Alison Moss, from Mrs Maxwell as follows:

Date 3 July 198–   Heading : Singapore visitors

Mr Tan and Mr Seah are arriving fr Singapore on Monday 10 July at about 11 am. As they are ~~very~~ important customers, could you please phone me the moment they arrive?

2 Then, Mrs Maxwell would like you to re-type the following letter to The Manager The Royal Oak Hotel Market Place Bromswood Lancs T91 3BC. Take 2 carbon copies of this letter, and, after you have taken them out of your typewriter, put one carbon copy back in the machine, and type on the top right hand corner: Accounts Dept. The reference on the letter will be: KB/LM. Date for 3 July 198-. Type an envelope.

Dear Sir

With reference to our telephone conversation yesterday, would you please reserve two single rooms (each with private bath) for the three nights of Monday 10 July, Tuesday 11 July and Wednesday 12 July. These rooms will be occupied by Mr Tan and Mr Seah from Singapore.

They will require transport from Heathrow on Monday 10 July to meet ~~them from~~ flight BA4610 arriving (british Time) at 9.30 am and also on Wednesday 12 July to take them back to Heathrow to catch flight BA 7003 leaving at 12.20 pm. They should be at the airport on 12 July at approximately 11 am.

Please send your account for accommodation and transport to the Accounts Department at ~~my~~ firm. (the above)

Yours faithfully
OFFICE EQUIPMENT SUPPLY CO LTD

K Benson
Sales Manager

Rules for word division

Compound words that already contain a hyphen should be divided at the hyphen – do not introduce a second hyphen.

Divide according to syllables: end-ings, improve-ment, sten-cils.

If there are two similar *consonants* in the middle of the word, divide between them: run-ning, sug-gest, excel-lent.

When words should NOT be divided

When they begin with a capital letter – proper names:
David, Lawrence, Bristol, Great Britain, Elizabeth

When the pronunciation would be changed:
coun-try, busi-ness, min-utes, mac-hines

When division would mean taking only 2 letters forward:
part-ed, mail-ed, typ-ed, correct-ed, frank-ed

This is because, after typing the hyphen at the right hand side, only one space is saved by dividing, so that word may just as well be completed on the same line.

Short words and words of one syllable:
was, can, from, now, did, through

Numbers and sums of money:
1534, £6,900, £34,650, 235,000

When completing a word at the right hand side (or typing the hyphen) use the **margin release** on your typewriter.

The test of good word division is that the meaning is clear to the reader from the first part of the word.

Word division should be avoided whenever possible – it is quicker to leave a space and type the complete word on the line below.

WHEN IN DOUBT – DON'T DIVIDE!

Practise word division

Type the following, indicating by a hyphen where you would be able to divide if you considered it necessary. Not all can be divided.

```
dispatched, valued, Manchester, £6778, straight, lost,

co-operate, borrow, embarrass, second-hand, equip, happen,

replied, getting, stewards, London, Elizabeth, £23,4000, unite,

await, worthwhile, valve, loyalty, youth, city, club, Derby.
```

Exercise 77

Type a memo with layout as in Exercise 76 on page 163 with one carbon copy. Date for 20 May 198-. The memo is from Robert Williams   Transport Manager, to Mrs Mary Dickens   Sales Manager's Secretary. The heading is the same as in Exercise 76.

Transport to Gatwick Airport on 2 June has been arranged for Mr Bryce — a car will collect him from his home at 0800 on that date. [Mr Bryce NP/ will be met at Gatwick on 28 June at 2100 and taken to his home. Flight numbers hv bn noted.

FOR YOUR TYPING FOLDER 11

Follow previous instructions for typing these exercises (see page 77).

MEMORANDA

1 Written communications between offices or branches of the same firm are typed on .... forms.

2 Memoranda (called "memos" for short) are similar to postcards, in that they contain no salutation, no .... and no inside address.

3 Usually, memos contain the name and title of the sender (or department) and name and title (or department) of ....

4 .... envelopes are typed for memos unless they are ....

5 The wording of memos is .... than that of business letters.

6 Memo forms are the same size as letterheadings, A4 or ....

7 A heading on a memo is helpful to the person reading it, when sorting the post, as ....

Exercise 22

Type the following on A5 landscape paper in double line spacing. Margins 1½″ left and 1″ right. Make your own line endings. Block the heading.

DURING AN INTERVIEW

The interviewer's job is to make you feel at ease, so you will be pleasantly surprised to find that you stop feeling nervous quite soon. Sit down when you are asked to do so. Talk naturally and avoid "you know". Nervous people often use this phrase out of sheer fright! At the end of the interview, the interviewer will usually say, "We will let you know." It is not often that a decision is given there and then. If you decide that you don't want the job anyway, don't say so, you might change your mind later on, or the job may not even be offered. Thank your interviewer for seeing you and say "Goodbye" with a smile. The last impression is just as important as the first.

FOR YOUR TYPING FOLDER 1

On a sheet of A4 paper, with margins 1″ both sides, turn up 7 (from alignment scale and top of paper) and centre:

Turn up 3 (leaving two *clear* line spaces).

Set tab stop for 4 spaces in from left hand margin.

Type numbers at margin; start sentences at tab stop.

Type in single line spacing, with double between sentences.

Fill in the gaps with the correct word (or words):

SPECIAL CHARACTERS

1   There is .... space after an oblique (sloping) stroke.

2   There is .... space after the £ sign before the figures.

3   The underscore is typed without turning up .... line spaces.

4   The @ sign is an abbreviation for the word .... and is used only in commercial documents such as ....

5   The & sign (the ....) is an abbreviation for the word ....; it is used only in: Mr & Mrs, addresses and registered names of firms.

Alternative placement of headings for memos

```
M E M O R A N D U M

To                                    Ref

From                                  Date
```

On the above memo form heading, "To" is placed before "From" and many firms prefer this layout.

Where memo forms are pre-printed, all the typist has to do is to use the layout provided. Where memo forms are not pre-printed, follow the layout preferred (carbon copies in the files will make this clear).

In examinations, candidates must be careful to type the correct names against "To" and "From" in case the headings are in a different place to that to which they are accustomed.

Both the layout above and the ones on pages 159–62 are correct. Which one is used is a matter of personal preference by the firm concerned.

Exercise 76

Type the following

```
M E M O R A N D U M

To  Mr Robert Williams  Transport Manager      Ref   MD/PK

From  Mary Dickens  Sales Manager's Secretary   Date   19 May 198-


SALES MANAGER'S FAR EASTERN TOUR JUNE 198-


Details of the above have now been finalised and are attached.
Mr Bryce will require transport to the airport on 2 June and also
from the airport on 28 June - times, flight numbers, etc, are on the
attached itinerary.


Enc
```

Warm-up drill

Margins 1″ left and ½″ right. Make your own line endings.

The zealous office junior quickly collected the incoming post and took it round to all the offices on the ground floor and first floor on Mondays, Wednesdays and Fridays. On Tuesdays and Thursdays, the post was taken first to the second floor, and the staff there expected it soon after 0900.

Preparation for accuracy/speed practice

Type each line 3 times.

receive receive receive receive receive receive receive receive receive receive
long-awaited long-awaited long-awaited long-awaited long-awaited long-awaited
decided decided decided decided decided decided decided decided decided decided
successful successful successful successful successful successful successful
discouraged discouraged discouraged discouraged discouraged discouraged
different different different different different different different different
experience experience experience experience experience experience experience

Accuracy/speed practice

Type on A5 landscape paper in double line spacing. Margins 1″ left and ¾″ right.
Make your own line endings.

	Words
SUCCESS OR FAILURE?	
If you receive the long-awaited letter offering you a job, reply at once	14
by letter accepting it, or tell them you have decided not to accept it,	29
if that is the case. You may receive a letter telling you that you have	44
not been successful. If so, do not be discouraged; every interview and	58
interviewer is different and adds to your experience. Next time you	72
will have a great deal more confidence.	80

TYPING THE DASH

The key used for the dash is the same as that used for the hyphen.

The dash is typed in sentences where a slightly longer pause is indicated than that given by a comma. The dash is typed with **one space** before and after.

Practise typing the dash

1 Come and have some coffee on Saturday - I'll tell you the time later.

2 The engineering firm has offered me a job - but it's not very well-paid.

3 My holidays are arranged to start on a Wednesday - which means easier journeys.

4 She was very clothes-conscious and up-to-date - which was why she never saved.

Alternative layout for memos

Block names after "From" and "To" and re-set left hand margin accordingly.

```
MEMORANDUM


From  Mary Morrison  Canteen Supervisor       Ref  MM/AV

To    Mr B Long  Assistant Buyer              Date  20 November 198-


      CLEANING EQUIPMENT


      The attached list gives prices, quantities and sizes of
      cleaning equipment needed in the canteen.

      As replacement of all these items is now an urgent matter, I
      would very much appreciate your co-operation.


      Enc
```

Exercise 75

On another of your memo forms, type a corrected copy of the following. Take 2 carbon copies. Date for today. The reference is AB/your own initials. The heading is: Expenses.

To   Mr Charles Ash Chief Accountant

From   Alan Blunt   Sales Manager

A copy of my expense account

(with receipts) sheet is attached for yr

Signature.

Enc

On *one* of the carbon copies, starting at the bottom left hand margin, about 1″ up from the bottom of the sheet, type: For the attention of Mrs Jane Carr   Assistant Cashier. The reason for this is to let Mrs Carr have her own copy.

162

Warm-up drill

Margins 1″ left and ½″ right. Make your own line endings.

1   The mountain climb zigzagged down steeply and the climbers quickly realised that they must get back to join the rest of the party before light failed.

Revise figures

2   Send cash by postal order to settle Invoice No GS/25438.

3   The meeting is arranged for 25 August 198- in Room 31 at 1700 hours.

4   So many people came to see the demonstration that 3 more rooms had to be opened, 102 more chairs borrowed and 4 more ticket collectors placed at the entrance.

5   Order No ZX 89215 was dispatched on 30 April last; it has not been received here up to today (24 May) and I would like you to telephone. The number is 664 317 Extension 48.

6   The first practicable typewriter was built in 1867, but typewriters were not sold until 1874. Tabulators were introduced in about 1898 and portable machines in about 1912.

Words with double letters

7   babble bobble Bobbie hobble gobble nobble rubbish rubber rubbed hobby

8   accede access accession succeed accessory accuracy account according

9   ladder laddie caddie addition coddle muddy wedded wedding hidden middle

10   bee been beef feed need needed seed seeded meet meeting feet three career

11   tiff piffle cuff cuffed puff puffed puffin tariff official differ staff

12   goggle gaggle mugged digger digging rugged bewigged ragged suggest jagged

13   will mill silly hill hilly valley fill filler pill excellent ball recall

14   grimmer swimming committee rummy comment programme commute common stemmed

15   penny runner funny bunny beginning keenness dinner thinner tinny personnel

16   loop cool pool fool wood stood soon good boost school smooth football

17   happy choppy shopping shopper dropped supplied apply applied appeal happen

18   merry sorry worry worried hurry hurried hurrying errors arrange referred

19   pass lass less toss amass dress dresses address addressing success business

20   petty little pattern bottle potter matter fitter better letter settle

21   puzzle dazzle drizzle drizzling buzz buzzer buzzing dizzy fizzy whizzed

22   babble accede ladder bee tiff goggle will grimmer penny loop happy merry

Exercise 73

On another of your memo forms, type a corrected copy of the following memo. Date it for today.

```
M E M O R A N D U M


From  J Boyett  Purchasing Officer        Ref JB/MM

To  Mrs F Hall  Stock Control Supervisor  Date  14 November 198-


A5 LANDSCAPE LETTERHEADING
```

I notice from the latest stocktaking figures that stocks of the above have remained ~~static~~ unchanged for some months. As A5 landscape letterheading is so little used, I suggest that you do not re-order; instead, use up present stocks by printing (on the reverse side) headings for memo forms.

Special notes:

> Leave 2 clear spaces between headings before starting to type.
>
> Turn up 3 after headings before typing the main heading (if there is one).
>
> Type memos in single line spacing.
>
> It is polite to add "Mr", "Mrs", etc, to the name of the person receiving the memo. This is not necessary for the name of the sender.

Exercise 74

On another of your memo forms, type a correct copy of the following draft memo. Take a carbon copy on plain A5 paper – in many offices this would be coloured bank typing paper, for identification purposes. Different coloured copies are sometimes sent to different departments.

```
M E M O R A N D U M


From  F Hall  Stock Control Supervisor   Ref  FH/PT

To  Mr J Boyett  Purchasing Officer      Date  15 November 198-
```

A5 LANDSCAPE LETTER HEADING

Remaining stocks of the above are now being reprinted in accordance w yr memo dated 14 Nov. When rec'd from Printing Dept they will be added to the balance in stock of memo forms. No further orders of A5 landscape letterheading will be processed. Members of staff will hve to be advised.

Preparation for accuracy/speed practice

Margins 1″ left and ¾″ right. Type each line 3 times.

annoyance annoyance annoyance annoyance annoyance annoyance annoyance annoyance

frustration frustration frustration frustration frustration frustration

important important important important important important important important

process process process process process process process process process process

difficult difficult difficult difficult difficult difficult difficult difficult

oldest oldest oldest oldest oldest oldest oldest oldest oldest oldest oldest

square square square square square square square square square square square square

uncreased uncreased uncreased uncreased uncreased uncreased uncreased uncreased

Accuracy/speed practice

Type the heading first (blocked).

PLACING THE PAPERS IN THE RIGHT FILE

	Words
Filing is done in order to find documents when needed. More	12
annoyance, frustration and waste of time are caused in firms	24
by not being able to find a paper that is needed than almost	37
anything else. Placing the papers in the right file is the	49
most important part of the whole filing process. A paper	61
placed in the wrong file will be very difficult to find and	73
could well be lost for ever. The most recent paper is always	85
placed on top of all the other papers in a file. These papers	98
will have been filed in date order, too, so that the oldest	110
paper is at the bottom, or back of the file. Papers should	122
be flat and square in the file so that they remain uncreased.	135
The other reason for placing papers carefully in a file is to	147
keep them clean and free from dust.	155

```
M E M O R A N D U M

From  Janet Black  Mail Room Supervisor        Ref  JB/KM

To  Mr A Simms  Company Secretary              Date  12 November 198-

REGISTRATION AND RECORDED DELIVERY


I attach for your approval (and alteration where you think
necessary) a draft notice in connection with the misuse of the
above, and recommendations regarding the alternative use of recorded
delivery.

When I receive the draft back from you, I will have copies
duplicated and sent to all offices concerned.

                              JB

Enc
```

To help staff sorting out incoming post (managers or secretaries) a heading is often typed on memos, as it indicates the contents at a glance.

Memos are often just initialled by the sender, instead of carrying a full signature.

An enclosure is indicated in the usual way, 2 clear line spaces under the last line of the body of the memo.

Exercise 72

Using carbon paper, make 6 copies of the memo form above on A5 landscape paper. Turn up 4 before typing the heading in spaced capitals. Turn up 3 under the heading. Set margins on 1″ left and ½″ right. Turn up twice between headings. Start "Ref" and "Date" on 70 (elite) or 75 (pica).

Make a copy of the memo at the top of this page on one of your memo forms.

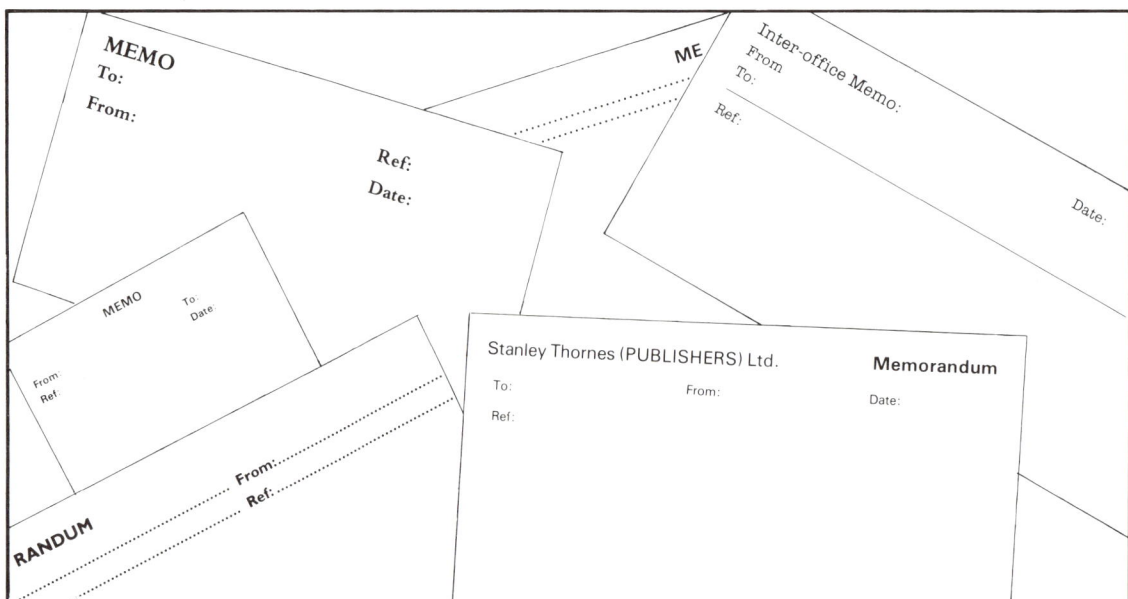

Carriage return drills

Return carriage smartly, without taking your eyes off your book. Type in double line spacing.

1. The receptionist's main job in a firm is to look after visitors.

   The receptionist may also:

   Type

   Operate a switchboard

   File

   Give out brochures

   Give out handbooks issued by the firm

   Open mail

   Be able to give simple first aid when necessary

2. Some of the qualities of a good receptionist should include:

   Politeness

   Friendliness

   Helpfulness

   Tactfulness

3. Callers who have made appointments might include:

   Applicants to be interviewed for vacancies

   Sales representatives

   Business people

   Visitors from overseas

4. Callers without appointments could be:

   People enquiring about vacancies

   Customers with complaints

   Sales representatives

5. Regular callers without appointments might be:

   Postal delivery people

   Security van drivers delivering cash for wages

   Delivery people from other firms

   Roadline delivery people

   British Rail delivery people

   Window cleaners

   Telephone disinfecting service staff

MEMORANDA

In most firms, written communications between offices or branches of the same firm are typed on memorandum forms called "memos". The correct word for "memo" is "memorandum" but this is rarely used.

Memos, because they are internal communications (sent round to the firm's employees), are simpler than letters, and contain no salutation, no complimentary close and no inside address.

Usually, they contain the name and title (or department) of the sender and the name and title (or department) of the recipient.

The wording of memos is less formal than that of business letters and in some firms, other staff are addressed by their forenames.

Memos are the same sizes as letterheadings – either A4 or A5.

No envelopes are typed for memos, unless they are confidential, in which case they would obviously be enclosed in an envelope marked "Confidential" in the usual way.

Carbon copies are taken of memos, for filing, and quite often other carbon copies are taken for distribution to other members of staff, for their information.

Memo forms may have printed headings, as shown below, but a memo is so simple in design that many firms do not have them printed, leaving the typist to type in headings. A typical typed memo form is shown on the next page.

MEMORANDUM

From   Ref
To   Date

FOR YOUR TYPING FOLDER 2

Follow previous instructions for typing these exercises (see page 77).

(see page 77)

CENTRING VERTICALLY AND HORIZONTALLY

1   A4 typing paper has .... typing lines from top to bottom.

2   A5 typing paper (landscape) has .... typing lines from top to bottom.

3   A5 typing paper (portrait) has .... typing lines from top to bottom.

4   A4 typing paper has .... typing spaces across (elite).

5   A4 typing paper has .... typing spaces across (pica).

6   A5 (portrait) has .... typing spaces across (elite).

7   A5 (portrait) has .... typing spaces across (pica).

8   A5 paper is .... the size of A4.

9   The centre of A4 paper (elite) is ....

Move margin back one space

10   The centre of A4 paper (pica) is ....

11   The centre of A5 (portrait, elite) is ....

12   The centre of A5 (landscape, pica) is ....

Warm-up drill

1 Jacob and Zeb very quickly picked the two dozen tulips and daffodils from behind
the big wall, and carried them back with them.

One-hand words

2 yolk ink zest oil upon are holy kink fear wed punk card fact tax was

3 lump saw acre ply pip get bad mum few him pup dew hip dew pup zest plump

4 were pink tweed pool was nook case jump daze map tweet saw were pink

5 sad only fare play exert mill exact pill fad kill gas mill look swear

Preparation for accuracy/speed practice

Type each line 3 times.

courteous courteous courteous courteous courteous courteous courteous courteous

pleasure pleasure pleasure pleasure pleasure pleasure pleasure pleasure pleasure

telephone telephone telephone telephone telephone telephone telephone telephone

conversation conversation conversation conversation conversation conversation

afterwards afterwards afterwards afterwards afterwards afterwards afterwards

romantic romantic romantic romantic romantic romantic romantic romantic romantic

computerised computerised computerised computerised computerised computerised

Accuracy/speed practice

DISAPPEARING LETTERS

	Words
A letter is one of the courteous gestures that gives pleasure	12
to friends and family, but it is gradually disappearing from	24
normal life. A telephone call from a friend gives pleasure	37
too - that is, unless one is in the bath, or in the middle of	49
cooking, or just on the point of going out to catch a train.	61
Even when there is time to spare to enjoy a conversation over	74
the telephone, there is nothing afterwards that can be enjoyed.	87
A romantic telephone call disappears literally into thin air	99
and cannot be kept in a chocolate box for years.	109
The arrival of the post now simply means unwanted advertising	122
material and computerised bills.	128

Warm-up drill

Margins 1″ left and ¾″ right. Make your own line endings.

Prices should be expected to be low in the sales, but dozens of bargains have been snapped up already, by shoppers who arrived quite early for the January sales.

Preparation for accuracy/speed practice

Type each line 3 times.

clerical clerical clerical clerical clerical clerical clerical clerical clerical
programmer programmer programmer programmer programmer programmer programmer
receptionist receptionist receptionist receptionist receptionist receptionist
business business business business business business business business business
separate separate separate separate separate separate separate separate separate
necessary necessary necessary necessary necessary necessary necessary necessary
personally personally personally personally personally personally personally
supervise supervise supervise supervise supervise supervise supervise supervise
functions functions functions functions functions functions functions functions

Accuracy/speed practice

Type on A5 landscape paper in double line spacing. Margins 1″ left and ¾″ right.
Make your own line endings.

The left hand margin should never be less than 1″.

THE PURPOSE OF THE OFFICE

	Words
An office is a place where any clerical work is done, and the word	13
"clerk" means any office worker − for example, typist, computer	26
programmer, receptionist. Offices exist in firms mainly to receive,	40
record and find information. In a small business, separate office	54
services will not be necessary. The manager can receive and give	67
all the information. In larger businesses, the managing director	81
cannot deal personally with all inward and outward communications	94
nor supervise everything that takes place. The office services are	108
there to carry out these functions on behalf of the management.	121

Exercise 23

Re-type the above accuracy/speed practice on A5 portrait paper with margins both
½″. Double line spacing.

4 Finally, you are asked to re-type the following, which is a draft of a notice to be sent to all the offices, after being approved by the Company Secretary.

One copy only, in double line spacing, with indented paragraphs, on A4 paper.

RECORDED DELIVERY ⟶ Centre

It has become more and more obvious during the last 3 or 4 months that registered post is being used unnecessarily for letters which contain, not valuables, but important papers. Registered post is an expensive service (because of the compensation paid by The Post Office when letters are lost) and also letters sent by registered post must be sent first class, which adds to the cost. The cheaper alternative is recorded delivery, by which letters can be sent first or second class, and which also gives proof of delivery and proof of posting. The question of compensation is hardly material in connection with important documents, as they could not be replaced in most cases so the registration fee is being wasted.

Obviously, anything that is valuable – money in the form of notes for example – must still be registered and in the event of any doubt, please ask the Mail Room Supervisor's advice before marking envelopes "Registered Post". The co-operation of everyone concerned will be much appreciated.

Leaflets issued by The Post Office on recorded delivery are available in the Mail Room if further information would be useful.

FOR YOUR TYPING FOLDER 3

Follow previous instructions for typing these exercises (see page 77).

(see page 77)

PUNCTUATION

1 .... spaces are left after fullstops, question marks and exclamation marks.

2 All other punctuation marks (commas, semi-colons and colons) have .... space after.

3 Headings have .... fullstops at the end.

4 There is .... space <u>before</u> the word typed after quotation marks and .... space after the last word <u>before</u> the closing quotation marks.

5 There is .... space between an opening bracket and the word typed after it, and .... space between the last word and the closing bracket.

6 A hyphen is used to separate two parts of a compound word and there is .... space before or after it.

7 A dash is used to indicate a pause in a sentence (slightly longer than that indicated by a comma) and there is .... space before and after a dash.

8 The .... key on the typewriter is used for the hyphen and the dash. It is a lower case key, and if typed continuously, it gives a .... line.

CARBON COPIES

Normally, one copy is taken of every document typed in an office. This carbon copy is used for filing. Sometimes, several carbon copies are taken and used for distribution to other offices, for information. Although it is becoming more common for firms to photocopy letters and memos, and file the photocopy, many offices still use carbon copies. Carbon paper is the cheapest way of producing copies, and the quickest, provided the typist is accurate and does not have to waste time erasing frequently.

Carbon copies are usually taken on thin typing paper (known as "bank" or "flimsy" – flimsy is slightly thinner than bank) which is often coloured, to make it easy to distinguish it from the white bond paper or letterheading used for top copies, which is a thicker paper.

Carbon paper is manufactured in many different strong colours. The colours in general office use are black, blue or purple.

Carbon paper should have the top left, or right hand corner cut away. This helps the typist to release the carbons when removing the papers from the typewriter, as they are held by the corner where the carbon has been cut off, shaken, and the carbons drop on to the desk. This saves handling carbons separately, and saves time.

3   The second letter is to be typed on A5 letterheading, with one carbon copy and an envelope. This letter will be delivered by hand, and is to be addressed to Mrs Emma Craven   12 Duke Street   Chelmsford   Essex   CM5 1JN. The letter will be signed by Miss Elizabeth Stevens   Personnel Officer.

Head the letter: Book-keeper. Date for yesterday.

Dear Madam

uc/ I noticed from yr advert in The Echo that you are interested in a

NP position as book-keeper. [There is a possibility of a vacancy here in the (near) future and I wd be pleased if

§ you wd ~~call~~ telephone & make an appointment to call & see me a s a p.

NP [The position is full-time, but consideration cd be given to part-time,

¶ if ~~preferred by you~~ you prefer.

Yrs ffly

Inserting carbons

a) Behind a sheet of white bond place a sheet of carbon paper, patterned side towards you. The plain side is the one that prints the copy.

b) Place a sheet of coloured bank or flimsy behind the carbon paper.

c) Straighten the papers so that the edges are level.

d) Insert them into your typewriter with the coloured paper *towards* you.

e) Use the paper release lever to ensure that the papers and carbon are uncreased and that the edges are level.

On a manual typewriter, an even touch is important as, if the typist is striking the keys unevenly, the carbon copies will show this clearly.

Correcting when using carbon paper

a) Insert a small piece of *thick* scrap paper, card, or a used envelope behind the carbon paper under the error and erase normally on the top copy (having first moved the carriage to left or right as far as it will go). Smudges on carbon copies indicate a lazy typist!

b) Take out the piece of scrap paper and erase the carbon copy with a soft pencil eraser.

c) Re-align the typing and re-type.

The maximum number of carbon copies is obtainable by using light-weight carbon paper and flimsy typing paper – about 8 or 9 readable copies on a manual typewriter. Using the same light-weight carbon paper and flimsy typing paper, an electric typewriter may possibly produce about 12 copies, with the pressure control set at maximum.

Using medium-weight carbon paper (which is the one most generally used in offices) and bank typing paper, a manual typewriter will produce about 6 readable copies.

Several copies produced by using carbon paper from one typing are often referred to as "manifolds" and typing a document with several carbon copies is known as "manifolding".

When several carbon copies are being typed, each carbon copy must be erased separately, with a piece of scrap paper underneath each sheet.

If an error is noticed *after* taking work out of the machine, each sheet must be erased and corrected separately. It is very difficult (almost impossible) to re-align even one carbon copy with the top copy once it has been removed from the typewriter. Typing directly on to a carbon copy does not match exactly, but as long as it is neatly aligned, it is acceptable. Avoid having to alter carbon copies separately by checking your work very carefully BEFORE you remove it from your typewriter.

PROGRESS TEST 3

1 You are working in the mail room of GPR Developments Ltd and one of your jobs is to fold the letters as they come from all the offices, and place them into the correct envelopes. If you notice an envelope that has been incorrectly typed, you type another, correct, envelope.

The following are five that you have spotted this morning. All the courtesy titles are either incorrect or have been omitted. Re-type them on envelopes if possible. If not, fold A4 paper into 3 lengthways

```
Messrs W D Fisher & Son Ltd        Philip J Marlow
23 Unicorn Hill                    2 Friar Street
Southend-on-Sea                    Penzance
Essex                              Cornwall
SS5 1HQ                            TR20 2JT


Mr H Graveney Esq                  S Black & Sons   Builders
The Laurels                        Studley Trading Estate
31 Market Place                    Rickmansworth
Warrington                         Herts
Cheshire                           WD5 1AJ
WA3 1SZ


Karen B Chester
189 King's Parade
Longeaton
Derbyshire
NG12 1JS
```

One of your other jobs is to help out occasionally in other departments when they are busy, and you have been asked today to type the following letters:

2 The first is typed on A5 portrait letterheading for GPR Developments Ltd (if this is not available, use A5 bond in the usual way) with one carbon copy and an envelope. This letter is to go by recorded delivery and is to be addressed to Simon Ladd   Kingfisher Cottage   Hankinson Way   Stockport   Cheshire SK6 1NF. Date for today. The letter will be signed by Mrs Jane Carr   Assistant Cashier.

Heading: Pension Fund   uc / us /

Dear Mr Ladd

Yr contribution to the firm's pension fund   uc/ will be refunded ~~to~~ you within a week or so,

stet   in accordance w ~~your~~ wishes in yr letter dated

NP   (date one week ago). [In the meantime, I enclose ~~a~~ the copy of yr birth certificate wh you ~~sent~~ to me with yr ltr.

Yrs sincerely

Enc

155

Carbon paper

There are two main types of carbon paper – "single" is coated on one side and "double" on both sides. Single carbon paper is the one most widely used and is available in various weights, ie thicknesses. Heavy-weight produces 1 or 2 clear copies only, but lasts a long time, medium-weight produces up to 5 copies at a time, and light-weight gives more than 5 copies but can be used only a few times before the copies are no longer clear.

Most firms today use what is known as "long-life" carbon paper, which is plastic coated and is clean, easy to handle and less likely to curl or crease. Coloured carbon paper is available, and is useful for identification purposes to send to a particular department, or person.

Each sheet of medium-weight or heavy-weight carbon paper can be used about 200 times. When the centre of A4 sized carbon paper is no longer producing good, clear copies it should be cut in half to give two sheets of A5. This will re-distribute the wear.

Double-coated carbon paper is used behind ink stencils (see Book II). A copy of the stencil is made on the backing sheet and, at the same time, an impression is made on the back of the stencil, enabling the typist to read (and check) what has been typed. Double-coated carbon paper used in stencils is usually discarded after one use ("one-time" carbon).

Other special instructions on letters may be:

By registered post
By recorded delivery
Airmail
Expresspost
By hand
Urgent

All these should be typed in capitals below the reference and above the date on both A5 and A4 business letters.

Registered post, recorded delivery, expresspost and airmail have either special envelopes or Post Office labels to stick on the envelope.

By hand – a letter taken by someone personally and not posted – and urgent letters have these words typed above the address in capitals on the envelope in the same place as "Confidential" is typed, with one clear line space between them and the address.

Exercise 71

Type the following A5 letter with one carbon copy and an envelope. Date for today. The letter is to go by registered post. It will be signed by Mrs Gina Thomas   Staff Supervisor.

Address the letter to Miss Annette Johnson   The Firs   75 Farnham Road   Reading Berks   RG1 8QD.

Dear Annette

I am enclosing your wages (£48.50) for the last week of your employment here, as I assume that you will not be

STET   returning to your ~~jobs here~~ position.   ⑧

NP   [I wish you every success for the future and hope you will find work to which you are more suited.

Yours sincerely

Enc

Warm-up drill

Margins 1″ left and ¾″ right. Make your own line endings.

1 The quaint old village proved an interesting place to visit, and a joint
expedition was arranged for two dozen people late in the year.

Practise shift lock

2 Names of books, newspapers and magazines are often typed in capitals instead of
between inverted commas: DAILY TELEGRAPH, DAILY MAIL, THE TIMES, EXPRESS,
SUNDAY TELEGRAPH and OBSERVER, are all examples of this.

3 Charles Dickens wrote NICHOLAS NICKLEBY and THE OLD CURIOSITY SHOP; Thackeray
wrote VANITY FAIR and Mrs Gaskell wrote CRANFORD. They are all examples of
Victorian novels and novelists.

4 The title of this book is TYPING SKILLS. The same author has written
TELEPHONE AND RECEPTION SKILLS and OFFICE SKILLS.

Preparation for accuracy/speed practice

Type each line 3 times.

important important important important important important important important
induction induction induction induction induction induction induction induction
introduction introduction introduction introduction introduction introduction
organisation organisation organisation organisation organisation organisation
procedures procedures procedures procedures procedures procedures procedures
information information information information information information
actually actually actually actually actually actually actually actually actually

Accuracy/speed practice

	Words
Your first day in an office is very important, and also rather alarming	14
to contemplate. It helps to get ready the evening before. What to wear	29
should be decided, clothes laid out, shoes cleaned, and alarm clock set	44
– it would never do to be late on the first morning! Many firms have	58
what is known as an induction course for new employees. An induction	72
course is actually an introduction to the firm, its departments and its	87
organisation and procedures. Many firms have a printed handbook which	101
will be given to you to keep with all this information contained in it.	115
It may be after lunch before you find out what you actually have to do	130
in the firm's office where you are to work. By this time, you will have	145
found out where the cloakrooms are and whether you clock in and out.	158
Some firms arrange a medical check-up for each new employee.	171

Exercise 69

Type an envelope for the stamped addressed envelope that would be enclosed with this letter. Mark this "Confidential" also, of course.

```
                  CONFIDENTIAL

Turn up 2
                  Mrs D Barnes OBE   Personnel Officer
                  Ernest C Williams & Co Ltd
                  Long Causeway
                  POOLE
                  Dorset
                  BH15 1DJ
```

Exercise 70

Type the following A5 portrait letter with one carbon copy and an envelope. Date it for today. Mark the letter and envelope "Confidential". Address them to
Michael Dobson BA   The Old Bakery   Middle Road   Truro   Cornwall TR1 4EW.
The letter will be signed by Michael Fowler   Chartered Surveyor.
Use your own initials for the typist's part of the reference.

Dear Mr Dobson

I wd be pleased if you cd call at my office asap to discuss the matter of the sale of yr land. I hv several people interested, but the price you are asking is ~~too~~ rather high.

NP [It occurs to me that you might be willing to reduce yr price if a sale cd be effected quickly

Yrs ~~faith~~ sincerely

Exercise 24

Type the following on A5 portrait paper, in double line spacing, with margins both
½″. Take two carbon copies. Make your own line endings.

CARE OF CARBON PAPER

Carbon paper should be stored flat, preferably in a box, away from radiators in
a cool place. Creased carbon paper produces "trees" on the carbon copies. A
treed carbon copy is the sign of a careless typist. Careful erasing prolongs
the life of carbon paper. Rubber dust should be brushed off the carbon paper
after erasing, away from the type basket on to the desk. The typewriter
carriage should be moved as far as possible to left or right before rubbing out.

Exercise 25

Type the following on A5 landscape paper, in double line spacing, with margins both
1″. Take two carbon copies. Make your own line endings.

"NCR"

NCR when used in connection with making copies means "no carbon required".
NCR paper produces copies by the use of chemicals, and is usually supplied in
sets, lightly attached at the top, thus saving the typist the job of inserting
and removing carbons. NCR paper will produce about 5 clear readable copies.
It is very clean to handle, quicker for the typist, and less storage space is
required for boxes of carbon paper in the stationery store cupboard. It is,
however, more expensive than ordinary paper plus carbon paper and it is very
difficult to make corrections on the copies - erasing is almost impossible and
it is necessary to use a special corrective which has to be painted on. It is
also very easy to mark NCR copies accidentally.

PARAGRAPHING

There are three ways to type paragraphs:

a) Blocked, where every line starts at the left hand margin. Blocked paragraphs are used by typists in many firms, as they are quick and easy to type. This is an example of a blocked paragraph.

b)   Indented, where the first line starts ½″ (5 or 6 spaces) in from the left hand margin. This is an example of an indented paragraph.

c) Hanging, where the first line starts at the left hand margin and the second and every following line starts 2 spaces in. This is an example of a hanging paragraph. Hanging paragraphs are used less frequently than block or indented, but are effective for sub-paragraphs, as they give emphasis to the first words.

One clear line is left between paragraphs in single line spacing (turn up 2).

SPECIAL INSTRUCTIONS ON BUSINESS LETTERS

One type of letter that would never be opened except by the person to whom it is addressed is a Personal or Confidential letter. It is therefore most important that not only is the envelope marked Personal or Confidential but the letter also.

Copy the following letter and envelope.

The Midland Secretarial Agency
Frederick Road
Edgbaston
Birmingham B15 4NX

Tel (021) 883215
Telex 29534

Your ref DB/MM   "Your ref" is the reference on the letter being replied to
Our ref MJ/JCK

CONFIDENTIAL

1 November 198-

Mrs D Barnes OBE Personnel Officer
Ernest C Williams & Co Ltd
Long Causeway
Poole
Dorset   BH15 1DJ

Dear Mrs Barnes

We have had an application from one of your employees,
Mrs Jane Knott, for a post as confidential secretary to a
director of a large local firm. Mrs Knott's application
states that she has worked for your firm as a secretary for
5 years and now wishes to move nearer home.

Could you please let us know if, in your opinion, Mrs Knott
would be a suitable person for the post of confidential
secretary? Any information you feel able to give will be
treated in the strictest confidence.

A stamped and addressed envelope is enclosed for your reply.

Yours sincerely

Mary Jefferson (Mrs)
Manager

Enc

Paragraphs in double line spacing

When typing blocked paragraphs in double line spacing, it is necessary to leave an extra line space between paragraphs, otherwise it may not be clear where the new paragraph begins.

Exercise 26

Type a copy of the following on A5 landscape paper, with margins both 1″, making your own line endings, in double line spacing with blocked paragraphs. While still in single line spacing, turn up 7 to type the heading, then turn up 3 and change to double line spacing.

PARAGRAPHS

A paragraph is a separate passage in a book, newspaper, magazine, etc, which divides up the chapter or article dealing with different topics. Paragraphs are intended to make the subject matter easier for the reader to understand. There is no general rule for the most suitable length for a paragraph, which will depend entirely upon the subject matter. Division into paragraphs gives "breathing space" to the reader.

Business letters especially should be set out in easily readable paragraphs, with short sentences that are clear and helpful in tone.

Exercise 27

Type a copy of the following on A5 landscape paper, in double line spacing with indented paragraphs. Because it is obvious where an indented paragraph starts, it is not necessary to leave an extra line space between paragraphs when in double line spacing. Margins 1½″ left and 1″ right. Make your own line endings.

INDENTED PARAGRAPHS

This paragraph is typed in indented form, with the first line starting ½" (5 or 6 spaces, according to whether the typewriter has elite or pica pitch) from the left hand margin. The tabulator should be set at this point, to save tapping the space bar each time a new paragraph is started.

No extra line space has been left before starting this new paragraph, as the indentation makes it clear where it began.

Warm-up drill

1   It was an amazing sight when the thousands of marathon runners started their long race through the city streets, and many of the spectators wondered how soon it would be before the first "stragglers" dropped out.

Common word drills

2   each early earth ease east education effect either electric electricity employ

3   end engine engineer English enough equal equally even event ever every example

4   except exchange exist expect experience expert express eye face fact fall family

5   far farm father fear February feel few field figure final find fire first fish

6   fly follow food foot for force form forward free frequent Friday friend from

7   front full fully further future

8   gave general generally gentlemen get girl give given go gold good govern

9   government great ground grow had half hand happen happy hard has have he head

10   health hear heart heat heavy heir help her here high him himself his history

11   hold hole home hope horse hour house how however hundred I idea if immediate

12   important importance impossible improve improvement in increase indeed industry

13   influence inform information instruction insurance interest iron is issue it

14   January judge July just keep kind king knew know knowledge many March mark

15   market marry mass master matter may me meal mean measure meat meet member

16   memory mere Mr method might mile milk million mind mine minute miss modern

17   moment Monday money month more morning most mother motor move much must my

Special character practice

18   Messrs Norton & Jones, Solicitors, have new premises at 56 & 58 Silver Street Leicester, but will not be moving in until later this month.

19   The invoice item wrongly gave the price of the sugar as: 35p per kg. It was corrected by the typist to: 9 kg sugar @ 33p per kg.

20   "Which way shall we go to the shops?" asked the girl, as they crossed the busy road. "I'm not sure," her friend replied, "perhaps the side streets will be less busy."

21   The holiday notice (for 198-) was posted in all the offices, and requests for special dates/weeks were asked for as soon as possible.

Indented paragraphs in single line spacing

An extra line space must be left between paragraphs in single line spacing, whether they are indented or blocked.

Exercise 28

Type a copy of the following on A5 landscape paper, in single line spacing with indented paragraphs. Make your own line endings; margins as for Exercise 27.

INDENTED PARAGRAPHS IN SINGLE LINE SPACING

This is an example of typing indented paragraphs in single line spacing, which shows that although each paragraph starts 5 or 6 spaces in from the left hand margin, it is still necessary to separate the paragraphs by an extra line space, for clarity of layout.

Business letters are typed in single line spacing, with an extra line space between paragraphs.

Exercise 29

Type a copy of the following blocked paragraph on A5 landscape paper. Margins 1½″ left and 1″ right. Make your own line endings.

BLOCKED PARAGRAPHS IN SINGLE LINE SPACING

This is an example of typing blocked paragraphs in single line spacing. As with double line spacing, it is necessary to leave an extra line space before starting a new paragraph, so that it is clear where it starts, when the blocked style is being used.

An experienced typist remembers this automatically, but it takes practice and time before a beginner always gets it right.

Typing hanging paragraphs

These are usually typed in single line spacing, with an extra line space between paragraphs. The easiest way to type them is to re-set the left hand margin after typing the first line and then use the backspacer and margin release to type the beginning of the first line of each new paragraph.

This is an example of two hanging paragraphs; they are not difficult to type, but require concentration, as it is easy to forget to backspace 2 for the first line of the new paragraph.

FOR YOUR TYPING FOLDER 10

Follow previous instructions for typing these exercises (see page 77).

TYPING BUSINESS LETTERS

1 A firm's first impression of another firm may be from a ....

2 The reference on a business letter consists of the initials of the person signing the letter and the initials of the person .... the letter.

3 The firm's name and address is printed at the top of the letterheading. The name and address typed on the letter is known as the .... address.

4 "Dear Sirs" is known as the ....

5 The complimentary close is ....

6 Many firms include their name (typed in capitals) immediately below ....

7 "For the attention of ..." on a letter is used to direct the letter to the right person in a firm where it is not permitted to address letters to ....

8 The heading in a business letter is typed under ....

9 After "Dear (followed by name)" the complimentary close is always ....

10 Margins on A5 (portrait) letters are often set on ....

Exercise 30

Type a copy of the following, in single line spacing with hanging paragraphs on A5 landscape paper. Margins 1″ left and ¾″ right. Make your own line endings.

PAYING YOUR TELEPHONE BILL PAINLESSLY

It is possible to budget for the next telephone bill by buying telephone stamps
from the post office. The stamps are available in values of £1 and £5 with a
stamp card to stick them on.

It is possible to buy as many as you like. Then when the next telephone bill
arrives you just take it with your stamp card to the nearest post office and
you only have to pay the difference.

It is possible to give telephone stamps as presents. There is an attractive
free gift card available at post offices which can be used to send stamps to a
relative or friend who has a telephone. They could make a very welcome
present.

Exercise 31

Type a copy of the following in double line spacing with indented paragraphs on A5 landscape paper. Margins 1″ left an ¾″ right. A writer indicates the start of a new paragraph by ⊏ and NP/ written in the margin. Centre the heading.

uc/
us/ Starting a new job

The right clothes will give you confidence.
This is particularly important for a new
job. Also, an outfit must be comfortable
when you are going to wear it all
day.

NP/ [All large firms have centrally heated offices,
and it is not necessary to wear thick
clothes indoors in the winter.

NP/ [Trousers, well-pressed and part of a
matched outfit, look smart, but any
old jeans and T-shirt will not do.

Exercise 68

The following letter is the one in reply to that on the previous page. Type it on A4 paper, with one carbon copy. Type an envelope.

The reference is PH/ followed by your own initials. Date the letter for 3 days from today.

The inside address is A L Carter & Company Limited   Trentham Trading Estate High St   Kirkcaldy   Fife   KY1 1LR

Mark the letter for the attention of Mr David Knight   Assistant Purchasing Officer.

Dear Sirs

Thank you for your ltr dated (insert suitable date) regarding the electronic postal scale BAL 8001 supplied against yr order NP no 7854/9. [We hv examined the std/ postal scale and find that there is a fault which is affecting the switch. A replacement scale has been dispatched to you today and we hope that this will function satisfactorily.

We apologise for the inconvenience you have been caused and enclose a cheque for £3.50 to refund your carriage charges.

Yrs ffly

Peter Hunt   Production Manager

149

Exercise 32

Repeat Exercise 31 in double line spacing with blocked paragraphs.

Exercise 33

Repeat Exercise 31 in single line spacing with indented paragraphs.

FOR YOUR TYPING FOLDER 4

Follow previous instructions for typing these exercises (see page 77).

CARBONS

1   Typing a document with several carbon copies is known as ....

2   Using medium-weight carbon paper and bank typing paper, a manual typewriter will produce about .... readable copies.

3   Carbon paper should be stored .... away from .... in a .... place.

4   Creased carbon paper produces .... on the carbon copies.

5   NCR paper produces copies by means of ....

6   Unfortunately, it is very easy to .... NCR copies.

7   Erasing is almost impossible when using NCR paper and it is necessary to use a ....

PARAGRAPHS

1   There are three ways to type paragraphs - blocked, indented and ....

2   With an indented paragraph, the first line starts .... in from the left hand margin.

3   When typing indented paragraphs in double line spacing it is .... to leave an extra line space between paragraphs.

4   When typing blocked paragraphs in double line spacing, it is .... to leave an extra line space between paragraphs.

5   When typing indented paragraphs in single line spacing, it is .... to leave an extra line space between paragraphs.

6   When typing blocked paragraphs in double line spacing, it is .... to leave an extra line space between paragraphs.

Exercise 67

Type the following letter on A4 paper, with one carbon copy. Type an envelope. The reference is DK/ followed by your own initials (as the typist). Date the letter for today. The inside address is GPR Developments Ltd   78 East Square   Chelmsford   Essex CM1 1JN. Mark the letter for the attention of Mr P Hunt   Production Manager.

Dear Sirs

We hv today returned by BRS the electronic postal scale BAL 8001 which you dispatched to us 2 weeks ago against our order No. 7854/9.

NP The m/c is giving us a great deal of trouble and we think it must be faulty in some way.

NP We shall be grateful if you will send us a replacement by return, as we hv scrapped our old scales and all our parcels now hv to be taken to the local post office to be weighed — a very time-consuming business, as you will realise. NP Your co-operation will be much appreciated.

Yours ffly

Doris Knight   Assistant Purchasing Officer

Warm-up drill

Margins 1″ left and ¾″ right. Make your own line endings.

The wheezy old accordion and the squeaky recorder made a noise which caused even the least musical in the crowd to jab their fingers in their ears.

Preparation for accuracy/speed practice

Type each line 3 times.

British Telecom's British Telecom's British Telecom's British Telecom's
precisely precisely precisely precisely precisely precisely precisely
solar solar solar solar solar solar solar solar solar solar solar solar solar
Observatory Observatory Observatory Observatory Observatory Observatory
nuclear nuclear nuclear nuclear nuclear nuclear nuclear nuclear nuclear nuclear
corrected corrected corrected corrected corrected corrected corrected corrected
clockmakers clockmakers clockmakers clockmakers clockmakers clockmakers

Accuracy/speed practice

TIME STOPPED

	Words
If you happened to phone the talking clock, British Telecom's Time Line,	15
at precisely 0100 on 1 July 1982, you heard nothing - no pips - no	29
female voice. In fact, time stood still all over the world at 0100 on	43
1 July 1982 to allow clocks everywhere to catch up with solar time that	58
had crept ahead because of the slightly uneven rotation of the Earth.	72
Every so often, even the most accurate clocks fall out of harmony with	87
the basic unit of measurement - solar time. It has happened 11 times	101
since 1972. The Bureau International de l'Heure in France, an inter-	116
national organisation, linked with the Royal Greenwich Observatory	130
decides on a date when the world should get back in step.	142
Extremely accurate nuclear clocks estimated that on 1 July 1982 we at	156
the Royal Greenwich Observatory would be exactly one second out of line.	171
The pause that corrected the difference made the last day of June 1982	186
a second longer than usual. Even Big Ben was attended by expert clock-	203
makers, early on the morning of 1 July to sweep the huge minute hand	217
forward a fraction.	221

Exercise 66

Type the following letter on A5 portrait paper, with one carbon copy and an envelope. Address the letter to LKJ Engineering Co Ltd   14 Camden High Street   Camden Town London   NW1 5JR. It is for the attention of Mr John Langford   Production Manager. Use today's date. The letter will be signed by Michael Rutherford   Purchasing Officer. Use your own initials for the typist's part of the reference.

Dear Sirs

Confirming our telephone conversation this morning (type date in) this is to confirm that we shall be pleased to see yr Production Manager a week from today (type date in) at 11 am to discuss the possible purchase of one of yr model XL 931 m/cs.

model

NP [Please ask him to report to reception on arrival.

Yrs ffly

CORRECTION SIGNS

Correction signs are used to give the typist instructions about alterations that are necessary in the work being copied. These special signs are written in the margin, alongside the line which contains the word, or words, to be corrected; there is also a sign under or over the word itself, so that there should be no possibility of misunderstanding, or overlooking, the correction. Much of a typist's work consists of typing from corrected copy, and it should be read through very carefully before starting to type, to make sure the correction signs are understood.

Some correction signs have already been used in this book:

uc/	upper case (capital letters)
caps/	as above
lc/	lower case (small letters)
us/	underscore
NP/	new paragraph
sp caps/	spaced capitals

The oblique stroke following the correction sign in the margin indicates that that is the end of that particular correction, because there may be more than one in any line.

Additional emphasis is given to correction signs by marking the word or words in the text, as follows:

one line under word (or words)	underscore
two lines under word (or words)	type in capitals (it **does not mean** underscore)
three lines under word (or words)	type in spaced capitals (it **does not mean** underscore)
square bracket in text	start new paragraph
one line under letter	change from lower to upper case or: change from upper to lower case

There are many other correction signs. Six more for your to learn are:

Sign in margin	Meaning	Sign in text
run on/	do **not** begin a new paragraph	
stet/	"let it stand" – ignore the alteration and type the word which has been crossed out	. . . . . under word to be typed
trs/	"transpose" – change word (or letters) around	round letters or words; sometimes numbered
d/	delete, omit, take out	word, or words crossed out
#	insert space	
◡/	close up space	◠

Exercise 65

Type the following business letter on A5 letterheading for the WTC Transport Co Ltd. If this is not available, turn up 10 before typing the reference. Take one carbon copy and type an envelope.

TE/ Type your own initials here

13 December 198-

The Transport Manager
Lamb's Furniture Co Ltd
35 Old Bedford Road
Luton
Beds   LU2 7HQ

Dear Sir

Thank you for your letter dated 12 December. Please accept our apologies for the difficulties you have had in contacting us by telephone. It has been out of order for some days and British Telecom are still trying to repair it.

We shall be pleased to transport the three-piece suites to Leighton Buzzard from your factory next week if you will let us know time of collection and number of suites.

Our rates for this type of load are on the attached sheet.

Yours faithfully
WTC TRANSPORT CO LTD

Thomas Evans
Manager

Enc

Special points   This letter is addressed to the Transport Manager as part of the inside
to note: address. This is an alternative to the attention line when there is no rule in
a firm about letters being addressed to individuals.

Exercise 34

Read through the following passage, to make sure you understand the alterations before starting to type. Type the passage on A5 landscape paper, in double line spacing. Margins 1½″ left and 1″ right.

<u>VACANCIES</u>

The employment exchange run by the Government's Manpower Services Commission is known as a Jobcentre. There is one in most of our cities and towns. There is also a Careers Advisory Centre for school and college leavers. Employers may notify Jobcentres of vacancies they wish to fill.

There are also employment agencies run by private firms. They keep a register of people who are looking for jobs, and put them in touch with firms who have vacancies. There is <u>no charge at all</u> to anybody looking for a job – it is the firms with the vacancies who pay, when a job is taken.

Advertisements in local papers are another source of information about jobs. vacancies.

Exercise 64

─────── A business letter on A5 letterheading (portrait) ───────

Lamb's Furniture Co Ltd   Tel (0582) 76590
35 Old Bedford Road   Telex 21154
Luton
Beds
LU2 7HQ

Our ref WO/FTJ

12 December 198-

WTC Transport Co Ltd
Grovebury Road
Leighton Buzzard
Beds   LU7 8SL

Dear Sirs

We have a large consignment of three-piece suites to
deliver to a firm in Leighton Buzzard early next
week and would like to know if you would be able to
undertake this for us. We have telephoned you on
several occasions but without success.

Please either telephone the undersigned by return or
write as soon as possible.

Yours faithfully
LAMB'S FURNITURE CO LTD

William Oliver
Transport Manager

Special points
to note:
Margins on A5 letters are usually set on ½".

As space is so limited on A5 paper, it is only possible to type a very short
letter; if there is an attention line, a heading and an enclosure indication,
A4 paper should be used, otherwise there will be insufficient space for a
signature.

FOLLOWING INSTRUCTIONS

Many marks are lost by candidates in typewriting examinations for not following the instructions printed (usually) at the top of a question.

These instructions may cover:

Line spacing

Margins

Paragraphs (blocked, indented or hanging)

How each heading is to be typed

Size of paper (and if A5, whether landscape or portrait)

Carbon copies (if any)

It is important to read through the question carefully, and mark (in pencil) these instructions *before* starting to type.

Alterations indicated by correction signs in the margins and in the text must also be noted carefully during this preliminary reading.

As you read, make sure that the passage makes sense; if it does not, you have misunderstood, or misread a correction sign.

Your dictionary (which is permitted in typewriting examinations at all stages by most examining boards) may help you here, if you cannot read the handwriting, or you are not sure of the meaning of a word which has to be corrected.

In the following exercise, the instructions are printed in CAPITALS so that you cannot miss them. This would not be done in an examination.

Exercise 35

Type the following passage on A5 LANDSCAPE paper with DOUBLE LINE SPACING. Take ONE CARBON COPY. MARGINS are 1½″ left and 1″ right. INDENT the paragraphs. CENTRE the heading.

Sp caps/   TELEPHONISTS

Another important post in a firm is that of the switchboard operator
trs/   or telephonist. Many of these are trained by British Telecom before going to work in a firm, as they must be efficient, tactful, polite, calm and helpful.

In some firms, the jobs of receptionist and switchboard operator are   stet/
combined and done by one person.   *telephonist*

The first person a caller speaks to in a large firm is always the switchboard operator and it is essential she gives the caller a good impression of her firm.

run on/   All telephonists should be trained to answer the telephone with a "smile" in their voices, even though it may be the end of a busy and
tiring day.

Exercise 63

Type the following business letter on A4 paper. Set margins as for the specimen letter and turn up 15 before typing the reference (if there is no letterheading). Take one carbon copy and type an envelope.

The Midland Secretarial Agency   Tel (021) 883215
Frederick Road   Telex 29534
Edgbaston
Birmingham B15 4NX

Our ref MJ/ *Type your own initials here*

Type today's date here

Line spacing as in example on page 143

Miss Anne Haynes
23 Dorridge Road
Dorridge
Solihull
West Midlands   B93 8BN

Turn up 3

Dear Miss Haynes

Turn up 2

VACANCY FOR WORD PROCESSOR OPERATOR

Turn up 2

I see from your record card that you have had some training on a word processor and that you would be interested in a job which included using one.

There is a vacancy for a word processor operator at a firm in Birmingham and they are prepared to send whoever is appointed on a fortnight's course so that they may become familiar with the type of word processor in use in their offices.

If you think this might be of interest to you, please telephone as soon as possible, and I will arrange an appointment for you with the Personnel Manager of the firm in question.

Yours sincerely

Mary Jefferson (Mrs)   *Woman's title in brackets after her name*
Manager

Special points to note: Heading over body of letter: this is in capitals without underscore – the modern way.

Complimentary close "Yours sincerely" – this is typed after "Dear" followed by the person's name and is a slightly less formal way of ending and starting a letter. It usually indicates either that letters have been written before or a telephone conversation has taken place.

144

Exercise 36

Type the following on A4 paper, with one carbon copy. Use double line spacing and indented paragraphs. Margins 1″ left and ½″ right.

LETTERS OF APPLICATION — lc and us

It is a good idea to type a letter of application for a job as a typist, but it is not essential, especially as many prospective employers like to see a specimen of an applicant's handwriting, even if their job is mainly typing. The letter, of course, should be written as clearly and neatly as possible, with spelling checked and double checked! It is a great saving of time and of considerable help to a prospective employer if a letter of application is short, with most of the information set out plainly on a separate sheet. This separate sheet should be headed "Curriculum Vitae" (which means "life history"). Curricula vitae can be duplicated (if this is possible) or typed with 5 carbon copies so that they are ready for sending out with letters applying for jobs. Making carbon copies of curricula vitae, or duplicating them, saves much time when many jobs are being applied for, and also avoids the possibility of omitting an important piece of information, but the covering letter must not be a carbon copy, even when a typewriter is available. Each letter of application must be separately typed. A carbon copy would not give a good impression to the person in the firm reading it.

Do not enclose a stamped and addressed envelope with letters applying for jobs. A firm that is genuinely interested in asking you to come for an interview will be prepared to pay for a stamp on the letter telling you this.

It may be necessary to send many letters applying for jobs before you are finally successful. Keep trying - eventually the opportunity will arise.

Exercise 62

A business letter on A4 letterheading

Set margin to follow printed heading where possible

The Midland Secretarial Agency
Frederick Road
Edgbaston
Birmingham B15 4NX

Tel (021) 883215
Telex 29534

Turn up 3

Our ref MJ/JCK

Initials of person signing letter followed by typist's initials

Turn up 3

23 October 198-

Turn up 3

John Parsons & Co Ltd
Holly Lane
Wishaw
Sutton Coldfield
West Midlands   B73 5RG

Inside address

Turn up 3

For the attention of Mr W Poole Office Manager

Attention line

Turn up 3

Dear Sirs

Salutation

Turn up 2

Thank you for your letter dated 21 October, advising me that you have appointed Miss Dawn Carr and Mrs Katherine Grayson as audio typists in your typing pool.

I note that Miss Carr and Mrs Grayson have been notified of their appointments and asked to report to you on Monday, 2 November at 9 am.

Our usual account in connection with our assistance in filling these vacancies is enclosed.

We are pleased to have been of service to your firm.

Turn up 2
Turn up 1

Yours faithfully
THE MIDLAND SECRETARIAL AGENCY

Complimentary close
Name of firm

Turn up 5

Turn up 1

Mary Jefferson (Mrs)
Manager

Name of person signing (initials in reference)
Job title of person signing

Turn up 3

Enc

Special points to note:

Attention line: this is typed on letters to direct it to the right person in firms where it is not permitted to address letters to individuals.

Complimentary close: this is followed by the name of the firm typed in capitals. Not all firms include this in their house style.

FOR YOUR TYPING FOLDER 5

Follow previous instructions for typing these exercises (see page 77).

CORRECTION SIGNS

1   The instruction "run on" in the margin means ....

2   The instruction "stet" in the margin means ....

3   The instruction "trs" in the margin means ....

4   #   in the margin means ....

5   ⌒/   in the margin means ....

FOLLOWING INSTRUCTIONS

1   Instructions at the top of a question on a typewriting examination paper may
     cover: line spacing, margins, paragraphs, size of paper, how headings are to be
     typed and ....

2   Before starting to type, read through the question carefully and ....
     special instructions.

3   If the passage does not seem to make sense as you read through, then you have
     .... or misread a ....

4   You are allowed to use an English dictionary in a typewriting examination which
     will help if you .... or you are not sure of the ....

MARGINS – MAKING UP YOUR OWN MIND

When no instructions are given regarding margins, remember the following:

the **left hand** margin must never be less than 1″*
the **right hand** margin must never be wider than the left

Therefore, if you are left to decide on your own margins, set the left hand
margin on 14 elite, 12 pica, to make absolutely sure that it is not less than 1″,
and set the right hand margin on 90 elite, 74 pica, to make sure it is slightly less
than 1″.

If no instructions are given about portrait or landscape, and you can make up
your own mind, choose landscape if at all possible (when typing a descriptive
passage, for example) as this avoids frequent, short lines and decisions about
line endings and possible word division.

Usually, it is obvious from the exercise that double or single line spacing should
be used – copy the line spacing used, when no special instructions have been
given. **When in doubt, follow the layout** is a useful rule, **but** do check
instructions very carefully before starting to type.

_____

*When typing on A5 portrait paper, usually ½″ margins must be set, because of
the narrowness of the paper.

TYPING BUSINESS LETTERS

A business letter is sent from one firm to another, and it is one of the most important jobs a secretary or audio typist has to do in an office. The letter must be typed without mistakes, and must be correctly spelt and punctuated. A firm's first impression of another firm may be from a letter.

Business letters are always typed on good-quality paper (it is not always white – some firms choose pastel colours) and have the firm's name, address, telephone and telex numbers printed at the top. In addition, the names of the directors appear, either at the top or bottom of the letterheading.

Two sizes are widely used – A4 and A5. The A5 size may be portrait or landscape.

Layout

There are many ways of setting out a business letter, and each firm has its own preference, known as the "house style". When starting a new job in a firm, the first thing a secretary or audio typist must do is to find out the house style, learn it, and follow it.

On the next page is an A4 business letter, with a fully blocked layout (every line starts at the left hand margin). Other layouts are explained in Book II.

Together with a fully blocked layout is combined "open punctuation". This means that there are no fullstops after abbreviations or at the ends of the lines in the address, etc. Open punctuation has been used all through this book; full (ordinary) punctuation, with fullstops after abbreviations, will be described in Book II. Open punctuation together with the fully blocked layout speeds up the output of a typist working on letters.

Type the letter on the following page on A4 bond and turn up 15 line spaces before typing the reference. Set margins on 1½" left and ¾" right.

Most business letters are typed in single line spacing, for economy reasons.

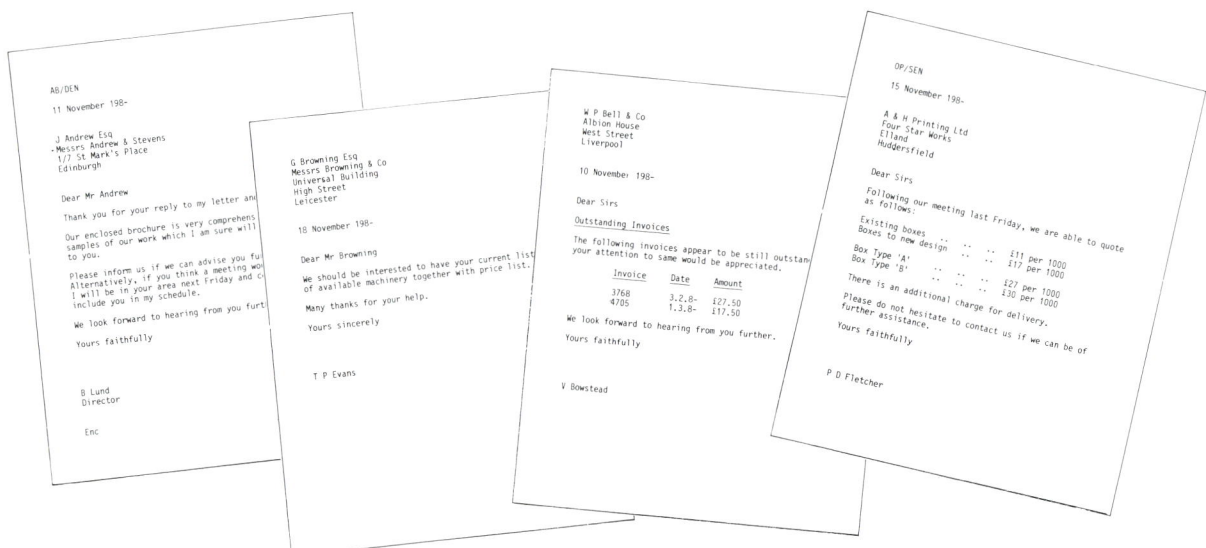

Warm-up drill

The girls looked puzzled as they tried to find the street which they had been
told was across the bridge and near to the houses being demolished.

Practice on the hyphen and the dash

The well-to-do man got out of his large car - it was obvious that he wished to
ask us a question - and we stopped to wait to hear what he said. Then, quite
unexpectedly, he made a U-turn and got back into his car. We looked at each
other, and walked on; the large car remained parked at the kerb - it was on
double-yellow lines so it couldn't stay for much longer - with the driver
sitting motionless. We noticed that the car was very mud-splashed.

Preparation for accuracy/speed practice

Type each line 3 times.

distinguished distinguished distinguished distinguished distinguished
published published published published published published published published
Debrett Debrett Debrett Debrett Debrett Debrett Debrett Debrett Debrett Debrett
PEERAGE PEERAGE PEERAGE PEERAGE PEERAGE PEERAGE PEERAGE PEERAGE PEERAGE PEERAGE
WHO'S WHO WHO'S WHO WHO'S WHO WHO'S WHO WHO'S WHO WHO'S WHO WHO'S WHO WHO'S WHO
Parliament Parliament Parliament Parliament Parliament Parliament Parliament
personalities personalities personalities personalities personalities
Esquire Esquire Esquire Esquire Esquire Esquire Esquire Esquire Esquire Esquire
abbreviated abbreviated abbreviated abbreviated abbreviated abbreviated

Accuracy/speed practice

A New Guide to Famous People by Debrett

DISTINGUISHED PEOPLE IN BRITISH LIFE

	Words
This new reference book on well-known British people still living was	14
first published in 1982 by Debrett, whose intention was to fill the gap	29
between DEBRETT'S PEERAGE and WHO'S WHO, with information about people	44
actively prominent in all walks of life - in other words, people whose	58
names appear frequently in the newspapers. As well as titled people,	72
DISTINGUISHED PEOPLE IN BRITISH LIFE includes Members of Parliament,	87
television stars, sports personalities and many others. Each entry	100
has an explanation of how to address correctly the titled and the un-	114
titled. Debrett is quite firm that every untitled male is an "Esquire"	132
(usually abbreviated to "Esq"), and every untitled, unmarried woman is	146
a "Miss" and not a "Ms".	155

Warm-up drill

1 Rex was amazed by the quite obvious errors in the manner in which the goalkeeper
played the game; his place was quickly taken by a newcomer who had proved his
worth in practice matches.

Practice on double letter words

2 see bee tree fee feet feel street meet meeting greet greeting deep

3 cannot accept offer cutting apple tariff approve success offer little

4 office staff happy annual dinner manner appear happen apply dapper

5 account accuse occur occurring affair affect effect affix affirm office

Preparation for accuracy/speed practice

Type each line 3 times.

outgoing outgoing outgoing outgoing outgoing outgoing outgoing outgoing

recognise recognise recognise recognise recognise recognise recognise recognise

answered answered answered answered answered answered answered answered answered

business business business business business business business business business

Accuracy/speed practice

BUSINESS LETTERS AND CARBON COPIES

	Words
When replies to business letters are typed, a carbon copy is typed	13
at the same time, and this is sent, with the letter which has been	27
answered, to the filing clerk. They are filed in the same file.	40
Carbon copies do not need release symbols, as they are copies of	53
outgoing letters.	57
A filing clerk would soon learn to recognise carbon copies, because	71
they are often on coloured paper, but also there is no printed name	84
of the firm at the top of the letter.	92
There is another type of business letter besides letters from	105
firms. This is a personal business letter – one sent from a	117
private individual to a firm. There would be no printed name	130
at the top of a personal business letter. Instead, there would	143
be a private address, either typed or written. Some people do	155
have their own printed notepaper, but this would still consist of	169
just an address and a telephone number (if they had one). There	182
would be no name at the top of the paper on personal notepaper.	195

Figure practice

1 The cost of the biscuits rose by 5p in 6 months.

2 Zoe is 17, Mark is 19, Sam is 18 and Sandra will be 17 next birthday.

3 We are planning to go to Greece on 5 May, before the weather becomes too hot.

4 In 1984, there may be a cable system of television which will provide 40 different channels.

5 In order to calculate exactly how many £50, £20, £10, £5, £1 notes and 50p, 20p and 10p coins will be needed a cash analysis has to be worked out.

6 Porterhouse Printers Ltd, of Cantwell Road, Plymouth, Devon, ordered exactly one week ago (order no 92746) 24 three-drawer metal cabinets, 90 cm high, with folding doors 180 cm high and fitted with rails for 5 rows of lateral filing. For the first item the stock code is 12/07/0169, at £20.70 each, totalling £496.80.

7 Two men helped the injured man out of the 1800 while Bob ran towards the nearest house. When the door opened, he quickly asked the woman to dial 999 as there had been an accident. The ambulance arrived 5 minutes later.

WORDS AND FIGURES IN SENTENCES

Words and **not** figures must always be used:

a) when the figure starts a sentence, eg Two people came to see me;

b) for the figure 1, eg We shall go one day to the show.

Figures and **not** words must always be used when typing:

sums of money and large numbers:	£38,950 709,881
dates	14 September 1982
post codes	B96 6TB
house numbers	45 & 46 Orchard Grove
percentages	15% or 15 per cent
before am and pm (indicating time)	8 am to 3 pm daily
weights	2 kg 25 g 4 lb 9 oz
measurements	20 cm 10 m 2 ft 6 in
invoice numbers	Invoice No 333421
quantity	250 boxes 10 rolls
prices	£12.50 each Total: £125 (no space after decimal point before pence)

One space between number and units except before and after units of money

3 Display the following on A5 paper with one carbon copy.

Sp caps/ Disco to be held by Ramblers Club on (date 4 weeks ahead) at
Castleton Country Club. 8 pm to 1 am.   Tickets: £3 which includes
Caps/ buffet supper.   No admission at door without a ticket.   Proceeds in
aid of the Mentally Handicapped.   It's a worthy cause — come and
give us your support!

4 Type a copy of the following in double line spacing with indented paragraphs on A5
landscape paper.

Centre → RAMBLERS CLUB uc & us/

*Stet
⟳*
The Ramblers Club was started in 1979 by a
group of keen enthusiastic walkers who were interested in
keeping paths and bridle ways open in &
around their town. An advert in the local
paper resulted in a membership of abt 70,
which settled down eventually to a steady 50.

*NP
⟋*
[New members are always welcome — the club
meets once a month in the Social Club
centre on the first Monday of each month,
at 8 pm. Rambles are arranged on Wednesday
evenings from May to August & at weekends
from September to April.

NP [The annual subscription is £1.

5 Type a copy of the following on A5 landscape paper, changing the blocked
paragraphs to hanging ones.

The Country Code is a guideline to inform visitors to the country
how to behave while they are enjoying their surroundings. Some of
the points in the Country Code are:

Enjoy the countryside and respect its life and work.

Use gates and stiles to cross fences, hedges and walls; take special
care on country roads.

Leave livestock, crops and machinery alone; protect wildlife, plants
and trees.

Keep to public paths across farmland; fasten all gates; keep your
dogs under close control.

Practice on words and/or figures in sentences

1   Twenty players attended the Annual General Meeting out of a total membership of over 50.

2   Mr and Mrs Keene live in a new house at 36 Lands End Road, Urmston, Manchester M34 3QT.

3   VAT is at present 15% of the value of the goods sold or bought.

4   We were asked to bring back 2 kg of potatoes, 8 oranges and 2 m of lining.

5   The amount owing (£25.60) was shown on Invoice No 309776.

6   The train was due at 8 am and the party planned to stay until 5 pm.

7   I paid £23.50 into my deposit account No 3109876 at the bank last Monday, 6 September 198-.

8   One hundred members of the audience paid £4.50 each for tickets for the concert last Saturday, but only 50 actually came to hear the new rock band.

9   Seven hundred and thirty-five rolls of wallpaper will be put into the sale at half price (eg £2.30 instead of £4.60) but there will still be 8500 in stock at the full price.

10 There will be a new school built in this district one day, but no one seems quite sure whether it will be in 2 years' time or 22.

11 Seventy-nine people only came to the concert, having paid £3.50 each.

12 First of all, I am going to call on my second cousin at 83 Gower Avenue, after which I shall visit my friends at 231 Springfield Gardens, where a party is to be held. One of my friends will be 21 on that day - the same day on which I shall be 18. Twenty-five people have been invited, but it it not expected that many more than 18 will arrive.

Exercise 37

Type a copy of the following passage, and correct the use of words and/or figures where you think they are used wrongly. There are 4 instances where they should be changed.

Today is the first September and most school pupils will be thinking about

returning in a few days' time. At this time of the year, the summer often

returns with warm, sunny days, which, even though they end around six pm, are

long enough to be enjoyed out-of-doors. 100's of schoolboys and girls will be

grumbling about going back to school, but most enjoy it when the initial "shock"

is over. Often, warm, sunny weather continues almost to the end of October, and

1 glorious week about that time will be half-term!

PROGRESS TEST 2

1 Type a personal letter (as follows) to Miss Sarah O'Malley   34 Woodside Road   Ballymena   Co Antrim   Northern Ireland   BT44 0SD. Date for today. Use your own address at the top of the letter and telephone number (if you have one). Sign the letter yourself. Type an envelope.

NP/ Dear Sarah [Delighted to hear from you and to learn that you enjoyed your holiday, in spite of the rather 'mixed' weather! We have had some hot days here, but nothing settled. [The disco is to be on   NP/
(date 4 weeks ahead) and you will be back in England by then, so do
try and come. It's in a good cause – the Mentally Handicapped.
NP/ [Guess what, I've been made secretary of the Ramblers Club (just
because I can type – no other reason!) and am feeling rather nervous
about it. I write everything out in rough first, before I type it.
Am just about to order disco tickets and feeling very important, as
you can imagine. Love to Kate.

As ever

2 Type a personal business letter to W & E Printing Ltd   Deal Industrial Estate   Deal   Kent   CT14 0HP. Take one carbon copy and type an envelope. Type your own address (and telephone number) at the top of the letter. Date for today.

Dear Sirs

Confirming our telephone conversation this morning abt tickets for the Ramblers Club Disco to be held next month I enclose a draft for you to use. I should like the layout the same as the draft with emphasis where I have used capitals + spaced caps.
The quantity to be supplied is 300, on pink card with black + gold lettering, at a price of £25. As mentioned on the telephone, we would like the tickets in a week's time. Yrs ffly (type yr own name) Ramblers Club Secretary
Enc

Warm-up drill

1 The zoom lens on a cine-camera enables the camera operator to change quickly from close-up to long shot. Thus "movies" can be made which are much more exciting and realistic than with the older types of camera.

Practise special characters

2 Because prices are rising so quickly (although inflation has slowed down in recent years) it is difficult to set aside sufficient money (say, 30% of income) to meet such payments as rent, electricity and telephone bills. Many people say "How can I budget when I never know, even roughly, how much the quarterly bills will be?" Banks will help with a budget account, if all expected bills are totalled and divided by 12, so that large cheques can be written at any time without worrying about being overdrawn. A cheque for £100 is a big amount out of one month's salary for most people. Bill, who works for Manson & Price Ltd, as a salesman, has a salary of £250 per month plus commission on sales. In addition, of course, he has a company car/petrol which is a great help.

Common word drills

3 name nation nature near necessary need neither never new news next night no nor north not note nothing November now number object observation October of off offer office official often oh oil old on once one only open operate opinion opportunity or order organise organisation other ought our ourselves out over owe owing own page paint paper part particular party pass pay peace penny people perfect perhaps person personal picture piece place plain plan plane plant play please pleasure point political poor position possible pound power present price principal principle probable probability product profit property provide public publish pull purpose put

4 quality quarter question quick quite radio rail rate rather reach read ready real really reason receive recent record red regard regret regular relate remark remember report represent require respect responsible responsibility rest result return right river road room round rule run safe said sail sale same satisfactory Saturday save say scene school science sea second see seem seen scene self sell send sense sent September serious serve service set several sew shall she ship short should show side sign simple since sir sit situation six size small so some sometimes soon sort sound south sow speak special specially spend spent stand start state station steal steel step still stone stop store story straight strange street strong subject success such suggest sum summer Sunday supply support sure surprise sweet system

FOR YOUR TYPING FOLDER 9

Follow previous instructions for typing these exercises (see page 77).

ABBREVIATIONS USED IN HANDWRITING

1   The abbreviation for "with" is ....

2   "shd" is the abbreviation for ....

3   "fr" is the abbreviation for ....

4   The abbreviation for "carbon copy" is ....

5   "m/c" is the abbreviation for ....

6   "hv" is the abbreviation for ....

7   "advert" is the abbreviation for ....

8   "asap" is the abbreviation for ....

9   "ffly" is the abbreviation for ....

10 "rect" is the abbreviation for ....

11 "th" is the abbreviation for ....

12 "wk" is the abbreviation for .... or ....

13 "&" should always be typed as .... except in registered names of firms, addresses and ....

14 Abbreviations when used as titles which are never typed in full are: Dr, Mr, Mrs, Ms, Esq and ....

15 Some other abbreviations that are never typed in full are: PS, am, eg, etc, and ....

16 The abbreviation for "about" is ....

17 The abbreviation for "yours" is ....

18 "shd" is the abbreviation for "shorthand" or ....

19 "received" is abbreviated to ....

20 The abbreviation for "for" is ....

21 A handwritten passage should always be .... before being typed, in order to get the sense of the ....

PROGRESS TEST 1

1   **Display the following notice on A5 paper:**

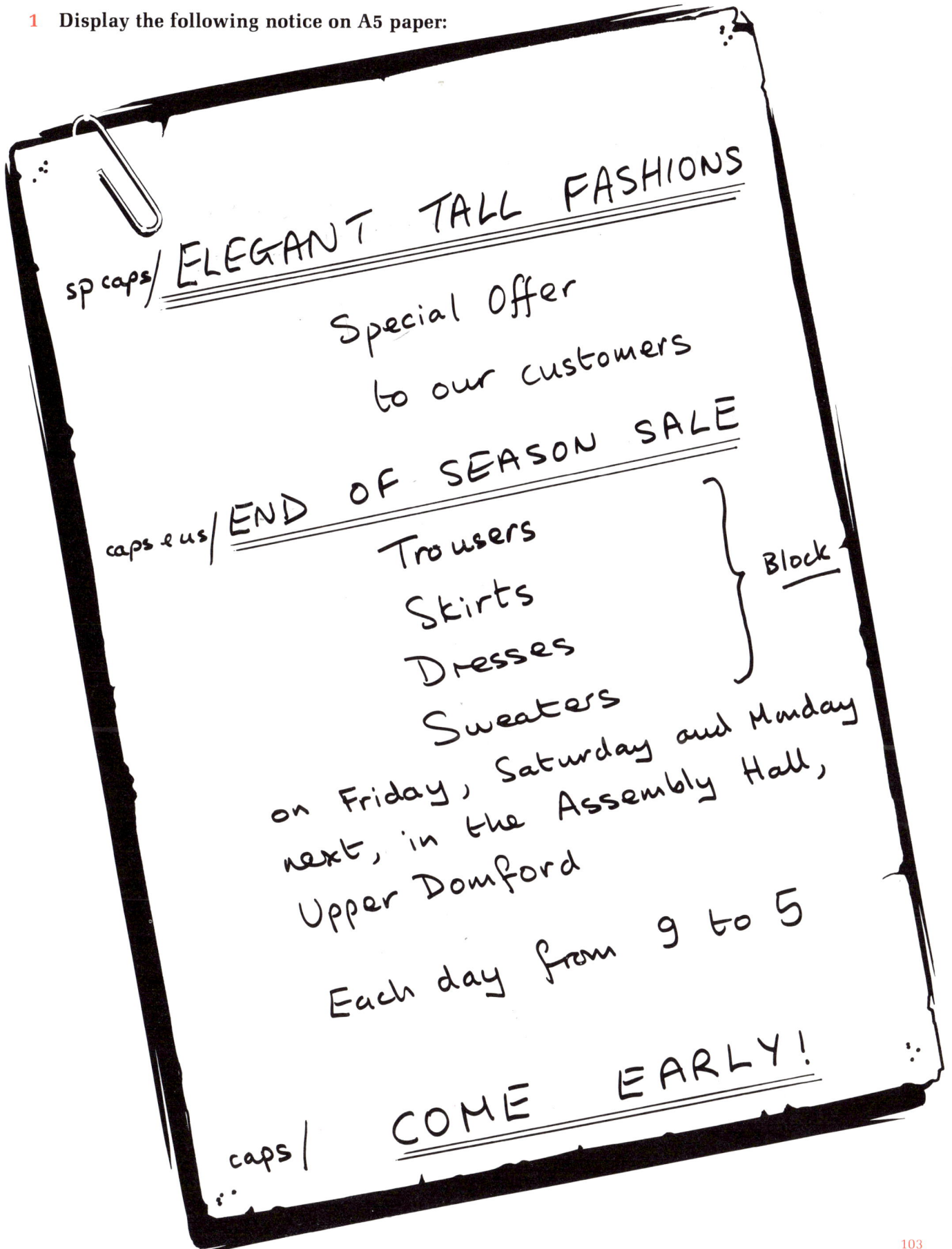

sp caps/ <u>ELEGANT TALL FASHIONS</u>

Special Offer

to our customers

caps & us/ <u>END OF SEASON SALE</u>

Trousers

Skirts

Dresses

Sweaters

} Block

on Friday, Saturday and Monday
next, in the Assembly Hall,
Upper Domford

Each day from 9 to 5

caps/ <u>COME EARLY!</u>

Exercise 61

Type the following letter on A5 portrait paper, with a carbon copy, to Mrs S Yardley Fern Lea   Hurstone Drive   Urmston   Manchester   M31 6PL. Type an envelope.

Fr   Miss Linda Holland
12 Fallowfield Drive
Sale, Cheshire M33 2UZ
Tel (0570) 319777

Dear Madam

I see from your advert in yesterday's "Evening Post" that you hv a typewriter (electric) for sale and I shd be interested to have info abt price etc. [NP I am an experienced typist and am looking for a reliable m/c in gd condition, as I am planning to wk from my own home.

NP [Please telephone or write to me & let me have full details asap.

Yrs ffly

137

2 Type the following on A5 paper, with one carbon copy:

<u>A CONTRACT OF EMPLOYMENT MUST SET OUT:</u>

Rates of pay (whether weekly or monthly)
Hours of work
Sick pay
Pension
Holidays and holiday pay
Length of notice to be given by either side
The right to belong to a chosen trade union
The right not to belong to a trade union
The person to whom a complaint can be made
Date of commencement of employment

3 Type a corrected copy of the following passage on A5 landscape paper, in single line spacing. Block the paragraphs.

Centre/
Sp caps/ DOGS

Dogs have been friends and companions of people since the very earliest times, as friezes on Egyptian temples illustrate. No other animal shows such affection and gives such faithful service. Dogs are used in hunting, looking after sheep, Arctic exploration, and guiding blind people. Dogs are also trained to track criminals. Frequently, they have saved people from drowning and from death by suffocation in snow drifts. The average life of a dog is about 10 to 14 years, though some live to be 20. The Kennel Club, founded in 1873, has more than 100 different breeds of dog registered, but the total of the various breeds all over the world is thought to be about 400, in addition to which there are still many types of wild dog in Africa, America, Asia and Australia.

4 Type the following passage on A5 landscape paper, in double line spacing. Indent the paragraphs.

<u>APPLICATION FORMS</u> — *centre*

Many firms send these to applicants for vacancies even though full details have been supplied to them on a curriculum vitae. The reason for this is that they may require the information in a certain order, or additional information to that given on the curriculum vitae. An application form must be completed and returned to the firm from whom it has been received as quickly as possible, with a brief "covering letter" stating simply that the completed application form is enclosed. Alternatively it can be handed in at the Personnel Department of the firm concerned.

Exercise 60

Type the following passage on A5 portrait paper, in double line spacing.

Referring to yr telephone call this morning we hv gone into the question of yr Order No 88192 dated of 11 October 198 - ~~and~~ to wh yr ltr dated 9 October refers.

We see f yr ltr th the goods you ordered hv not bn recd. The package shd have arrived at yr wks on 10 May by BRS and we do not understand the delay. NP/ [We are looking into the matter and will telephone you asap when any info is available.

SECTION 4

Typed Communications

ABBREVIATIONS IN LONGHAND (HANDWRITING)

Dr, Mr, Mrs, Esq, PS (postscript), am, pm are all examples of abbreviations that are **never** typed in full.

Some other examples are:

> eg (exempli gratia, meaning "for example")
>
> etc (et cetera, meaning "and so on")
>
> ie (id est, meaning "that is")

There are other abbreviations which are used when writing out drafts for typists to copy from, and these should *always* be typed in full:

abt	about
advert	advertisement
&	and (except in names of firms, addresses and, occasionally, Mr & Mrs)
asap	as soon as possible
bn	been
cc	carbon copy *or* copy circulated
f	for
ffly	faithfully
fr	from
gd	good
gds	goods
hv	have
info	information
ltr	letter
m/c	machine *or* machinery
recd	received
rect	receipt
shd	should, shorthand
th	that
w	with
wk	work, week
wks	works, weeks
yr	your
yrs	yours

There are many more of these; *always* read through a handwritten (longhand) passage before you start to type, to get the sense of the abbreviations.

TYPING PERSONAL LETTERS

People who are able to type, quite often type letters to friends – it is quicker and, in many cases, easier for the recipient to read! The size of the paper used depends on the length of the letter – it is wasteful to use A4 paper for a short note, for instance – A5 would be much more suitable.

A5 personal letters

The A5 paper can be either portrait or landscape; it is not important which one is used.

A5 portrait letters

Set margins on ½". Use single line spacing.

Turn up 4 and type your own address, with a separate line for each line of your address. Start each line at the margin (block them).

Turn up 3 and type the date, starting at the margin.

Turn up 3 and, starting at the margin, type "Dear", adding the name.

Turn up 2 and start the letter, at the margin.

Block each new paragraph.

After the last paragraph, turn up 2, and type whatever you decide to finish your letter with – "Kind regards", "Yours ever", "With love", etc., starting at the margin.

Finally, sign it (do not type your name).

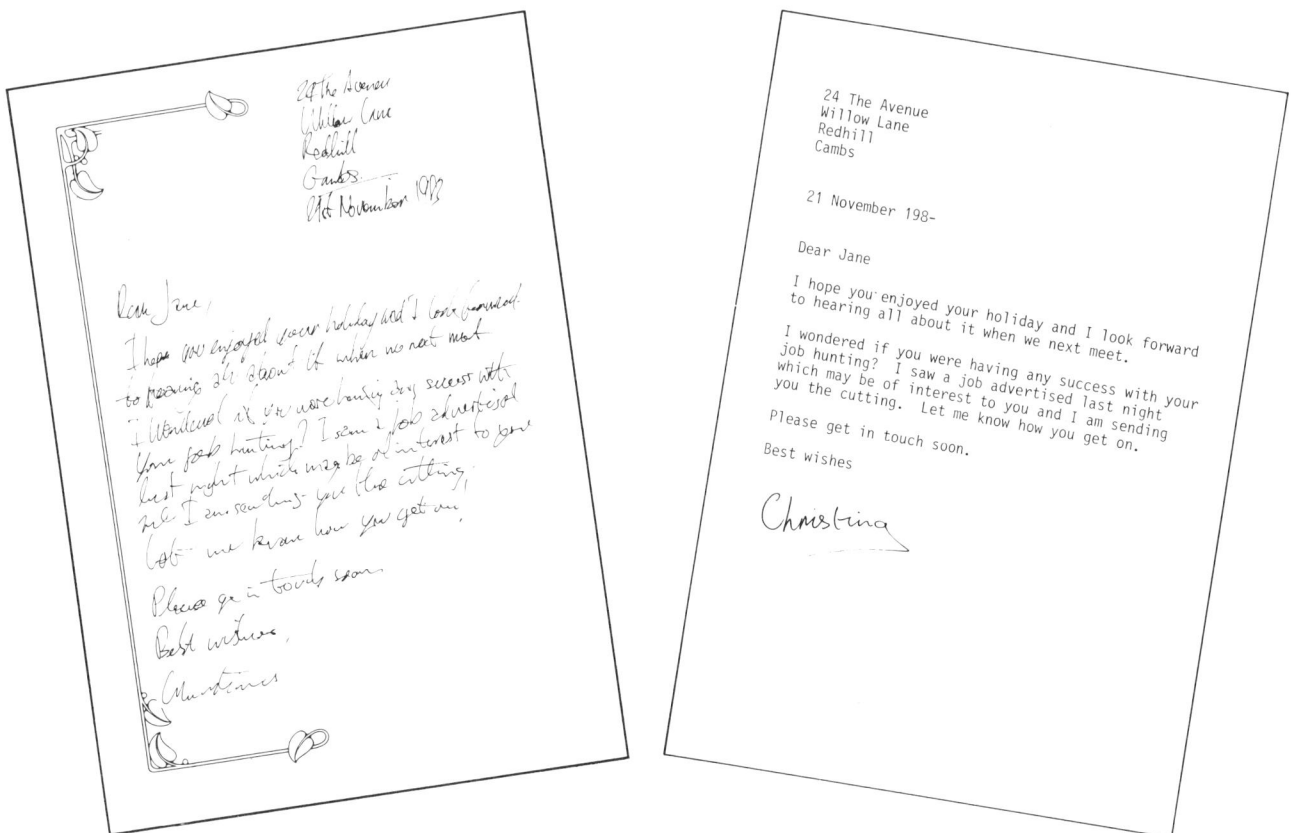

Preparation for accuracy/speed practice

Type each line 3 times.

Cancellation Cancellation Cancellation Cancellation Cancellation Cancellation
attractiveness attractiveness attractiveness attractiveness attractiveness
commemorate commemorate commemorate commemorate commemorate commemorate
essential essential essential essential essential essential essential essential
mechanical mechanical mechanical mechanical mechanical mechanical mechanical
minimum minimum minimum minimum minimum minimum minimum minimum minimum minimum
defacement defacement defacement defacement defacement defacement defacement
philatelists philatelists philatelists philatelists philatelists philatelists
throughout throughout throughout throughout throughout throughout throughout
hand-stamping hand-stamping hand-stamping hand-stamping hand-stamping

Accuracy/speed practice

POST OFFICE SERVICE FOR STAMP COLLECTORS

	Words
Cancellation of stamps on envelopes (franking) by The Post Office often	15
affects the attractiveness of stamps, which seems a pity when often a	29
great deal of work has gone into the design of the stamps to commemorate	44
events of national and international importance. This is a source of	58
great annoyance to stamp collectors. Unfortunately, the cancellation of	73
stamps is an essential part of conducting postal business and where, as	87
in the case of the British Post Office, 34 million letters of varying	102
shapes and sizes, are handled every day, the mechanical equipment used	116
for the purpose of franking cannot be finely adjusted to provide minimum	131
defacement of the stamps by delicate cancellation.	141
The Post Office is aware, however, of the needs of stamp collectors	155
(philatelists) and there is a special postal facility at 26 post offices	170
throughout the country providing hand-stamping. On the first day of	184
issue of new stamps, this service is made available at more than 200	198
post offices.	201

Exercise 38

Type a copy of the following personal letter on A5 portrait paper. Set margins on ½″ left and right and start typing on the 4th line from the top edge of the paper. See page 106 for line spacing.

---

53 Arndale Avenue
Underbank
Stockport
SK3 8NF

24 October 198-

Dear Marilyn

As you can see, I have made progress with my typing lessons and today we have practised typing personal letters, which will be very useful to my friends, who will not have to read my awful handwriting any more.

I hope to be coming to Wigan one weekend soon so perhaps we could meet - have lots of news for you and am dying to hear yours.

Will let you know exact date later.

In the meantime

Much love

Tina

Warm-up drill

Dozens of people crowded into the meeting to hear a speaker on the latest methods of slimming. The majority of the audience did not appear to be overweight, but there were quite a few jokes about "Billy Bunters" and "fatties" bandied around, and many promises to attend further meetings to report on dieting progress.

Common word drills

1 an and able about above according account across act add advantage advertise advertisement after afternoon again age ago agree air along also altogether am among amount animal announce another answer any appear April are arm art as ask at attempt attention August authority away awe baby back bad balance bank base be beautiful because become bed before begin behind belief best better between beyond big black blue board body book both bought boy brake bread break bring brother brought build built buoy business but buy by

2 call came can capital car care carry case cause cell certain change character charge cheap check cheque chief child children city clean clear coal coarse cold colour come comfort commit common company competition complete condition connect consider continue control copy cost could country course cover credit cry custom cut danger date day dear December deep degree deliver delivery demand depend desire detail develop die differ difference different difficult difficulty direct discover distance distribute division do door doubt down

Practise hanging paragraphs

Type the following on A5 landscape paper, in single line spacing with double between paragraphs.

POST OFFICE GUIDELINES ON METHODS OF ADDRESS

Do not use the name of the house instead of the number. Where the house bears a number, the name of the house is unnecessary.

Do not use the words LOCAL, BY or NEAR.

Do not use the name of the county town in place of the name of the county, for example, Warwick for Warwickshire, Durham for Co Durham, as there is a risk of circulation to the county town instead of to the office of delivery.

Do not use country names in the addresses of items posted within the UK for delivery within the UK.

Exercise 39

Type the following letter on A5 portrait paper. Make your own line endings.

Turn up 4 from top edge of paper

Holmlea
Alexandra Road
Redruth
Cornwall
TR16 4NT

Turn up 3

21 August 198-

Turn up 3

Dear Sally

Turn up 2

Thank you for your letter telling me all about the
disco. I was wild about missing it, but had transport
problems (as usual).

Turn up 2

I think that raising £76 was marvellous - is it a
record?

Turn up 2

Am starting a part-time job next week (helping in a
newsagent's shop) so shan't be able to get to see you
until school starts, but look forward to catching up
with all your news then.

Turn up 2

With love

Debbie

Exercise 40

Type the following personal letter on A5 landscape paper. Margins on 1″. Make your own line endings.

Turn up 4 from top edge of paper

Cliff Cottage
Greenfield Terrace
Camborne
Cornwall
TR14 6JX

Turn up 3

Alternative place for date, ending on right hand margin   28 August 198-

Dear Debbie

Turn up 2

Thanks for your news - glad to hear about the part-time job, you are
lucky. Not much doing here, although I am baby-sitting several
times a week, which, although it's dead boring, brings in some cash.

See you back at the dear old daily grinding shop -

Lots of love

Sally

FOR YOUR TYPING FOLDER 7

Follow previous instructions for typing these exercises (see page 77).

PERSONAL BUSINESS LETTERS

1   A carbon copy should always be taken of a personal business letter as it keeps an .... record of its contents.

2   An example of a personal business letter is an application for a job, or a letter to someone asking if ....

3   The name is typed 4 clear line spaces below "Yours faithfully" on a personal business letter in case the .... is difficult to read.

4   When a woman or a man signs a letter which she/he has typed, she/he signs over her/his typed name with .... or .... after it in brackets.

5   The title that might be used when it is not known whether a woman is married or single is ....

6   An alternative place for the postcode on a letter is ....

7   An indication that there is an enclosure with a letter is .... typed two clear line spaces below the typed name of the sender.

FOR YOUR TYPING FOLDER 8

Follow previous instructions for typing these exercises (see page 77).

ADDRESSING ENVELOPES

1   The part of the address on an envelope that is <u>always</u> typed in capitals is the ....

2   The last line of an address on an envelope is <u>always</u> the ....

3   The name of the county in which the post town is situated is necessary as this helps The Post Office with the ....

4   Exceptions to this are county towns and certain very large cities such as London, Manchester and ....

5   Some county names may be abbreviated and there is a list of correct abbreviations in .... which is published by ....

6   The postcode is used in the .... sorting of mail. Every address in the United Kingdom has a ....

7   Addresses are typed on envelopes parallel with the .... edge and should be approximately in the ....

8   There are many sizes of envelopes available; the Post Office Preferred sizes (POP) are within 90 mm x 140 mm (3½" x ....) and 120 mm x 235 mm (4¾" x ....).

Personal letters with telephone numbers

If you are on the telephone at home, include it at the top of your letter after the address. Turn up 2 before you type it.

Exercise 41

Type the following personal letter on A5 landscape paper. Make your own line endings.

```
Old Farm Cottage
Whitecross
Penzance
Cornwall
TR20 8HN

Tel (0736) 553 279                          1 September 198-


Dear Sue

Tried to phone you several times last week, but finally
guessed that you must be away.  Great news!  I'm engaged!
Dying to tell you all about it so decided to write and ask
you to ring me as soon as you get back.  I want you to be a
bridesmaid, of course, but we'll talk about that on the
telephone.  Date for wedding probably Christmas.  Isn't it
exciting?

Hope you are now quite well and over your accident.  We must
meet soon - we'll make all our plans when you ring.

Much love

Mo
```

Exercise 42

Type the following personal letter, using your own address, today's date, and signing the letter yourself. Type your telephone number too, if you have one. Don't forget your postcode.

```
Dear Kate

I was so sorry to hear about your brother's accident the
other day and that he is in hospital.  You must all have
been terribly worried.  I do hope that he is now getting
better and will soon be home again.  Please give him all
our best wishes when you see him.

I was wondering if he would like any visitors.  Dave would
like to come, and Tim.  Let me know also times of visiting,
and whether Pete would like anything to read.

Lots of love
```

Exercise 59

Type the following personal business letter, with one carbon copy, on A5 paper. Type an envelope. Date for today. Use your own address at the top of the letter. Add your telephone number – if you are not on the phone, invent one.

The Matron

Sea View Old People's Home

Cupressus Road

Mayfield, Dalkeith

Midlothian   EH22 5HA

Dear Madam   GRANT

        My aunt, Mrs Nancy Grant

wrote several weeks ago to tell us that

uc   she would be moving to your home

      soon after she sent her letter to us.

                    replied

⌿   I am I wrote back, addressing my   stet

⌿   letter to you my aunt at your Home.

        Since then, we hv not heard

fr   my aunt and are wondering if

she is ill and cannot write to

NP   us. [I would appreciate some news of her

asap either by letter or telephone.

        Yours faithfully

131

Exercise 43

Type the following personal letter, using your own address and telephone number. Choose either A5 portrait or A5 landscape paper. Date it for today. Sign your own name.

Dear Sue

Thanks a lot for the super birthday present and card. The scarf is exactly the right colour to go with my new jacket — great!

I was sorry you couldn't get to my party — it seemed to go well and I think everyone enjoyed it.

See you soon. I'll give you a ring when I'm next in South Shields.

Love

Exercise 57

Refer to page 114 for an example.

Type the following personal business letter on A5 paper. Use your own address. Type today's date. Address the letter to The Branch Manager   Farflung Building Society High Street   Anchester   Avon   AR9 7DY. Make your own line endings. Type an envelope. Don't forget to type your name.

```
Dear Sir

I would be pleased to receive leaflets, and any other information
you may have regarding regular savings schemes.

I have just started work and would like to save regularly from the
beginning of next month, as I plan to get married in two or three
years' time.

Please also send me details of any savings schemes you have for
future mortgages.  Could you also tell me whether I should be given
any preference for a mortgage as a saver with your Society?

Yours faithfully
```

Exercise 58

Type the following personal business letter, using today's date and your own address, on A4 paper; add your phone number if you have one. Make your own line endings. Take one carbon copy. Sign the letter yourself. Don't forget to type your name. Type an envelope.

Turn up 7

```
The Personnel Manager
Messrs Laidlaw & Lamson Ltd
Saltmeadows Road
Blyth
Northumberland
NE24 2NJ
```

Turn up 3

```
Dear Sir
```

Turn up 2

```
Thank you for your letter asking me to attend for an interview on
(type date here 7 days ahead).  Unfortunately, I shall be taking
examinations that day and unable to attend.  Would it be possible
for me to come on (type date here 14 days ahead) at the same time?

I apologise for any inconvenience which this may cause, but feel
sure you will understand the importance of my examinations.
```

Turn up 2

```
Yours faithfully
```

Turn up 5

Warm-up drill

1 The expert was amazed and puzzled by the contents of the small black box, which contained jewels of an unusual brilliance, size and hue.

Practise figures

2 One of the main reasons for the 24-hour clock is to avoid any misunderstanding about time; when am or pm is used, it can be confusing.

3 The bargain price of the shoes is £9.99; originally they were £14.99 a pair, as invoice No 5578 dated 12 March 1985 shows.

4 One day last month, 5731 cars passed along the High Street.

5 A large percentage of the pupils in the class (85 per cent) preferred to take sandwiches for lunch.

FORMS OF ADDRESS

When writing to *individuals*, always give them a title – Mrs, Miss, Ms (when it is not known whether a woman is married or single, or when a woman chooses to be addressed this way), Mr. An alternative (rather out-of-date) title for a man is Esq (abbreviated from Esquire) but this is being used less and less frequently today. When "Esq" is used, it is typed *after* the name.

The titles Dr, Rev (abbreviation for Reverend), Captain, Professor replace any of the titles mentioned above.

Letters after a person's name are typed without spaces in between: JP OBE MP MA. If there is more than one set of letters, they are typed with one space between each set of abbreviations.

Firms should be addressed as Messrs only when their names *do not* include Limited, the abbreviation Ltd, or PLC (Public Limited Company). Firms whose names start with the word "The" or when a title is included in the name – Sir William Watkins & Co – should not be addressed as Messrs.

Exercise 44

Type the following addresses on A5 paper, adding the correct form of address in each case. Capitals for towns. Type along one line.

6 Jennifer K Binns 18 Hereford Road Worcester WR1 5RL

7 James Timothy Furlong MA 16 Fosse Way Banbury Oxon OX1 2AD

8 D J Curtis & Sons (Builders) 131 Abbotts Wood Close South Shields Tyne and Wear NE35 1QD

9 D J Wilmott Ltd Cobleigh Hill Wigan Lancs WN1 1NR

10 The JLC Finance Company Sutton House Wrexham Clwyd LL13 6LH

Warm-up drill

The quiz panel felt very nervous as they faced their audience and waited for the first questioner. It was a new experience for most of the panel members, and although they had all been reading up on their subjects, they were still worried about speedily recalling the right answers.

Preparation for accuracy/speed practice

Type each line 3 times.

immune immune immune immune immune immune immune immune immune immune immune
detectors detectors detectors detectors detectors detectors detectors detectors
succession succession succession succession succession succession succession
ordinary ordinary ordinary ordinary ordinary ordinary ordinary ordinary ordinary
letter-bomb letter-bomb letter-bomb letter-bomb letter-bomb letter-bomb

Accuracy/speed practice

DETECTING LETTER BOMBS

	Words
No person or company in the public eye is ever immune from the danger of	14
letter-bombs. An unfamiliar postmark or a misspelt name should act as a	29
warning that the envelope may contain an explosive device.	41
There are now detectors available which will sense explosives through a	56
substantial bundle of papers, or even a packet over two inches thick.	70
It is possible to put through handfuls of letters, in rapid succession,	84
or packages up to 16 inches wide. Films and magnetic tapes are not	98
affected. Most detectors are simply plugged into an ordinary 13 amp	112
power point and are very easy to use.	120

FOR YOUR TYPING FOLDER 6

Follow previous instructions for typing these exercises (see page 77).

(see page 77)

FORMS OF ADDRESS

1   Firms are addressed as "Messrs" only when their names do not include
     .... or .... or ....

2   Firms whose names start with "The" or when a title is included in a name, should
     .... be addressed as "Messrs".

3   Individuals must always be given a title - Mr, Miss, Mrs or Ms. A rather
     out-of-date title for a man is ....

4   The titles Dr, Rev, Captain, Professor replace ....

5   Letters after a person's name are typed .... without spaces in between.

6   If there is more than one set of letters they are typed in order of
     ....

7   When it is not known whether a woman is married or single, the courtesy title
     .... should be used.

Exercise 56

Rule four rectangles as before, and set out correctly the following addresses.

1. Mr R Marshall

    17 Haig Avenue

    Wimborne   Dorset

    BH22   0JR

2. Mr Peter T Delaney
    278 Nottingham Road

    Keighley   West Yorkshire

    BD22   0LY

3. Dr G M Hall
    74 Telford Road
    Halstead   Leicester   LE7 3RD

(Leicester is another city where the county may be omitted from the address on an envelope.)

4. Miss Wendy Pike
    Walnut Cottage
    Buckingham Road

    Lingwood   Norwich

    NR16 1NG

(Norwich is another example.)

128

TYPING PERSONAL BUSINESS LETTERS

A personal business letter is one that is sent to a firm or an individual about a business matter. An example is an application for a job, or a letter to someone asking if their name may be used as a referee.

A carbon copy should always be taken of a personal business letter, to keep an exact record of the contents. It is, therefore, important to include on the letter, below your own address, the name and address of the person, or firm, to whom the letter is to be sent, otherwise the carbon copy will not contain this information. The correct name for this is the "inside" name and address which goes on all business letters, whether personal or typed on behalf of an employer.

Exercise 45

Type a copy of the following personal business letter and keep it in your typing folder for future reference. Use A5 portrait paper. Set margins on ½″.

Turn up 4 from top of paper

34 Saltmeadows Road
Blyth
Northumberland
NE24 2NJ

Turn up 3

13 September 198–

Turn up 3

The Manager
Sunglow Holidays Ltd
Newgate Street
Newcastle upon Tyne
NE4 8NS

The "inside" name and address – the person to whom the letter is being sent

Turn up 3

Dear Sir

Turn up 2

Please send me any information you have on one-week holidays in Norway in July 198–.

Turn up 2

Yours faithfully

Turn up 5

Anne West

Anne West (Miss)

The name of the person sending the letter is typed below it in case the signature is difficult to read.

A woman types after her name whatever title she wishes to be addressed by (she may, after all, be "Dr"). If she does not add a title, a typist replying to her should use "Ms".

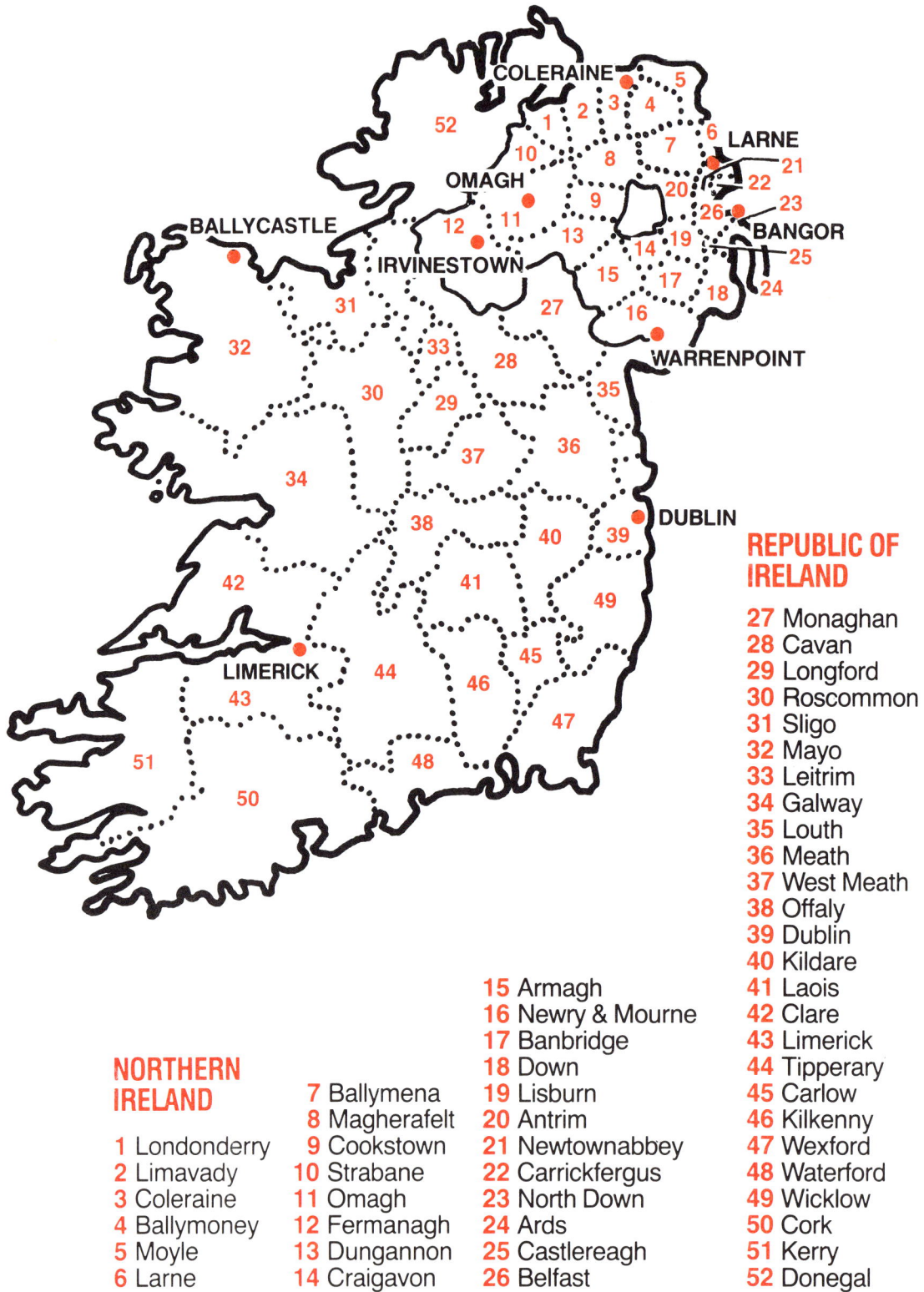

COLERAINE
5
52
3 4
1 2
OMAGH
10 7
6 LARNE
8
21
20 22
9 26 23
BALLYCASTLE
11 BANGOR
12
13 14 19 25
IRVINESTOWN
15 17 24
31
27 16 18
32
33 WARRENPOINT
28
30
29
35
37 36
34
38 DUBLIN
39
42
40
41
49
45
LIMERICK
44 46
43 47
51
48
50

REPUBLIC OF IRELAND

27 Monaghan
28 Cavan
29 Longford
30 Roscommon
31 Sligo
32 Mayo
33 Leitrim
34 Galway
35 Louth
36 Meath
37 West Meath
38 Offaly
39 Dublin
40 Kildare
41 Laois
42 Clare
43 Limerick
44 Tipperary
45 Carlow
46 Kilkenny
47 Wexford
48 Waterford
49 Wicklow
50 Cork
51 Kerry
52 Donegal

NORTHERN IRELAND

1 Londonderry
2 Limavady
3 Coleraine
4 Ballymoney
5 Moyle
6 Larne
7 Ballymena
8 Magherafelt
9 Cookstown
10 Strabane
11 Omagh
12 Fermanagh
13 Dungannon
14 Craigavon
15 Armagh
16 Newry & Mourne
17 Banbridge
18 Down
19 Lisburn
20 Antrim
21 Newtownabbey
22 Carrickfergus
23 North Down
24 Ards
25 Castlereagh
26 Belfast

Exercise 46

Type a copy of the following personal business letter on A5 landscape paper. Make your own line endings.

Turn up 4
from top
of paper
24 Oakworth Close
Coventry
West Midlands
CT4 C78

Turn up 3

15 October 198-

Turn up 3

The Secretary
Hill View Drama Club
19 Dene Grove
Coventry
West Midlands   CT5 B65   *An alternative place for the postcode –
leave 6 spaces before starting to type*

Turn up 3

Dear Sir

Turn up 2

I am interested in joining the Hill View Drama Club. Would you please send me details of times and dates of meetings?

Turn up 2

Yours faithfully

Turn up 5

Martin Corder

Martin Corder

It is only possible to type very short personal business letters on A5 paper, because the inclusion of an inside address as well as the sender's address reduces the amount of space available for the actual message. If you are in any doubt at all about a letter fitting on to A5 paper, then type it on A4. You can always widen the margins, so that the letter is attractively set out on the paper.

When anything is enclosed with a personal business letter, it should be indicated by typing "Enc" two clear line spaces below the sender's name. If there is more than one enclosure (as in the next letter) "Encls" (the abbreviation for "Enclosures") should be typed. Another abbreviation for "Enclosures" is "Encs". Both are equally correct.

The reasons why a typist should type "Enc" at the foot of the letter are:

a) as a reminder to whoever seals the letter

b) as a reminder to whoever opens the letter that there should be an enclosure with it.

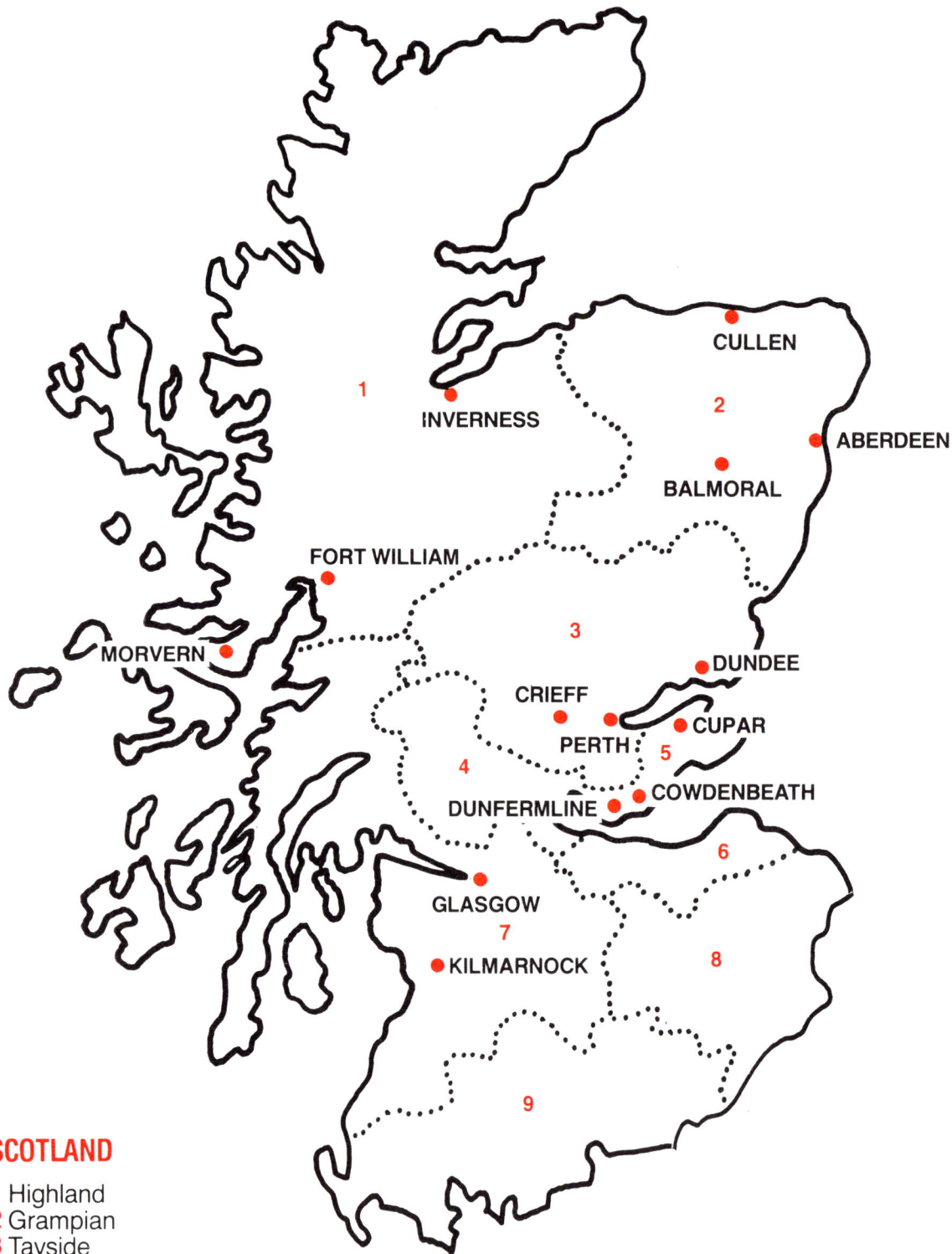

SCOTLAND

1 Highland
2 Grampian
3 Tayside
4 Central
5 Fife
6 Lothian
7 Strathclyde
8 Borders
9 Dumfries & Galloway

Map labels:
CULLEN
INVERNESS
ABERDEEN
BALMORAL
FORT WILLIAM
MORVERN
DUNDEE
CRIEFF
CUPAR
PERTH
COWDENBEATH
DUNFERMLINE
GLASGOW
KILMARNOCK

Exercise 47

Type a copy of the following personal business letter on A4 paper. Set margins on 1½″ on the left and 1″ on the right. Make your own line endings.

```
JUNIOR
SECRETARY

We are looking for a junior
secretary with good short-
hand/typing to assist in busy
purchasing/ director's office of
motor components' manufac-
turer and distributor. Starting
salary £3,500.
Please write or telephone in
the first instance to:

The Office Manager,
Millard & Perkins Ltd,
St Christopher's
Trading Estate,
Bromswood, Essex
B45 5TB
```

Turn up 7 from top edge of paper

33 Linford Road
Streatham
London
SW9 75J

Turn up 3

19 May 198-

Turn up 3

The Office Manager
Millard & Perkins Ltd
St Christopher's Trading Estate
Bromswood Essex
B45 5TB

Turn up 3

Dear Sir

Turn up 2

I am interested in your advertisement in today's issue of the "Daily News" for a junior secretary, and enclose details of my education and training, together with a photocopy of my latest school report.

Turn up 2

I am 18 years of age and have finished my examinations; I shall be able to leave college at the end of June.

Turn up 2

If you would like me to attend for an interview, I shall be pleased to do so on any day and at any time to suit your convenience.

Turn up 2

Yours faithfully

Turn up 5

Joanne M Davidson

Joanne M Davidson (Miss)

Turn up 3

Encls

115

WALES

22 Gwynedd
23 Clwyd
30 Powys
42 Mid Glamorgan
43 Gwent
46 South Glamorgan
47 West Glamorgan
61 Dyfed

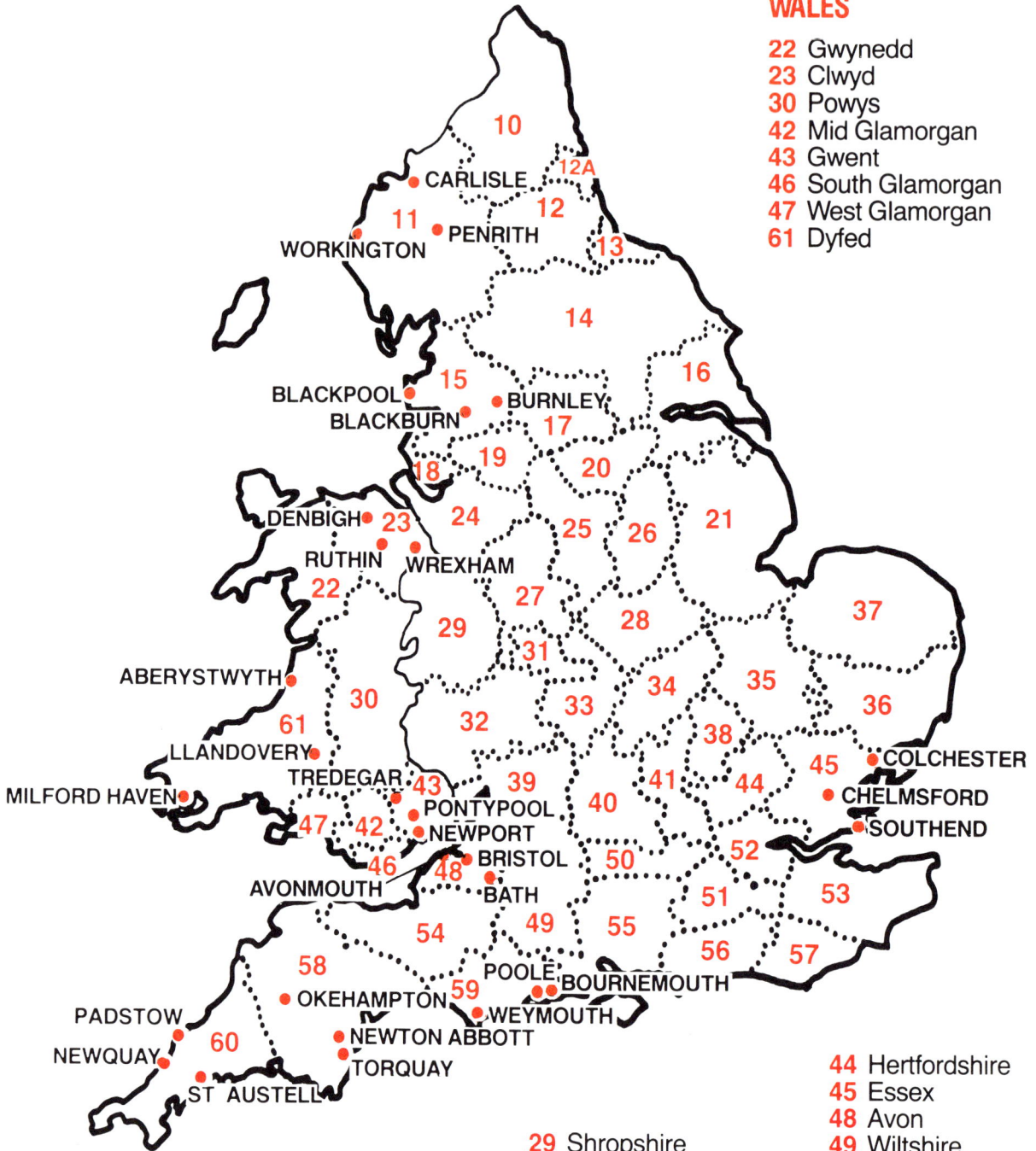

ENGLAND

10 Northumberland
11 Cumbria
12 Durham
12A Tyne & Wear
13 Cleveland
14 North Yorkshire
15 Lancashire
16 Humberside

17 West Yorkshire
18 Merseyside
19 Greater Manchester
20 South Yorkshire
21 Lincolnshire
24 Cheshire
25 Derbyshire
26 Nottinghamshire
27 Staffordshire
28 Leicestershire

29 Shropshire
31 West Midlands
32 Hereford & Worcester
33 Warwickshire
34 Northamptonshire
35 Cambridgeshire
36 Suffolk
37 Norfolk
38 Bedfordshire
39 Gloucestershire
40 Oxfordshire
41 Buckinghamshire

44 Hertfordshire
45 Essex
48 Avon
49 Wiltshire
50 Berkshire
51 Surrey
52 Greater London
53 Kent
54 Somerset
55 Hampshire
56 West Sussex
57 East Sussex
58 Devon
59 Dorset
60 Cornwall

125

Exercise 48

Type the following personal business letter on A4 paper, with one carbon copy. Make your own line endings. Set margins on 1½″ left and 1″ right. Use your own address. Type today's date. Address the letter to Mawson's Mail Order Fashions   Chapel Street   Murton-on-Thames   Middx   TW12 2EG

Dear Sirs

I see from your advertisement in yesterday's "Daily Echo" that you stock extra-long skirts, trousers and dresses, and I would be pleased to receive your latest catalogue.

Enclosed are stamps to the value of 25p to cover the cost of postage, as requested in your advertisement.

As I shall be going on holiday next month and staying quite near to Murton-on-Thames, would it be possible for me to call and try on anything in your catalogue which interests me? Perhaps you will let me know when you send your catalogue.

Yours faithfully

Your signature here

Type your own name here, adding your correct title, ie, Miss, Ms, etc

Enc

Exercise 49

Type the following personal business letter on A4 paper, with one carbon copy. Make your own line endings. Set margins on 1¼″ on left and ¾″ on right. Use your own address. Type today's date. Address the letter to: The Chairman   Hipvalue Fashions Skirt House   Murton-on-Thames   Middx   TW12 2EH

Dear Sir

On 3 July 198-, (at your branch) in High Street, Trumpton, I bought a blue linen size 14 skirt, style 141170, price £14.99.

NP [On 7 July the zip broke as I put the skirt on, and when I took it off, I noticed a large tear in the hem. I complained to Miss Gregory (your branch manager) on 10 July but was refused an exchange of skirt or a refund.

run on (I still have the damaged skirt and the receipted bill. A photocopy of the bill is enclosed.

NP [Could you please look into the matter for me?

Yours faithfully

Enc

Practise finding the right county

Type the following sentences, completing them by adding the correct county name from the maps on pages 125–7.

ENGLAND AND WALES

1   Newquay, Padstow and St Austell are in the county of ....
2   Torquay, Newton Abbott and Okehampton are in the county of ....
3   Weymouth, Bournemouth and Poole are in the county of ....
4   Bristol, Bath and Avonmouth are in the county of ....
5   Pontypool, Tredegar and Newport are in the county of ....
6   Milford Haven, Llandovery and Aberystwyth are in the county of ....
7   Denbigh, Ruthin and Wrexham are in the county of ....
8   Blackpool, Blackburn and Burnley are in the county of ....
9   Carlisle, Workington and Penrith are in the county of ....
10 Colchester, Chelmsford and Southend are in the county of ....

SCOTLAND

1   Glasgow and Kilmarnock are in the county of ....
2   Cupar, Cowdenbeath and Dunfermline are in the county of ....
3   Aberdeen, Balmoral and Cullen are in the county of ....
4   Crieff, Perth and Dundee are in the county of ....
5   Inverness, Fort William and Morvern are in the county of ....

NORTHERN IRELAND

1   Coleraine is in the county of ....
2   Bangor is in the county of ....
3   Omagh is in the county of ....
4   Larne is in the county of ....

REPUBLIC OF IRELAND

1   Warrenpoint is in the county of ....
2   Dublin is in the county of ....
3   Irvinestown is in the county of ....
4   Limerick is in the county of ....
5   Ballycastle is in the county of ....

Warm-up drill

The cliff path wound among the rocks until it vanished dizzily into the heights. The climbers toiled upwards until they too were out of sight of the watchers on the beach.

Preparation for accuracy/speed practice

Type each line 3 times.

modernise modernise modernise modernise modernise modernise modernise modernise
postcoding postcoding postcoding postcoding postcoding postcoding postcoding
consists consists consists consists consists consists consists consists consists
surrounding surrounding surrounding surrounding surrounding surrounding
precisely precisely precisely precisely precisely precisely precisely precisely
Electronic Electronic Electronic Electronic Electronic Electronic Electronic
destination destination destination destination destination destination
automatic automatic automatic automatic automatic automatic automatic automatic

Accuracy/speed practice

POSTCODE DOTS ARE ANYTHING BUT DOTTY!

	Words
The Royal Mail's drive to modernise the post depends on postcoding.	14
Every address in the country has a postcode, which consists of two	28
groups of letters and figures.	34
The first group is the outward part; it tells where, in a post town	48
or its surrounding area, a letter has to be sent. The second, inward	62
group, says precisely where the address can be found when the letter	76
has reached the post town.	81
Machines cannot yet read postcodes as we can. So the postcode is	95
"typed" on to the face of the envelope in the form of blue dots, by	109
operators using a keyboard similar to a typewriter. Electronic eyes	123
read the dots and then direct the mail to its destination through	136
automatic sorting machines, which operate at a speed of 16,000 per	149
hour.	152

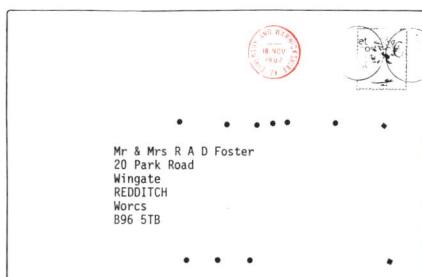

Mr & Mrs R A D Foster
20 Park Road
Wingate
REDDITCH
Worcs
B96 5TB

Exercise 55

Rule four rectangles 90 mm × 140 mm (3½″ × 5½″) and type the following addresses in the correct position.

1 Ms Patricia Ellis
   Albion Avenue
   South Lambeth
   LONDON
   SW8 1BX

Type postcodes as shown here

2 The Manager
   The Forward Manufacturing Co Ltd
   14 Jameson Road
   WARLEY
   West Midlands   B69 9PF

3 Mr A C Edge
   Swallow Cottage
   Swindon Bank
   HARROGATE
   North Yorkshire   HG3 4QZ

4 Mrs Maureen Moore
   Oakdene
   17 Abbeygate Road
   AXMINSTER
   Devon   EX13 15XF

5 Mr Stephen Sands
   18 Christian's Close
   COVENTRY
   CV2 3GJ

(Coventry is one of the cities which, provided the postcode is typed or written on the envelope, need not have the county added.)

ADDRESSING ENVELOPES

A correct postal address consists of:

      Name of person to whom letter is being sent

      Number of house (or name if it has no number)

      Name of street, road, avenue, crescent, lane, etc

      District (where it applies), or name of village, in the country

      Post town

      County

      Postcode

Of the above, the post town is very important. This is where the mail is sorted out for a particular district and is the basic unit of the postal system. It must *always* be included in the address and shown in BLOCK CAPITALS on the envelope.

The name of the county in which the post town is situated is necessary as this helps with sorting. Exceptions to this are county towns and certain very large cities such as London, Manchester and Birmingham. Some county names may be abbreviated and there is a list of correct abbreviations in **Postal Addresses And Index To Postcode Directories**, which is published by The Post Office.

The postcode is used in the automatic sorting of mail and must always be the last part of an address. Every address in the United Kingdom has a postcode.

Figures should be used in typing postcodes for "zero" and "one".

The example illustrated below and on page 119 is reproduced courtesy of The Post Office.

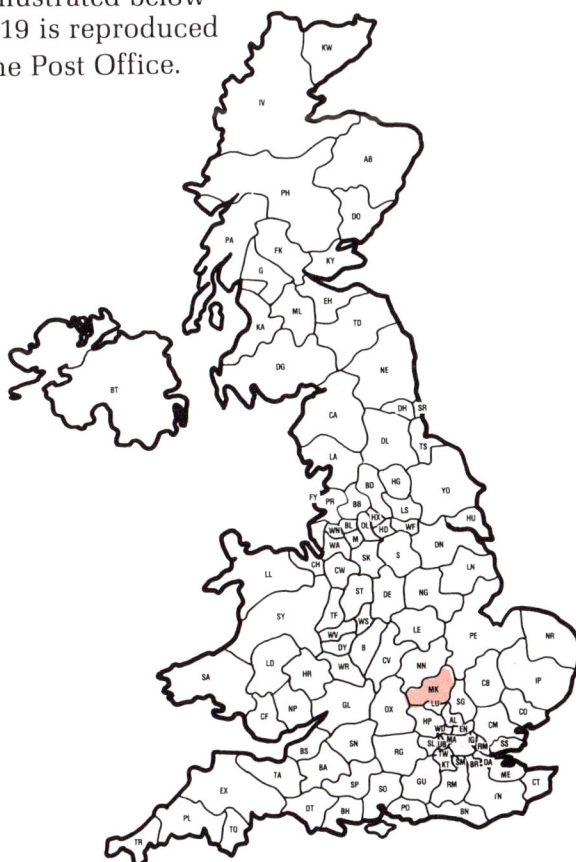

Exercise 52

Type the following addresses correctly on rectangles ruled 90 mm × 140 mm
(3½″ × 5½″), or fold A5 paper once (top edge to bottom edge portrait size) which will
give you rectangles just slightly larger than this size. Use all four sides.

1   Mr D Wheeler   6 Lenton Crescent   Coalville   Leicester   LE6 3LA

2   Mr W Gordon   3 Winter Crescent   Llantarnam   Cwmbran   Gwent   NP44 3TX

3   Mr A Taylor   22 Albion Drive   Minworth   Sutton Coldfield   West Midlands   B76 9YU

4   Messrs William Brown & Co   53 Embridge Square   London   W1V 5FZ

5   Miss F C Wallace   70 Faulkland Road   Glastonbury   Somerset   BA4 6BE

Exercise 53

Type envelopes for the letters you have typed so far from this book on rectangles
ruled as in Exercise 51, or on A5 folded paper.

Exercise 54

Type envelopes correctly addressed to yourself and four other members of your class.
If you don't know your postcodes, try to find out for your next lesson and make a note
of them somewhere until you can remember them.

Rapid typing of envelopes

When you have some real envelopes to practise on, try "feeding" them into your
typewriter as follows, which makes it much quicker:

Open the envelope flap and feed it into your machine, flap downwards:

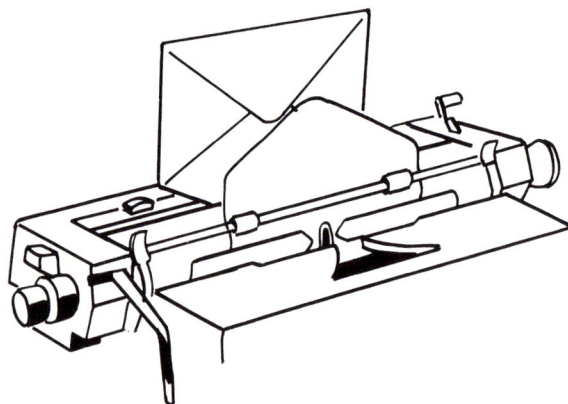

Type the address in the correct position.

As you turn the cylinder knob to remove the typed envelope, feed in the next
one to be typed, flap downwards, as before. This brings the blank envelope into
position for typing, as the typed envelope is removed. It is known as "chain"
feeding.

If you have hundreds of envelopes to type, it is a great time-saver!

Envelope sizes

The Post Office prefer envelopes (and postcards) not less than 90 mm × 140 mm (3½″ × 5½″) and not larger than 120 mm × 235 mm (4¾″ × 9¼″). The Post Office have powers to make an extra charge for letters outside this range – either smaller or larger. Window envelopes are accepted by The Post Office as POP (Post Office Preferred) but aperture envelopes (with cut-out address panels not covered by transparent material) are not. POP envelopes can be sorted automatically by The Post Office.

Mrs F G Cranleigh
High Gables
198 Greengate Street
EASTBOURNE
Sussex
BN21 3AJ

235 mm×100 mm (9¼"×4")

Exercise 51

Rule up a rectangle as above and type the address as if on an envelope.

Two of the most commonly used envelope sizes (both POP) are: 90 mm × 152 mm (3½″ × 6″) and 229 mm × 102 mm (9″ × 4″).

Addresses are typed on envelopes on the *longer edge* and should be in the lower half of the envelope, approximately in the centre. It is not necessary to measure this – guessing will do – but it is important to leave **at least** 38 mm (1½″) clear over the address for The Post Office to postmark the envelope and cancel the stamp.

Each part of the address should be on a separate line, with the postcode last. The postcode should have no fullstops and should not be underscored.

In the case of a long address, the postcode may be typed on the same line as the county, with 6 spaces between.

Envelopes are usually typed in single line spacing, except on very large envelopes, when double line spacing may be clearer.

Blocked layout (each line starting at the margin) is quicker and is the one usually adopted.

There are many sizes of envelope available, apart from the two given above, and in many qualities of paper. Firms match envelopes to their letterheading.

A correctly addressed envelope: suitable for A5 letterheading

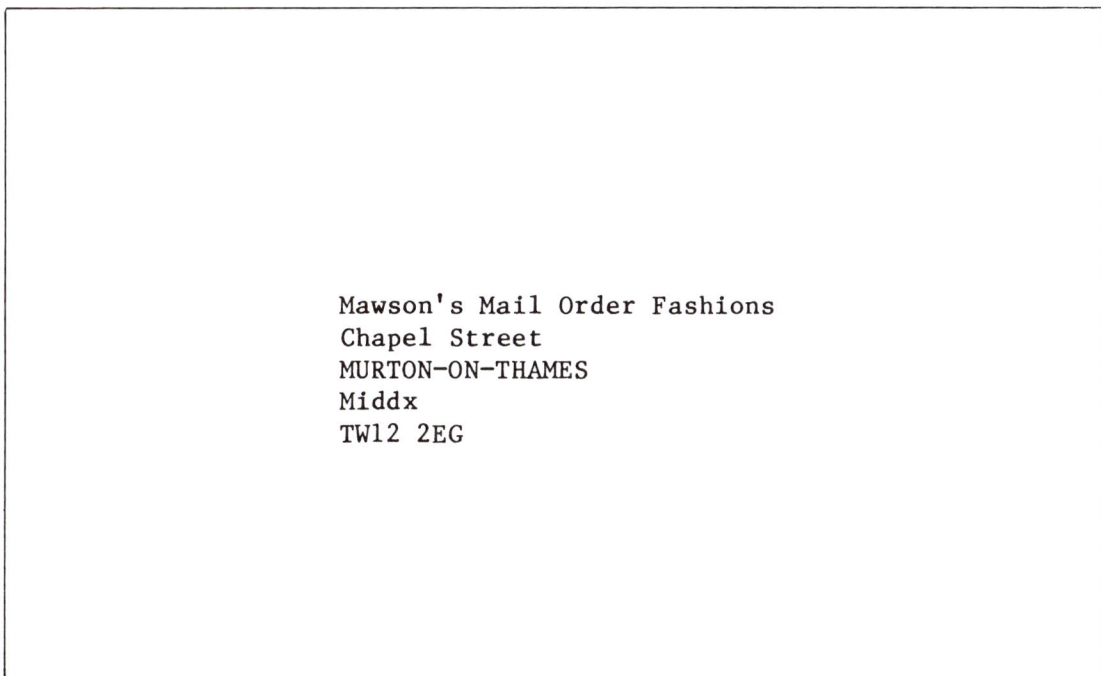

```
Mawson's Mail Order Fashions
Chapel Street
MURTON-ON-THAMES
Middx
TW12 2EG
```

150 mm×90 mm (6″×3½″)

Middx is the correct abbreviation for Middlesex and is one of the abbreviations for county names accepted by The Post Office.

Exercise 50

Rule a rectangle 150 mm × 90 mm (6″ × 3½″) and type the address above, correctly placed as if on an envelope.

Typing Skills

PAGES 121 to 240

Index

INDEX